The NATIONAL CONSUMER LAW CENTER

GUIDE TO

The Rights of Utility Consumers

Other National Consumer Law Center Publications

BOOKS FOR CONSUMERS
NCLC Guide to Surviving Debt
NCLC Guide to Mobile Homes
Return to Sender: Getting a Refund or Replacement for Your Lemon Car

LEGAL PRACTICE MANUALS

Debtor Rights Library
Consumer Bankruptcy Law and Practice
Fair Debt Collection
Foreclosures
Repossessions
Student Loan Law
Access to Utility Service

Credit and Banking Library
Truth in Lending
Fair Credit Reporting
Consumer Banking and
    Payments Law
The Cost of Credit
Credit Discrimination

Consumer Litigation Library
Consumer Arbitration Agreements
Consumer Class Actions
Consumer Law Pleadings

Deception and Warranties Library
Unfair and Deceptive Acts and
    Practices
Automobile Fraud
Consumer Warranty Law

Other Publications for Lawyers
The Practice of Consumer Law
Stop Predatory Lending
NCLC REPORTS Newsletter
Consumer Law in a Box CD-Rom

The NATIONAL CONSUMER LAW CENTER

The Rights of
Utility Consumers

From

THE NATIONAL CONSUMER LAW CENTER
America's Consumer Law Experts

Charles Harak
Olivia Bae Wein
Gillian Feiner

For reprint permissions or ordering information, contact
Publications, NCLC, 77 Summer Street, 10th Floor, Boston MA 02110,
(617) 542-9595, Fax (617) 542-8028, E-mail: publications@nclc.org

Library of Congress Control No. 2006921868
ISBN-13: 978-1-931697-87-3
ISBN-10: 1-931697-87-6

10 9 8 7 6 5 4 3 2 1

Printed in Canada
Cover design and illustration by Lightbourne, copyright ©2006.

Table of Contents

About the Authors   vii
Acknowledgments   viii
Introduction and How to Use This Book   ix

Chapter 1   An Overview of Utility Service and Regulation   1

Chapter 2   Issues in Obtaining Service: Deposits, Prior Bills, Bills of
Others   5

Chapter 3   How to Get Help Paying or Lowering Your Bills   13

Chapter 4   Restrictions on the Termination of Service   25

Chapter 5   Late Charges and Reconnection Charges   35

Chapter 6   Asserting Consumer Rights at the PUC and Elsewhere   39

Chapter 7   A Brief Primer on Telephones and Water   43

Chapter 8   Unregulated Deliverable Fuels: Heating Oil, Propane,
Kerosene, Etc.   47

Notes   51

Appendix A   Utility Terminations: Consumer Protections and
Time Frames   61

A.1   Seasonal Termination Protection Regulations   61

A.2   Serious Illness and Age-Related Protections   73

A.3   Termination Time Frames   83

Appendix B   Selected Utility Regulations   93

B.1   Deposits, Selected Regulations   93

B.2   Limitations on Grounds for Disconnections and Denying Service,
Selected Regulations   94

B.3   Payment Plans, Selected Regulations   95

B.4   Landlord-Tenant Procedures, Selected Regulations   101

Contents

Appendix C Utility Contact Information   103

    C.1 Weatherization Assistance Program   103

    C.2 2005 State LIHEAP Directors   108

    C.3 State Utility Commissions   116

Appendix D Serious Illness Certification   125

    D.1 Sample Serious Illness Certification and Sample Response to
Utility That Refuses to Grant Serious Illness Protection   125

    D.2 Physician Certification of Serious Illness or Life Support   126

Appendix E State Utility Regulations   129

Appendix F Federal Poverty Guidelines   141

Appendix G Consumer's Guide to Intervening in State Public
Utility Proceedings   143

    Bibliography   181

    Index   187

About the Authors

The National Consumer Law Center (NCLC) is the nation's expert on the rights of consumer borrowers. Since 1969, NCLC has been at the forefront in representing low income consumers before the courts, government agencies, Congress, and state legislatures.

NCLC has appeared before the United States Supreme Court and numerous federal and state courts and has successfully presented many of the most important cases affecting consumer borrowers. NCLC provides consultation and assistance to legal services, private, and government attorneys in all fifty states.

NCLC publishes a nationally acclaimed series of manuals on all major aspects of consumer credit and sales. (For a complete list of NCLC publications, go to the Bibliography at the back of this guide.) NCLC also conducts state and national training sessions on the rights of consumer borrowers for attorneys, paralegals, and other counselors.

Charles Harak is an NCLC staff attorney focusing on low-income energy and utility issues. He previously worked at the office of the Massachusetts Attorney General and at the Massachusetts Law Reform Institute, and has worked on utility and housing issues for over 20 years. He also serves as the President of the board of the Tri-City Community Action Program.

Olivia Bae Wein is an NCLC staff attorney focusing on low-income energy and utility issues. She serves on the board of directors of the National Low-Income Energy Consortium, co-chairs the LIHEAP Coalition, and serves on the Steering Committee of the Campaign for Safe and Affordable Drinking Water. She previously worked at Consumers Union.

Gillian Feiner was a consumer law fellow of the National Consumer Law Center and is presently an attorney with Klein, Roddy, & Ryan in Boston.

Acknowledgments

The Rights of Utility Consumers builds on materials developed for a practice package made possible through support from the Administration on Aging, Department of Health and Human Services. (The points of view and opinions expressed both in the practice package and in this guide are entirely NCLC's.) The authors are very appreciative of the contributions of all who have helped with this guide: Julia Devanthery and Kay Joslin for their work on Appendix A; Shirlron Williams for her work on Appendix C; and John Howat for his work on Appendix G.

Special thanks to: Denise Lisio for editing the book and production work; Nathan Day for editorial and production assistance; Donna Wong for production advice and assistance; Mary McLean for indexing; Julie Gallagher for design and typesetting; and Lightbourne for cover design.

Introduction and How to Use This Book

This book was born out of our experience in providing advice to individual consumers about their utility service. We saw a need for a simple, how-to guide for both utility customers and the front-line social services workers and advocates who assist them.

At the National Consumer Law Center (NCLC), we have been helping utility consumers for thirty years on a broad range of utility and energy problems. We advise individuals on their problems, such as making payment plans and avoiding utility service termination. We also work on larger-scale issues, like opposing utility rate hikes, advocating for the adoption of low-income discount rates, and designing programs that make it easier for low-income families to afford their utility bills. For many years, we have published *Access to Utility Service*, a legal treatise that contains hundreds of pages of in-depth analysis and detail that lawyers and experienced advocates need to represent their clients.

Over the years, we have also seen the need for a short, simple, and practical guide designed primarily for customers as well as advocates who do *not* specialize in utility issues. We hope that this guide will provide a handy, straightforward reference source for consumers and non-experts. This introduction provides an overview of what is contained in the following chapters and how best to use the materials.

WHO SHOULD USE THIS BOOK?

This book is about how to avoid utility terminations, locate financial assistance to help pay utility bills, and how to otherwise confront utility problems. It is designed for consumers and those in front-line positions who help individuals with any number of consumer, financial, or family problems. Such front-line workers include: social workers at government and private agencies and hospitals; advocates for the elderly; legal services staff; those who work for housing agencies; and fuel assistance and weatherization agency employees. We hope that even experienced utility advocates will find something of value in this volume as well.

WHAT TYPES OF UTILITY SERVICES DOES THIS BOOK COVER?

This book focuses on gas and electric service—the services that many people use to heat, cool, and light their homes and run various appliances. Although water and telephone service are covered, there is less extensive discussion of them. Every state in the country regulates, in one form or another, gas and electric companies, and those state regulations contain important consumer protections. By becoming more familiar with state regulations and protections, consumers and their advocates will be able to solve many (but by no means all) of the utility problems they encounter.

Chapter 1 is an overview of the nature of gas and electric utility regulation. Chapter 2 is about obtaining service, including deposit requirements, the use of "credit scoring" to determine deposit amounts, and requirements that bills be cleared up from prior addresses. Chapter 3 explains how to reduce utility bills by applying for fuel assistance, discount rates (where available), weatherization assistance, and assistance from other programs. Chapter 4 examines the often very powerful protections against termination of utility service that exist in most states. Chapter 5 discusses late fees and service restoration fees. Chapter 6 explains how consumers and their advocates can assert rights before state public utility commissions.

Chapter 7 addresses telephone and water service. In general, there are fewer rules governing telephone service than for gas and electric service. As for water service, a large percentage of consumers are served by municipal or other local governmental water agencies, which, as a general rule, are not regulated by state public utility commissions. Therefore, the discussion of the rights of water customers in this guide is limited.

Finally, Chapter 8 briefly discusses "deliverable" fuels and their protections: home heating oil, propane, wood, and coal. Few regulations anywhere in the country cover these fuels and there are therefore few protections.

We caution those who use this book that rules governing utility service vary quite widely by state. It is therefore impossible to provide detailed advice that applies in every state. When using this book, you should make sure to check the local rules in your state; this book provides advice on how to do that. The appendices at the end of this guide provide a great deal of useful information. Appendix C.3 contains a list of each of the state utility regulatory commissions, including contact information. Most states' utility commission web pages provide links to the regulations governing billing and terminations, or at least a summary with cross-references where you can find the complete regulations. In addition, Appendix E.1 contains citations to each state's utility regulations, as well as links to the websites where they can be found. While we cannot adequately describe the regulations in each of the 50 states in this one book, the chapters and appendices should provide a roadmap that will help consumers and advocates in every state develop strategies to address utility problems.

Anyone interested in a more detailed discussion of the topics covered in this guide should use National Consumer Law Center, *Access To Utility Service* (3d ed. 2004 and Supp.), which may be ordered on-line at www. consumerlaw.org. That website also contains information about NCLC's utility and energy initiatives, by clicking on "action agenda."

We welcome any comments you may have about this book, sent to publications@nclc.org or by phone at 617-542-8010.

1

An Overview of Utility Service and Regulation

Gas and electric service in the United States is primarily regulated by state-level Public Utility Commissions (PUCs),[1] not by the federal government. In every state, Investor Owned Utilities (IOUs), which are private and quite often large corporations, are much more closely regulated than municipally-owned or other government-owned entities (known as munis) or rural electric cooperatives (known as co-ops). IOUs include Pacific Gas & Electric (PG&E) in California, Commonwealth Edison (ComED) in Illinois, Consolidated Edison (ConEd) in New York, and the Southern Company in the South. PUCs generally regulate the rates and consumer practices of the IOUs. Based on the assumption that *publicly owned* entities do not need to be regulated by the state, however, the PUCs almost never regulate munis' or co-ops' rates and regulate few, if any, of their consumer practices.[2] This book therefore focuses primarily on the rules that apply to IOUs.

While large IOUs are owned by their stockholders, just like any other corporation, they are considered "public" utilities because they are obliged to serve the public pursuant to rates and rules approved by the state PUC. Public utilities are required to provide service to every member of the public within their service territories, except when specific rules allow them to deny service. This is the case, for example, with rules allowing them to refuse service to customers who refuse to pay a reasonable deposit or who fail to clear up a bill for prior utility service.

Historically, most utility companies were granted a "monopoly franchise" or license to serve an exclusive geographic area, in exchange for which the utility was generally required to serve all customers. For example, a family

1

that lives within Alabama Power's service territory can only purchase its electric power from Alabama Power. No other company is allowed to sell electricity to residential customers in its territory. The rates of companies that have a monopoly franchise are set by the state PUC, and many of their customer practices are also regulated: how much they can charge as an up-front deposit; the types of payment plans they must offer customers; and the timing of termination notices.

In approximately a dozen states, electric utilities have undergone what is usually called restructuring or deregulation.[3] To understand what restructuring means, it is important to understand the difference between electric generation service and electric distribution service, and how they can be provided separately. Until the 1990s, utility companies almost always provided generation and distribution services bundled as a single package. The utility would own both the power plants that generated the electricity, whether these were coal, oil, nuclear or hydroelectric plants, and also provide all of the related distribution services: building and maintaining the lines that transport the power from the power plants and distributing power to homes and businesses; reading meters and sending bills; answering phone calls and providing customer service; and keeping up with maintenance and repairs.

In California, Massachusetts, New York, Texas, and elsewhere, utility companies have been either required or allowed to divest their power plants, that is, sell them off to independent, unregulated owners. The utility companies still remain in the distribution business—delivering power to houses and businesses, reading meters and sending bills, etc.—but they now buy power on the wholesale market. This is similar to a restaurant that does not own its own farm or greenhouse and buys its produce on the wholesale market before delivering meals to customers. For those familiar with the crisis in the California electricity markets around 2001, restructuring resulted in that state's major utilities selling off their generation plants and then having to buy power in the wholesale market.[4] When prices in the wholesale market skyrocketed, utilities were forced to double or even triple their prices. One large utility, PG&E, was forced into bankruptcy.

While all of this may seem very abstract to consumers in states that have not restructured their electricity markets, real and adverse affects have resulted for consumers in states that have. Consumers living in states that have restructured may be allowed or even required to choose from among a number of "competitive" generation suppliers. Those consumers should choose carefully after learning about each company's prices, deposit requirements, and billing terms.

➡ **POINTER:** Find out from your state utility commission whether consumers who stay with their original regulated company instead of choosing a new, competitive supplier gain additional protections.

In many of the states that have restructured, the state capped rates for residential customers for a set period of time. In almost every restructured state, the PUC (and sometimes the state energy or consumer affairs office) will have information describing the restructuring process and choices available to consumers, both on the Internet and in printed brochures.

2

Issues in Obtaining Service

Deposits, Prior Bills,
Bills of Others
(Landlords, Prior Occupants,
or Family Members),
Identification Questions,
and Line Extensions

WHEN DEPOSITS ARE REQUIRED AND
ALTERNATIVES TO DEPOSITS

Utilities in every state except Massachusetts may require applicants and existing customers to pay a security deposit in order to receive utility service. They do so as a means of assuring payment for the utility services they provide. Deposit regulations vary in their specifics from state to state, but most permit utilities to require applicants and customers having payment-related issues to pay deposits in order to receive or continue to receive utility service.[1]

Arkansas' deposit regulation is typical.[2] It allows utilities to require a deposit if the applicant:

- Cannot provide satisfactory payment history for the same kind of service during the previous 12 months;
- Has an undisputed past-due unpaid account for previous utility service;
- Did not pay bills from the utility by the close of business on the due date either twice in a row or three times in the last 12 months;

- Gave the utility two or more checks for previous service within the preceding 12 month period that were returned unpaid for reasons other than bank error;
- Experienced a suspension of service during the last 24 months for non-payment of any undisputed past-due bills;
- Misrepresented his or her identity in obtaining service;
- Failed to reimburse the utility for damages due to negligent or intentional acts or obtained, diverted, or used service without the utility's authorization or knowledge; or
- Provided materially false information that is relevant to the conditions of obtaining service upon application for service or within the preceding two-year period.

Although the specifics may vary, most state regulations include some or all of the above provisions.

In addition to utility payment history, utilities often consider other factors when assessing a customer's creditworthiness: an applicant's record of home ownership or purchase; proof of regular income; and, increasingly, applicants' commercial credit reports, which is discussed below. Missouri's regulation provides a good example. It states that credit can be established with a record of home ownership or purchase, a record of one year of full-time employment or an adequate, regular source of income, or references from commercial creditors.[3] However, at least several state regulations specifically prohibit utilities from determining creditworthiness based on some of the above-mentioned factors.[4] Furthermore, the federal Equal Credit Opportunity Act (ECOA) prohibits utilities from demanding a deposit on the basis of an applicant's race, color, religion, national origin, sex, marital status, age, or income based in whole or in part on a public assistance program (including SSI, TANF, and LIHEAP).[5] Consumers who believe their utility is requiring deposits on the basis of any or all of these prohibited factors should contact a legal services attorney.

UTILITIES' USE OF CREDIT SCORES TO DETERMINE WHETHER TO REQUIRE A DEPOSIT

One serious downside to modern technology and the growth of data harvesting industries is that utilities can now easily and quickly access a consumer's credit history. While credit scores have traditionally been used to determine whether to grant and how much to charge for mortgages, car loans, and credit cards, utilities are now turning to credit scores for determining payment risk. But there are issues with the appropriateness of using commercial credit scores to determine credit risk in the utility context,[6] including the facts that credit reports are notorious for including errors and that consumers have a tendency to treat utility bills differently than other types of debt. A handful of states have rules that specifically prohibit or restrict the use of credit scores for determining whether utilities are allowed to ask for a deposit.[7]

Unless state regulations specifically allow the use of credit scores, one could argue that the use of credit scores to determine whether to require a deposit is prohibited. If a credit score triggers a deposit requirement, the utility should be required, under the federal fair credit reporting law, to provide consumers with a notice that its decision was based, at least in part, on a credit report and the name of the credit bureau that issued the report.[8] This right exists so that consumers can check their credit reports to make sure they are accurate and to dispute inaccurate information.

HOW DEPOSITS ARE CALCULATED

Utility regulations typically provide that a deposit is not to exceed an estimated charge for two to three months of service. Quite a few utilities allow customers to pay deposits in monthly installments.[9] While regulations regarding payment of deposits in installments vary, a typical installment-related provision may permit customers to pay deposits in three consecutive monthly installments: 50% in the first month followed by two equal 25% payments in the second and third months. Keep in mind that deposit requirements may be more flexible for elders,[10] low-income consumers,[11] and during the winter months.[12]

LIMITS ON DEPOSIT COLLECTION
AND RETENTION

Utility deposit regulations generally place limitations on utilities with respect to how the utility collects and keeps customers' deposits. Although state utility deposit regulations vary, most require that utilities:

7

- Keep records of deposits and issue receipts for those deposits to their customers;
- Return deposits within a time period specified by regulation if the customer has maintained a good payment record; and
- Pay interest on the deposit at a specified rate.

Some utilities will honor a customer's request to return a deposit early when the customer making the request has a good payment record.

Questions to Ask When Confronting a Deposit-Related Issue:

- **Utility payment history:** How far back can the utility look? Are the utility's payment history records accurate?
- **Credit score:** Which credit agency did the utility use? What was the customer's credit score? What is the minimum credit score necessary to avoid a deposit? Is the credit report accurate?
- **If you are an elder, receive public assistance, or the utility is seeking a deposit during the winter months:** Are there special rules that limit or prohibit a deposit request?
- **Maximum deposit:** What is the maximum deposit the utility can require and how is it calculated?
- **Installments:** Can the deposit be paid in installments?
- **Return of deposit:** How soon and under what conditions will the utility return the deposit?

ALTERNATIVES TO DEPOSIT

Instead of a deposit, some utilities accept the signature of a cosigner (sometimes called a "guarantor") who agrees to be responsible for payments that the utility consumer fails to make. However, this approach must be carefully considered by the co-signer or guarantor because this person will be liable for the unpaid bills. Another limited alternative to the barrier of paying a deposit is to seek housing where the utilities are included in the rent.

BILLS OWED BY OTHERS OR
FROM PRIOR ADDRESSES

Utilities often refuse an applicant's request for new service because of a debt the applicant owes from another address or because of bills the utility believes are due from another household member such as a roommate, relative, or spouse. Similarly, utilities often deny tenants service because of a landlord or prior tenant's unpaid bills. It is therefore crucial that applicants for service be aware of their rights in these situations.

➡ **POINTER:** If the company denies you service at a new address, find out why. If the reason is that you owe for utility service at a prior address, ask the company if you can make a payment plan on that amount or pay a deposit to get your service turned on, instead of having to pay the old bill in full immediately. If you do not get a satisfactory answer from the company, call your Public Utility Commission's consumer division for help. To find your local Public Utility Commission, go to Appendix C.3 at the back of this guide.

Bills from a Prior Address. Traditionally, some states do not allow a utility to deny an applicant service at a new address based on the fact that the applicant owes a bill for service at a prior address.[13] However, most state utility regulations permit utilities either to deny service to, or require a deposit from, an applicant who has unpaid utility bills from a prior address.[14] Despite the regulations, many of those states will still provide utility service at the new address if the consumer pays off the unpaid amount, the consumer enters into a payment plan to repay the past-due amount (sometimes called an "arrearage"), or shows that he or she has a legitimate dispute regarding the past-due amount pending at the Commission.

Bills of the Landlord or Prior Occupant. The law in most states is clear that a utility company cannot deny an applicant new service simply because there is an amount due either from a prior unrelated occupant of the dwelling[15] or from the owner of the property.[16] In the case of a landlord's failure to pay the utility bills, tenants typically have the right to notice of the delinquency and pending termination have the right to request service in their own name.[17] Some states allow for receivership[18] (where a judge appoints another entity, a "receiver," to collect rent and manage and maintain the building) and rent withholding.[19] If the utility denies service on these bases, contact the Public Utility Commission's consumer division. To find your local Public Utility Commission, go to Appendix C.3 at the back of this guide.

Bills of a Roommate, Spouse, or Household Member. The rules about denial of service because of the debt of a roommate, spouse, or household member are a little more varied. Many states follow the rule that a utility cannot deny an applicant service based on someone else's debt, whether that third party is a completely unrelated prior tenant or a close family member. However, several state Public Utility Commissions (PUCs) have adopted rules which allow the utilities to collect bills owed by an applicant's roommate, spouse, or household member before starting new service.[20] For example, the PUC may allow the utility to collect the third party's debt if the applicant and third party lived at a prior address together and also will be living at the new address together.[21] Similarly, the utility may be allowed to collect the debt owed by the spouse of the applicant from a prior address.[22] Since the rules regarding when a utility can deny service based on a debt owed by the applicant's roommate or spouse vary by state, customers who face this problem should contact the PUC's consumer division and ask what the state's rules provide.[23] To find your Public Utility Commission, go to Appendix C.3 at the back of this guide.

IDENTIFICATION ISSUES

Most utility companies require applicants for new utility service to verify their identities, although the practices vary widely. In some instances, a utility may accept the customer's request for new service over the phone, with the customer simply stating his or her name and address as sufficient proof of identity. This may be particularly true at addresses and in neighborhoods where customers have generally paid their bills in the past. However, some companies may require a written application, a Social Security number (SSN), and other proof of identity before establishing service. Such requirements are particularly likely if the company believes that person owes for service at a prior address, or simply if the person is applying for service in a neighborhood where many customers have bad payment histories.[24]

Public Utility Commissions rarely have rules that specifically address what type of proof of identity a company may require. For example, the Wisconsin Public Service Commission has detailed rules about the deposits that may be required from customers seeking new service,[25] but the rules are silent about an applicant for service having to prove his or her identity. Similarly, Texas has detailed rules governing "Requests for Service"[26] that address how quickly a company must respond to a request to initiate service and the circumstances in which a company must extend its electric or gas lines to serve a

---

Three Things Applicants for Utility Service Should Know About Proof of Identity

1. There is generally no requirement that an applicant for service be a lawful resident of the United States to obtain service. This is important because many applicants who do not legally reside in the country are fearful about applying for anything that requires proof of legal status.

2. We are aware of no state that requires a customer to produce a Social Security number even though many companies routinely request this because they find it a useful identifier. This is again especially important information for immigrants who do not have Social Security numbers and legal status in this country.

3. An applicant for new service should be able to prove identity through any reasonable means: driver's license, passport, ID card provided by a government benefits program, etc. *If the utility company is asking for a form of identification that is not available, the applicant should contact the Public Utility Commission's consumer division for assistance.* The applicant should explain that he or she has reasonable proof of identification and that the company is insisting on some other form of ID, and should ask the consumer division to direct the company to accept the customer's available proof of ID. To find your local Public Utility Commission, go to Appendix C.3 at the back of this guide.

---

new customer. But those rules are silent on what, if anything, a customer must do to establish his or her identity. New Jersey represents one of a small number of states whose rules address the types of identification that a utility may require an applicant to produce.[27]

Often, states establish their policies not through regulations but through individual cases, a practice which makes it more difficult for consumers to learn about their rights. For example, the New York PUC has formally adopted regulations that allow a utility to "establish non-discriminatory procedures to require an applicant to provide reasonable proof of the applicant's identity" and to deny service "to applicants who fail to provide reasonable proof of identity."[28] However, those regulations do not define what is "reasonable proof" of identity. In a 1998 decision, the Commission ruled that companies cannot insist on obtaining only one particular form of identification, SSNs, and must be flexible in accepting any reasonable proof of identity, such as driver's licenses, Resident Alien Cards, public assistance registration cards, etc.[29] Unfortunately, there is no way of knowing if utilities routinely comply with this old order, and individual consumers would have a hard time locating it even if they knew it existed.

11

A similar situation exists in Iowa. Iowa utilities were routinely refusing to provide utility service to customers who would not produce a Social Security number. When customers complained that requiring SSNs was unfair and not specifically allowed by the rules, the PUC orally responded that companies could not require SSNs. It further urged customers to complain if any company demanded SSNs. The problem, of course, is that customers do not know that companies cannot demand SSNs if the PUC does not say so in its own rules. Few customers will therefore know to complain.

Whether or not a PUC's rules or decisions directly authorize companies to request proof of identity, the companies will often do so as a matter of practice, unless the Commission has explicitly prohibited it. In some cases, the company will have included the identification requirement in its "tariffs."[30]

LINE EXTENSION CHARGES

In most states, an electric or gas company can refuse to provide service to an applicant where there is not a gas or electric line close to the applicant's house. In many areas of the country there simply is no gas service, and companies are not required to extend their gas lines into parts of the state where there have never been gas lines. (This is a much less common problem for people seeking electric service.) Even where there are gas or electric lines somewhat nearby the applicant's house (say, one hundred yards away), most states have some rule that allows the company to charge a "line extension" fee if the company would have to extend its existing lines to provide service to the applicant.[31] (Alternatively, the details about how close an applicant must be to the nearest line to get service without paying a line extension charge may be included in each company's tariffs,[32] depending on the state.) Customers who live beyond the distance where connections must be provided for free will either have to pay the line extension fee or go without utility service.

3

How to Get Help Paying or Lowering Your Bills

ELECTRIC, GAS, AND HOME-HEATING FUELS (OIL, PROPANE, WOOD, ETC.)

Introduction. Home heating assistance comes in a variety of different forms and from many different sources. Consumers having difficulty paying for heating their homes should investigate each of the programs and sources discussed below and apply for help.

Every state has programs for low-income consumers who need help paying bills related to home heating, whether the source of heat is electricity, natural gas, heating oil, propane, or any other fuel. Another source of heating assistance offered by many states is discounted rates to low-income consumers for gas and electric service. Finally, some states and utility companies have programs that offer services that will help reduce the wasteful use of energy, which in turn reduces bills and actually increases comfort.

LIHEAP.[1] The Low Income Home Energy Assistance Program (LIHEAP) is a federal program that makes *actual* payments for qualified low-income consumer's heat-related bills. In some states, LIHEAP will help with cooling as well. While the federal government provides most of the funding for LIHEAP, individual states establish the rules about who is eligible and about how payments are made. Therefore the rules and application procedures may be slightly different from state to state.

Most states decide who can receive LIHEAP payments based on household income. In order to qualify for LIHEAP assistance, most states require that household income must be at or below 150% of the federal poverty level (roughly $29,000 for a family of four as of 2005). But, in some states maximum eligibility might be higher (for example, 200% of the poverty level) or lower (for example, 125% of the poverty level). To find out what your state requires for LIHEAP assistance or to apply for LIHEAP assistance, contact your local LIHEAP office by using the contact information in Appendix C.2 at the back of this guide. To review the federal poverty levels, go to Appendix F at the back of this guide.

➡ **POINTER:** Consumers having difficulty paying their heating costs should apply for LIHEAP even if they are not certain whether they are eligible.

A large percentage of families who receive LIHEAP have *earned income,* in other words, they are working households who do not receive any other form of government assistance. Too many households exclude themselves from applying even though they may in fact be eligible. LIHEAP serves elders and young people, families and single people, those who receive government assistance, and those who work but whose earnings are low. In many states, families who are not citizens and whose legal status in the U.S. is unresolved are still able to receive LIHEAP payments.

Depending on the state's rules, LIHEAP assistance may come in two different forms:

- A one-time payment to a utility company or heating oil dealer; or
- Several payments over the course of the winter as bills become due.

Some states may even make payments to landlords, if heat is included as part of rent.

Furthermore, because electricity is needed for the thermostat and heating system controls, some states may direct some of the payments toward electric bills even where the heating system uses oil or natural gas. In those circumstances, it is important for the consumer to budget how much of the LIHEAP assistance should be used on electric bills, rather than on heating fuel bills. (In some states, consumers may not have this choice; the LIHEAP agency will decide how to divide the payments.)

The overall amount of the LIHEAP payments varies widely, from as low as $150 to $200 per household to as high as $800 to $1,000 per household. Northern states tend to offer higher payments; southern and western states tend to offer lower payments. States are also required to offer payments for so-called "energy crisis intervention," which means that the state must offer the consumer assistance within 18 to 48 hours, depending on how serious the consumer's crisis is.

While the federal government provides LIHEAP grants directly to the 50 states, most states make arrangement with more local agencies (usually called "community action agencies," "community action programs," or CAPs) to accept applications and make the LIHEAP payments.

To find out where to apply for fuel assistance in your area

- Call the LIHEAP program in your area listed at the back of this guide in Appendix C.2.
- Ask your local utility company for this information. Utility companies are often in contact with the agencies that offer LIHEAP in their areas.
- Contact the National Energy Assistance Referral service (NEAR), a free service for persons who want information on where to apply for LIHEAP help. NEAR can be contacted by e-mail at energyassistance@ncat.org (please include your city, county, and state in your message) or by using NEAR's toll-free phone number 1-866-674-6327 (or 1-866-NRG-NEAR).

LOW-INCOME WEATHERIZATION AND ENERGY EFFICIENCY PROGRAMS

Introduction. Many low-income households live in older and sometimes poorly maintained homes and apartments. Energy bills in these homes may be higher than necessary because of air leaks from cracks and openings around windows and doors or from poorly sealed attics and basements. A poorly insulated home means a less comfortable home in both winter and summer. However, consumers can take some steps to better insulate their homes, which can reduce heating and cooling costs.

By properly maintaining heating and cooling equipment, adequately insulating roofs and walls, lowering the thermostat on the water heater as well as insulating it, and, where possible, installing energy efficient appliances, consumers can make better use of the energy that they are purchasing.

Consumers should be very cautious before investing more than a few dollars in any weatherization or conservation efforts with a contractor, however. While it might make sense in the long run for households with extra cash, it is often not the wisest use of funds for households that are struggling to pay for rent and food. To know whether an energy conservation investment is a good use of money, you must analyze the cost of the investment against how

15

long you expect to live in this residence and your anticipated energy savings. This type of analysis should be done by an expert.

Government Sponsored Weatherization Programs. The Low Income Weatherization Assistance Program (WAP) is funded by the federal government and administered by the federal Department of Energy. (In some states, a portion of the LIHEAP funds is sent directly to WAP so that more homes can be weatherized.) Similar to the LIHEAP program, each state designs and implements its own WAP using the federal funds provided. States often contract with the same community action agencies that run LIHEAP programs to deliver WAP services at the local level, although some states contract with housing agencies to deliver WAP services. As with LIHEAP, consumers must be income-eligible to receive weatherization assistance, which in many states means that a consumer's income will need to be at or below 150% of the federal poverty level (although some states go as high as 200% of the poverty level or a little higher). To find out what your state requires for WAP assistance or to apply for WAP assistance, contact your local WAP office using the information in Appendix C.1 at the back of this guide. To review the federal poverty levels, go to Appendix F at the back of this guide.

One major difference between WAP and LIHEAP is that WAP generally has a waiting list in most areas. Many states will have priorities for the elderly, families with young children, or households with very large heating bills.

➡ **POINTER:** It is still worth applying even if you will be placed on a waiting list.

Consumers often assume that they cannot receive weatherization assistance if they rent their house or apartment rather than own it. This is not true. While there are somewhat different rules, *renters are still eligible* to receive weatherization assistance and should apply.

Weatherization can make a huge difference. Detailed studies have shown that families who receive weatherization assistance see their heating usage decrease by an average of 30%. In a cold state, this can reduce annual heating bills by $600 or more.

Many states add their own funds to increase the amount of money that is available to weatherize low-income homes. Also, many gas and electric utilities offer their own low-income energy efficiency programs. These utility programs can take two basic forms: (1) the utility may give money directly to the same agencies that administer the federal WAP assistance, and thus just "piggy back" on the federal program by adding more dollars; or (2) the local utility may offer services that WAP does not offer in a particular state or local area, such as replacing old and inefficient refrigerators or installing energy-efficient lighting.

Find Out Where to Get More Information About WAP:

Appendix C.1 at the back of this guide includes contact information for each state's weatherization assistance program. Similarly, the Department of Energy has an easy-to-use website for learning more about WAP in each state. If you have access to the web, go to www.eere.energy.gov/weatherization/state_contacts.html. You will find a map of the U.S. with links to each state's WAP office and information on where to apply for the program.

Discounts on Electric and Natural Gas Rates. Many states require some or all of their natural gas and electric companies to offer discounted rates to consumers, while some companies around the country now offer low-income discounted rates voluntarily. The discounts may be offered to a broadly-defined group of low-income households (for example, all customers with incomes at or below 150% of the poverty level), or to customers who already receive some form of government assistance (for example, LIHEAP), or to low-income elders. While the discounts vary quite widely in their precise terms, there are a few basic types:

- *Your bill is reduced by a certain percentage.* Often, this type of percentage discount only applies to a small portion of your bill. For example, the company may reduce your bill by 10%. However, percentage discounts often apply *only* to the distribution or base rate charges on your bill, not to the actual "cost of fuel" or "cost of gas" charges. Distribution or base rate charges are the company's non-fuel costs, in other words, the costs of billing, reading meters, answering customer calls, making repairs, performing maintenance, and operating trucks and equipment. Cost of fuel charges cover the cost of fuels burned in electric power plants; cost of gas charges cover the cost of natural gas the utility purchases for its customers. Percentage discounts rarely apply to cost of fuel or cost of gas charges. The bottom line is that percentage discounts *do* give consumers a discount, but it is usually a small one.
- *You are billed at on a separate, low-income rate.* Many companies use a completely separate and lower rate for their eligible low-income consumers.

17

■ *You are required to pay a percentage of your income toward your bill.* A few states have taken a much more detailed approach to offering lower rates to low-income consumers based on their actual need. For example, a state may decide that low-income households should not pay more than 3% of their income on electric bills and 5% of their income on gas (heating) bills. If the household has $10,000 in income annually, the household would only be required to pay $300 annually for electricity and $500 for gas. In these states, the utility would have to collect the balance due from LIHEAP or other sources.

There are a few ways to find out if companies in your area offer low-income discount rates

1. The easiest way is to call your local electric or gas company and ask. Most companies also place this type of information on their web pages.

2. Contact your state utility commission. Appendix C.3 at the back of this guide contains contact information for each state utility commission. Many state utility commissions include information about discount rates on their web page and may be able to provide information on discount rates over the phone.

3. Go to the NCAT LIHEAP website, where there is a listing of many state and local utility discount programs: www.liheap.ncat.org/Supplements/2004/supplement04 .htm. If there is a dollar amount listed in the "utility rate assistance" column, then discount rates are probably offered in your state. Be aware, however, that there may be additional utility discount programs in your state that are not listed in the "utility rate assistance" column.

Self-Help Weatherization and Water Conservation. If you are unable to find or qualify for any of programs through your utility or the government, there are still a number of practices which may help reduce your usage. In some situations, people are surprised how much these relatively inexpensive procedures reduce energy and water bills.

On a windy day check for leaks of air around your windows and doors. You can use a lit stick of incense to detect leaks around windows and doors by moving the stick around the frame and watching to see if there is any wind blowing the smoke.

If you are a tenant, try to get the landlord to fix these leaks properly. If the landlord does not fix the problems, or you own your own home, try a number of homespun fix-ups.

■ Use caulk or weather stripping for air leaks around windows. In the winter you can seal windows with heavy-duty clear plastic sheets or clear plastic film. In a pinch you could use clear plastic tape to seal the cracks.

■ For leaks around doors, leave a rolled up towel next to the bottom of the door. If necessary, to stop leaks around the top and sides of doors, use weather stripping or tack up a blanket or large towel.

■ If there are holes in the walls, try to plug them up by stapling plastic sheeting over the holes and caulking the edges of the plastic. You will be surprised how much warmer a house or apartment can be without the heat loss from cracks between openings and walls.

■ If you have a fireplace, make sure the flue is tightly closed. As the home warms up, you can consider turning down the heat.

■ Turn off lights and heat or cooling when not at home.

■ Close the door for any rooms you are not using, and don't try to heat or cool them.

Toilets are often the largest source of water use inside a home. Leaks from the toilet and the faucet waste water and money. Remember that your sewer bill is generally determined by how much water you consume. By saving water, you are saving twice—on your water and your sewer bill. Your water utility may provide free toilet leak detection kits. You can also purchase several inexpensive leak detection dye tablets at the hardware store. The hardware usually necessary to fix a toilet leak can cost from just a few dollars to around $20.00. If you have water leaks that you can not afford to fix, call your water company. Many water companies have programs that assist homeowners with low-cost plumbing problems.

Turn off the water while you are brushing your teeth.

➡ **POINTER:** If you think that your home or apartment is wasting a lot of energy, whether due to an old heating system or drafty doors and windows, you should apply for assistance from the Low Income Weatherization Assistance Program (WAP).

TELEPHONE BILLS

Low-income households in every state are eligible for the federally-mandated Lifeline and Link-Up programs. Lifeline is designed to reduce the monthly cost of having basic landline service. Link-up is designed to reduce the initial, one-time charge a family pays to install landline phone service. Each state gets a certain amount of money from the federal program and must offer a minimum level of discount to eligible consumers. But many states supplement the federal Lifeline program with their own low-income telephone assistance program, which results in even larger discounts.

➡ **POINTER:** In general, you will pay about $10 less each month for your basic phone service if you qualify for Lifeline and your state does not offer additional assistance. In states that do offer extra assistance, the discount may be almost $20 per month.

➡ **POINTER:** Special rules apply to low-income residents of tribal lands, where the Lifeline and Link-Up discounts are even larger.

Where to Go for More Information About Lifeline & Link-Up:

- *Call your local phone company.* Local phone companies can be a helpful resource for information about Lifeline and Link-Up. However, be aware that some companies might make it difficult to apply for Lifeline/Link-Up. Don't stop here if you don't get your questions answered.
- *Contact your state utility commission.* Most utility commissions can quickly tell you which companies offer Lifeline and Link-Up discounts. Use Appendix C.3 at the back of this guide to locate information about your utility commission. If the person answering the phone isn't sure how to transfer your call, ask for the "consumer division" or "customer assistance" staff, or the "rates" division.
- *Contact the Universal Services Administrative Company.* The Universal Services Administrative Company administers the federal Lifeline and Link-Up funds. Go to their website at www.lifelinesupport.org, where you will find a map of the U.S. with links to participating phone companies in each state; then, under the heading "Low-income households," click on "Find a Service Provider in Your State." Consumers without web access can call (888) 641-8722 for more information.

WATER BILLS AND WATER CONSERVATION

Assistance Programs. There is no federal program that provides assistance to low-income households for their water bills. There are a very small number of water utilities that provide low-income water rate discounts. This may change as water bills start to increase to help pay for maintenance and replacement of aging pipes and treatment facilities as well as new treatment technologies.

➡ **POINTER:** Call your local water company to see if there are any discount rates available, but the answer will often be "no."

Crisis Funds. There are also local *fuel funds* and, in some areas, *water funds* that raise charitable donations from utility customers, utility shareholders, and other private and corporate donors. These crisis funds help households that do not qualify for LIHEAP or who need additional help paying energy or water bills. Fuel fund programs are run by a range of organizations including government agencies, non-profit organizations, the Salvation Army, community action agencies, and religious organizations. While most of these funds will only make payments on electricity, natural gas, or home heating oil bills, it is possible that the fund would occasionally make payments on water bills. The best way to find out if there is a fuel fund in your area is to ask the local fuel assistance agency or local utility company.

Conservation and Maintenance. On average, almost 3,500 gallons of water per person are wasted each year due to leaks in the home. While one study found that two-thirds of homes lost around 10 gallons or less of water each day due to leaks, a small number of homes were responsible for most of the water lost to leaks. Water companies, especially those in areas where water is scarce, may offer free leak detection (for example, dye tablets to test for leaks in the toilet) and water conservation devices (for example, low-flow showerheads, faucet aerators, and bags for toilet tanks so that they use less water to flush).

➡ **POINTER:** If you pay for your water, ask your local water company for information on water conservation and for any programs they offer, such as free faucet aerators or low-flow showerheads.

OTHER PROGRAMS THAT MAY OFFER HELP

There are other programs that may be used to cover utility bills where the household is facing disconnection of services. However, these programs vary widely from state to state and even from locality to locality within a state. There is no certainty that these programs are available in your area, so you will have to check with local agencies or offices.

- The *Federal Emergency Management Agency (FEMA) Emergency Food and Shelter Program (EFSP)* may, under certain circumstances, provide funds for up to one month's utility payment. FEMA funds may be administered by the same agency that administers fuel assistance (LIHEAP) in your area, by some other non-profit agency, or by your local city, town, or county government. The agency that administers FEMA-EFSP funds has wide discretion in determining how the FEMA-EFSP funding is to be used in the community. In most areas, your local fuel assistance agency will be able to tell you who administers FEMA-EFSP in your community.

- *State domestic violence agencies, and non-profit agencies that work with domestic violence victims,* sometimes help domestic violence victims set up new apartments or homes away from the abuser. Those agencies may offer assistance for paying off old utility bills so that the person can move into a new apartment and get utility service there. If you are a victim of domestic violence and an agency is helping you, ask if they have funds available for utility bills.

- *State child welfare, social services, and human services agencies* may also have access to discretionary funds to help families avoid eviction, or to help house families who have been evicted. Sometimes these funds can be used to pay utility bills. If you or anyone in your family is a client of one of your state's child welfare, social services, or human services agencies, you should ask whether that agency has any funds available to help pay utility bills.

- *Local churches, temples, and mosques* often have discretionary funds available to help people in need. Sometimes, you do not need to be a member of that religious organization to get help. If your utility service has been terminated or you are facing a termination, ask around in your community to find out if there are any religious groups that offer help on utility bills. Also ask if there are any community or civic organizations that help families with financial problems.

BILLING STRATEGIES TO AVOID LATE FEES

Introduction. You may be able to avoid paying late fees on your bills by making your payments more evenly from month to month using what is called budget billing or levelized payments and by choosing a payment date that is easier for you to meet. However, these strategies will not solve your problem if your bills are simply too high month after month.

Budget Billing or Levelized Payments.[2] Many families incur late fees because they cannot pay their bills on time. Families who live in cold climates often have huge, unaffordable bills in the winter; families in hot climates may have the same problem in the summer.

One billing strategy to help households with their energy bills is called budget billing (or levelized payments). With budget billing, instead of billing for the actual monthly usage, the utility company will send out estimated bills each month for the average monthly bill based on the last year's total charge. In this way higher winter or summer costs are spread out over the course of the year. Usually, at some point during the year, the utility will reconcile the actual usage with the estimated usage so that by the end of the year the consumer is billed for what was actually used. Where estimated bills are greater than the actual bills, the accounts will be credited with the difference. Conversely, where the estimated bills were less than the actual bill, the consumers will be charged for the difference. Almost every company offers budget billing. Call your company to find out the details.

Moving the Due Date of Bills.[3] Some utilities allow consumers whose utility bill comes due before a regular payday to change the payment due date. These plans are sometimes referred to as "preferred payment date" programs. Such plans can help households with very tight cash flows avoid late charges.

▶ **POINTER:** Even if your utility company does not formally offer such a preferred payment date program, call them to see if you can make an arrangement to have your bills arrive on a day of the month when you generally have more cash available.

4

Restrictions on the Termination of Service

STEPS A UTILITY MUST TAKE BEFORE DISCONNECTING SERVICE

Introduction. In most states there are laws that provide a variety of significant protections when utility companies threaten termination of utility service. Many of the larger utilities are regulated by commissions called Public Utility Commissions (PUCs) or Public Service Commissions (PSCs). A regulated utility company can only shut off a customer's service if it has met the requirements set out by these laws and commission rules. When a utility fails to follow correct termination procedure, a customer may demand that the utility start over and re-initiate the entire termination process.

By far the most common cause of utility termination is non-payment of utility bills. Regulations typically permit disconnection for non-payment of bills exceeding a certain amount ($50 or more, for example) or of bills that have been unpaid (sometimes called "in arrears") for more than a specified number of months.

The Payment Period. Utility payments are generally due within a certain number of days after the bill is generated or mailed, depending on the state. This period is called the "payment period." Payment periods vary widely by state.[1] If a customer fails to pay during the payment period, the utility may send a shutoff notice. The shutoff notice must generally be separate from other mailings, be clearly marked as a shutoff notice, be clearly written in English,[2] and contain information about options that could eliminate the need to disconnect service, such as discount programs, payment plan options, and other protections against termination. Additionally, shutoff notices should include information about what to do if the customer is disputing a portion of the bill (see *Non-Payment of Disputed Bills*, later in this chapter) and the process for appealing a termination.

The Termination Notice Period. Once the customer receives the shut-off notice, the termination clock, or "termination notice period," starts. As with payment periods, termination notice periods vary widely among the states. As a result, service termination can occur within as few as 15 days or as many as 40 to 50 days from the time a customer receives a bill.[3]

It is important for advocates to note that many state regulations require utilities to provide repeat written notice, phone notice, or in-person notice prior to disconnecting service.[4] In addition, some states' regulations provide for several extra days when the termination notice is mailed. These additional notice requirements may extend the termination time frame and should figure into termination time-frame calculations.

Limit on the Times or Days When Shut-Offs Can Occur. In general, utilities cannot legally disconnect service during non-business hours (for example, weekends and holidays). As a result, a customer in a state whose termination time frame is 20 days long may actually have 22 days if the 20th day falls on a Saturday. In addition, many states further restrict the hours the utility may disconnect. For example, Maine's rule, which is typical, provides that utilities may disconnect from Monday through Thursday, 8 A.M. through 3 P.M., and may not disconnect on Fridays, on the day of a legal holiday, on the day before a legal holiday, or on a day the utility is closed to the public.[5] These extra limits ensure that a customer whose service is about to be, or has been, disconnected is able to resolve disputes with the utility and get service restored without having to spend a night, weekend, or holiday without service.

Termination Time Frame
Utility sends bill → Payment Period ends without payment → Utility sends Shutoff Notice → Termination Notice Period ends → Final written, phone, or in-person termination notice (required in some states) → Utility many disconnect during specified business hours

When Termination Notices Lose Their Power. Some states' utility regulations provide that termination notices lose their legal power after a given period of time.[6] This is often referred to as "becoming void." In other words, if the utility fails to disconnect within that given time frame, the utility must start the termination notice procedure over again. Generally, a utility that disconnects service after the termination notice has become void must restore service and re-initiate the termination procedure.

Exceptions to Termination Protections. In certain situations, regular disconnection notice provisions do not apply. For example, customers who fail to keep up with payment plans may not be entitled to the standard termination notice period.[7] In addition, many states' regulations permit utilities to terminate service *without any notice* under certain circumstances, including: meter tampering, fraud, circumstances under which continuation of service poses an immediate hazard, and non-compliance with utility rules.

When the Landlord Is Providing Utility Service. Tenants whose landlords are responsible for providing utility service usually have some protections when faced with disconnection due to their landlord's non-payment of utility bills. Almost every state's utility regulations require utilities to notify tenants of impending terminations even when the *landlord* (not the tenant) is the utility's customer. Typical tenant notice provisions require utilities to post termination notices in common areas and/or mail notices to individual tenants. In general, tenants are entitled to the same number of days' notice as their landlord.

➡ **POINTER:** Before you withhold rent, you should contact a legal services attorney or other person knowledgeable in your state's housing law. You may suffer adverse consequences if your state does not allow rent withholding or if you do not carefully follow rent withholding procedures.

In addition to notifying the tenants of an impending disconnection, most state regulations require utilities to notify tenants of their options for continuing service. These options vary according to the way the premises are metered. Meters are the devices the utility uses to measure the amount of energy used by the customer. If the premises are metered individually then customers will usually have the option to continue service in their own name. If the premises are master-metered (in other words, there is one meter for the entire building), the utility will generally provide tenants with the option of continuing service by grouping together to pay new bills as they come due.

This can become complicated in large buildings because it requires tenants to organize and strategize. In either case, whether the premises are individually metered or master metered, tenants who opt to continue their utility service may deduct those payments from their rent in most states.

Finally, tenants are generally not responsible for the landlord's debts to the utility company (sometimes called "arrearages"). Tenants only become responsible for utility payments once they enter into an individual or group agreement with the utility company under which they agree to pay all *future* utility bills.

➡ **POINTER:** Notify the utility company that the landlord is not the person using the utility service.

Utility companies may not always know that the person they send the bills to is a landlord and not necessarily the person using the utility service, especially where smaller buildings are concerned. Tenants who think their landlords have stopped or may stop paying utility bills should consider informing their utility service providers that the landlord is not the person using the utility service in order to prevent service disconnection without notice.

Illegal Shut-Off by Landlord. In most states, landlords who are responsible for providing utility service cannot disconnect their tenants' utility service as a means of evicting them. This type of eviction is called "self-help" eviction and is generally illegal; landlords must go through the courts to evict tenants. Tenants can usually stop self-help evictions by going to court. In addition, tenants may be entitled to recover damages for the landlord's illegal actions. Tenants dealing with landlords engaging in this type of self-help eviction should contact their local legal services office.

NON-PAYMENT OF DISPUTED BILLS

In general, state regulations prohibit utilities from terminating service for non-payment of *disputed* amounts. This prohibition typically continues until the utility resolves the dispute or, if the customer is dissatisfied with a utility's resolution of a dispute and decides to appeal, until the customer has used up all of his or her appeals.

A minority of states' utility regulations provide that customers may be required to put disputed amounts into an escrow account pending dispute resolution.[8] In those states, a customer's failure to place the disputed charges in escrow during the course of a dispute investigation could lead to service termination. Customers disputing a *portion* of a bills must pay the undisputed portions to avoid shutoff. In addition, they should write a note to the utility indicating which portion(s) of the bill the partial payment is intended to cover and the amount in dispute.

OTHER PROTECTIONS AGAINST TERMINATION

Financial Hardship. Many of the restrictions discussed below will only apply in cases where the customer can demonstrate "financial hardship." Financial hardship can usually be shown by providing proof of income below a certain percentage of the federal poverty levels,[9] or proof of receipt of public assistance (including SSI, TANF, and fuel assistance like LIHEAP). More specific information about eligibility and financial hardship application forms should be available directly from the utilities. To review the federal poverty levels, go to Appendix F at the back of this guide.

Serious Illness or Disability.[10] Many utilities will postpone utility disconnection if it would threaten the health or safety of one of the household's occupants. This restriction is often referred to as a serious illness protection. As mentioned above, some states' serious illness provisions may only apply to households experiencing financial hardship. Customers who postpone termination based on the serious illness protections remain responsible for their past and current utility bills and may be required to enter into payment plans as a condition of postponing termination.

Utilities that allow customers to postpone termination of service based on the fact that someone in the household has a serious illness or a disability will require proof of that illness or condition. That proof is usually called "certification."[11] A letter from a licensed physician is generally acceptable. In addition, most utilities also accept certifications from nurses, other licensed health care practitioners, public or private agencies providing mental health care services, public health officials, and, in Delaware, Christian Science practitioners. Furthermore, most utilities will accept an *initial* certification over the telephone on the condition that the professional providing certification mails the utility *written* confirmation within a given period. Determining whether a utility will accept a certification over the phone is especially important when a service termination is imminent.

In general, serious illness certifications are only valid for limited periods of time and usually expire after 30 or 60 days. Customers seeking to continue the postponement must obtain another certification and re-submit it after the initial certification expires. Some utilities limit or prohibit renewal even when the illness persists.[12] To review sample serious illness letters and a sample certification, go to Appendix D at the back of this guide.

➡ **POINTER: About the term "serious illness":** Serious illnesses are not necessarily limited to those that are visible to the outside world or even to those that are life-threatening. On the contrary, chronic illnesses like diabetes or asthma, as well as mental illnesses, may suffice for establishing eligibility for the protection, depending on how the state's serious illness provision is worded. When obtaining a serious illness certification, customers should request that the doctor or health care provider include the term "serious illness" and also inform the doctor of the potential need for re-certifications down the road.

Age-related protections for elders and infants.[13] In addition to the serious illness protections described above, quite a few states have enacted age-related protections. Most of the specific age-related protections apply to elders. Some states' age-related protections are more far-reaching than others, as illustrated by the examples listed below:

- Customers 65 and older shall not have service terminated due to non-payment during the winter months if they sign up for and stick to a payment plan;[14]
- At least five days prior to terminating service to elderly or disabled customers, the utility must submit a written report and investigation to the PUC;[15]
- Utility may not discontinue service to households where all residents are 65 and older without written approval of the PUC.[16]

Not all age-related protections apply to elders, however. At least one state[17] specifically prohibits utilities from disconnecting or refusing to restore a customer's service for non-payment if there is a child under the age of 12 months and service has not been terminated for non-payment before the child's birth.

Furthermore, several states' regulations prohibit the utility from disconnecting service when doing so would threaten the well-being of a member of the household due to age. These more general provisions could be helpful when advocating on behalf of both elderly clients and clients whose households include young children. Finally, remember that customers taking advantage of age-related protections usually have to enter into payment plans as a condition of obtaining the protection. To find out what kind of protections your state has, go to Appendix A.2 at the back of this guide.

➡ **POINTER:** Many states whose regulations provide serious illness or age-related protections also have provisions protecting customers with life-threatening illnesses or customers with disabilities. Examine all of your options. Depending on the nature of the illness and/or disability and your state's particular provisions, use of one type of provision over the other may be preferable.

Special Notification for Elders. A number of states provide elderly customers with special termination notification, which requires the utility to notify the elder or a third-party of the impending termination, either in-person or by phone. In addition, many utilities offer third-party notification programs under which elderly customers may request that shutoff notices be sent to a third-party, often a relative, in addition to the customer. This may be useful if an elderly customer falls behind on bill payment as a result of extended illness or hospitalization.

Cold Weather Protection.[18] Many states have winter utility termination rules in effect that prohibit utilities from terminating or refusing to reinstate services due to non-payment of heat-related utility bills. Most winter protection provisions apply during a several month period, typically from mid-November through mid-April. Although this period is usually set by regulation, Public Utility Commissions will often extend these periods when cold weather starts early or persists. Several states also extend the winter protection rules to 24-hour periods not falling within the winter months for which the national weather service has predicted temperatures of below 32 degrees Fahrenheit. To find out what kind of protections your state has, go to Appendix A.1 at the back of this guide.

Some winter protection provisions apply exclusively to customers who are experiencing financial hardship, while others also apply to households which include children, the elderly, the infirm, or disabled individuals. Almost all winter protection provisions require customers taking advantage of

31

the protection to enter into payment plans as a condition of continued service. Finally, even when the winter protection provisions that prevent utility termination do not apply, perhaps because of lack of financial hardship or because no one in the household is elderly, disabled, or infirm, regulations typically call for enhanced termination notification procedures during those months.

Hot weather protections. A few states also have rules prohibiting service disconnection for 24-hour periods during which the National Weather Service is predicting unusually high temperatures. Eligibility for protection from termination under the hot weather provisions may depend on financial criteria. To find out what kind of protections your state has, go to Appendix A.1 at the back of this guide.

➡ **POINTER: Temporary weather regulations:** Utility commissions often extend cold and hot weather protections when warranted by unusually severe weather conditions. Check with your utility commission to see if they have issued any temporary cold or hot weather moratoria on utility shutoffs. To find your local utility commission, go to Appendix C.3 at the back of this guide.

RIGHT TO A DEFERRED PAYMENT PLAN

Most states require utilities to offer customers the option of entering into a deferred payment plan before shutting off utility service. A typical deferred payment plan requires the customer to pay new bills as they come due while paying a portion of past-due amounts or "arrearages" each month. Some states' utility regulations include specific requirements for entering into payment plans. For example, they may require customers to pay a certain portion of the past-due amount up front and limit the time the customer has to bring the account up to date, most often to a period of 6 or 12 months, or even require the customer to make a showing of financial hardship.[19]

Utilities are generally eager to bring accounts up to date as quickly as possible and they may pressure their customers to enter into aggressive payment plans. However, utilities may be flexible in their payment plan negotiations as long as they are assured some monthly utility payment. For example, they may be willing to:

■ Overlook past-due amounts and/or accept less than the current bill amount for customers whose financial circumstances are dire; or

- Accept different payments each month. For example, seasonal workers may want to pay less toward past-due amounts in the winter and more in the summer, or vice versa.

It is worth noting that some states' utility regulations permit utilities to provide less termination notice to customers who are breaching their payment plans.[20]

➡ POINTER: Only negotiate realistic payment plans!

The utility company may push for a payment plan that requires larger payments than you or your client can afford. Such a plan is not in anyone's best interest. It renews the risk of shutoff and it lessens the utility's hopes of getting any payments at all. Furthermore, many states' utility regulations provide that the utility is not obligated to renegotiate the plan if the customer fails to fulfill her part of the agreement (usually by missing payments).

UTILITIES THAT SELL APPLIANCES

In addition to selling utility service, many utility companies also sell or lease utility appliances such as water heaters and ranges. Non-payment for merchandise is *not* an appropriate reason for the utility to disconnect or refuse to connect utility service.[21] However, many utility companies that sell and lease appliances bill these items together. This type of billing can create problems for customers who cannot afford both payments. For instance, a utility company might apply its customer's utility payments to the appliance portion of the bill rather than to the utility portion thereby creating a past-due amount in the utility portion of the bill. If this happens, customers or their advocates should call the utility and ask them to apply the payment to the utility bill. If the utility refuses, an appeal to the Public Utility Commission may be necessary. Finally, be aware that while non-payment of appliances should not lead to utility disconnection, it could lead to repossession of the appliance. To contact your local Public Utility Commission, use the information in Appendix C.3 at the back of this guide.

BANKRUPTCY

Consumers who are having difficulty paying their utility bills are often experiencing other major financial difficulties. Some will look to bankruptcy for relief.[22] While the bankruptcy law protects these consumers from utility shut-off because of past-due bills and requires the utility to reconnect disconnected utility service, customers will still be responsible for current bills as they come due. Furthermore, it is worth noting that several states' utility regulations permit utility companies to require customers who have filed for bankruptcy to pay a deposit as "adequate assurance" that future bills can be paid. Deciding to seek bankruptcy protection and the actual filing of the petition can be a highly complicated process. Utility customers considering filing for bankruptcy should consult a legal aid attorney or a private attorney specializing in bankruptcy law.

MUNICIPAL UTILITIES

Municipal utilities are agencies or departments of cities or towns that own and provide utility service such as water and electricity. Municipal utilities, while typically not regulated by the state utility commission, are subject to constitutional due process duties. The U.S. Supreme Court, in the case *Memphis Light, Gas and Water Division v. Craft,* held that due process requires a municipal utility to provide its customers with at least notice of the disconnection, the reason for the disconnection, a hearing prior to the termination, and notice of the availability of a procedure for protesting that a proposed termination is unjustified.[23] Because the due process rights and obligations stem from constitutional law as opposed to state law and utility commission rules, you should seek help from a legal services office or a private attorney if you did not receive adequate notice or an opportunity for a hearing.

For other problems with a municipal utility, you should contact your representative in the municipal government and seek his or her help. These problems might include facing a pending disconnection or refusal by the utility to allow you to enter into a reasonable payment plan. If you find more broad-scale problems that affect a large number of consumers, you should consider organizing other constituents to pressure the local government to change how the municipal utility handles consumer issues such as a right to a reasonable payment plan, low-income and vulnerable consumer protections, and extreme-weather shut-off protections.

5

Late Charges and Reconnection Charges

LATE CHARGES

Introduction. Utilities often impose late charges on customers who do not pay their bills on time. Such charges are generally intended to compensate utilities for its costs as a result of the late payment or to provide incentive for households to make timely payments. Many state utility regulations authorize utilities to impose late charges on their late-paying residential customers in the form of a percentage of the unpaid balance. The average late charge is about 1.5% per month but can be as high as 5%.

As mentioned in the previous chapter, the "payment period" can vary from state to state, but one thing all states' payment periods have in common is a final due date. If a customer does not pay his or her bill by the final due date, the utility will often view the bill as "delinquent." When a customer's bill is delinquent, the utility may apply late charges to the customer's bill and can eventually terminate the customer's service. Many states have regulations that require utilities to provide a grace period before a utility can call a bill delinquent. For example, the regulations in Illinois require that the due date printed on the bill must be at least 21 days after the post mark on the bill; if the utility receives the customer's bill by mail 2 days after the due date, the Illinois regulations require the utility to treat the customer's bill as being on time. Illinois has a 2-day grace period for bills the utility receives by mail.[1]

Additionally, most state regulations provide that the payment period begins when the bill is mailed (i.e., postmarked). But, some states provide that the payment period begins when the utility generates the bill.[2] In those states, customers could incur late charges if the utility mails the bill late! A customer who receives a late bill and is assessed late charge should call the utility immediately and request that the late charge be removed.

35

Late Charges on Disputed Bills. As discussed in the previous chapter, most states' regulations prohibit utilities from terminating service for non-payment of *disputed* amounts.[3] Similarly, utilities are prohibited from assessing late fees on disputed amounts. Thus, the utility should not impose a late charge on the portion of the balance that is in dispute and is unpaid.

➡ **POINTER:** Remember, some states' utility regulations do require customers who are disputing their bill to pay the disputed amount into an escrow account pending dispute resolution.[4]

Imposing Late Charges on Unpaid Late Charges, or "Pyramiding."[5] "Pyramiding" is a term used to describe the practice of assessing late payment penalties on other unpaid late charges. Pyramiding can arise in several different scenarios, one of which is prohibited by federal law. Other types may be unlawful under one or more state laws.

Federal law[6] prohibits utilities from assessing a late charge solely because a customer did not pay a previously imposed late charge. For example, Joanne is assessed a $5.00 late charge for failing to pay her $100 January bill within the payment period. Joanne sends her $100 payment late, in early February, and then pays her February bill, also $100, on time. The utility applies the payments as follows:

- The first $100 is applied to the $100 January bill; and
- The second $100 is applied to the late charge ($5) and $95 of the February bill.

Because of the way the utility applies the second payment, the utility assesses another late fee on the unpaid balance ($5) of the February bill. Even if Joanne pays all of her future bills on time and in-full, the utility could continue to impose late charges on the unpaid late charges that accumulate. Note that this type of pyramiding may occur when third parties such as charities and fuel assistance programs are paying current bills but are unwilling to pay unpaid late charges.

Two other kinds of pyramiding may be unlawful under state laws, depending on the consumer's state:

1. State law may prohibit utilities from imposing multiple late charges for the same delinquency. For example, if a customer pays her February, March, April, May, and June bills on time but never pays her January

bill, state law may prohibit the utility from collecting multiple late charges for the January delinquency.

2. State law may prohibit utilities from calculating new late charges using a balance that includes not only past-due amounts but previous late charges as well.

Customers who believe their utility is engaging in one of these types of pyramiding practices should first collect all recent bills or, if those bills are not available, ask the company for a printout of all bills rendered and payments received for the past 6 or 12 months.

➡ POINTER: Contact your local legal services office or other agency that is familiar with state laws governing the pyramiding of late charges.

RESTORING SERVICE AND RECONNECTION CHARGES

Customers whose service has been terminated can get service restored by:

- Eliminating the reason for disconnection (for example, by paying past-due amounts, entering into a reasonable payment plan to pay past-due amounts, or by providing a guarantee of payment from a federal, state, or local agency);
- Showing the utility commission or regulatory authority (for example, the city council if it is a municipal utility) that the disconnection was wrongful; or
- Demonstrating that a legal protection applies to the customer (for example, the household is eligible to benefit from a seasonal, age-related, or income-related restriction against termination).

Many states' regulations require utilities to reconnect service within a certain amount of time once the reason for the disconnection has been fixed, often within 12 or 24 hours. At least one state requires the utility to reconnect service immediately when the disconnection was improper.[7] In addition, at least one state provides that failure to restore service without good cause may result in the utility paying a $25 per day penalty to the customer ($50 a day if the circumstances involve: a medical emergency; service to the elderly, blind, or disabled; heat-related service in the winter; or if the utility had no-tice of risk of serious impairment to the consumer's health and safety).[8]

Most utilities charge a fee to reconnect service. However, utilities may waive or reduce that fee under certain circumstances. For instance, in a New York case, the Public Service Commission approved a settlement agreement that waived a reconnection charge for any customer who agreed to have their utility bill paid directly by their social services provider, or who showed that they were SSI recipients or had received LIHEAP benefits within the prior year.[9] Some Public Utility Commissions or Public Service Commissions may also require that customers be offered a chance to pay these reconnection charges as part of a payment plan.

6

Asserting Consumer Rights at the PUC and Elsewhere

INDIVIDUAL RIGHTS

Introduction. Each of the 50 states has a Public Utilities Commission or PUC.[1] The name of these commissions may vary from state to state. For example some states may have a Public Utility Commission (PUC) while others have a Public Service Commission (PSC). This book refers to all of these commissions as PUCs. All of the PUCs accept complaints from consumers. This chapter provides a road map for how to go about asserting consumer complaints at the PUC and elsewhere.

1. Always Contact the Utility Company Before Going to the PUC. In many states, the first question a customer will hear when calling the PUC's consumer division is: "Have you already called the utility and tried to work this out with them?" You will save yourself time by going to the utility first. However, that does not mean that you should agree with or accept whatever the utility company says. Particularly when trying to negotiate payment plans or deposits, you should remember that you always have the option of going to the PUC. The utility company's goal is to get the highest possible payment or largest deposit. Your goal will often be to get by with a small deposit (or no deposit) or a long-term payment plan. Because the company has the power to shut off service, you may have a hard time insisting on a reasonable payment plan or deposit. You should feel free to say "no" to the company's offer on a payment plan or deposit amount and ask the PUC's consumer division for help negotiating if necessary.

2. Always Be Prepared to Discuss Payment Plan Details and Have Any Necessary Documentation Ready. If the issue is a payment plan amount, make sure you have worked out your budget and expenses *before* you call the company. For example, if you're trying to get a 10 month payment plan on a $1,000 arrearage, make sure you can demonstrate to the company that you can afford to pay $100 a month so that the overdue amount will be paid off in 10 months, and that you cannot afford the $200 a month the company wants. If you can convince the company that you can truly afford to pay the current bills and $100 each month on the arrearage, but that agreeing to pay $200 on the arrearage will guarantee that the payment plan will fail, you're more likely to get the payment plan you're looking for. Similarly, if you're trying to assert a serious illness, make sure that your doctor is willing to send a serious illness certification letter and that you have any other documentation you may need on hand.[2] Finally, if you're raising a dispute about the amount of your bills, make sure you have those bills handy.

3. Find Out Who Handles Complaints at the PUC. Complaints are almost always handled by a division of the PUC with a name like "Consumer Division" or "Consumer Affairs" or, occasionally, "Complaints." The contact information should be on the PUC's web page.[3] Go back to point #2, "always be prepared discuss payment plan details and have any necessary documentation ready," and make sure you have everything you will need to speak to the consumer division. Sometimes, you may need to present the consumer division with some additional documentation after you have spoken to the company, for example, any letter from the company denying your complaint.

4. Don't Give Up! When you contact the utility, you will usually be dealing with a front-line customer service representative (CSR). These CSRs handle dozens of calls daily and are often working from scripts that instruct them how to structure payment plans and deposits. They generally won't deviate from those scripts. If you are not satisfied with the results you get from a front-line CSR, ask to speak to a supervisor or, where available, a "billing specialist" or "credit specialist." These representatives deal with customers having a hard time paying their bills routinely and may (or may not!) be more understanding. Similarly, don't give up with the first person who answers your call at the PUC's consumer division. They, too, have supervisors, and you can ask to speak to a supervisor if you're not getting the result you were hoping for.

5. Look for Someone to Help You. It's not at all unusual to feel intimidated by having to call up the utility company or Public Utilities Commission. You may want to locate someone more experienced in utility matters to provide guidance and support. In some cases—particularly those involving terminations of service and the risk of harm to young children, elders, or the seriously ill—legal services programs, councils on aging, charities, or other non-profit groups may be willing to offer help in calling on behalf of the customer. Or, someone at your local fuel assistance (LIHEAP) agency may have a lot of experience negotiating with your utility company. Don't be shy about asking for help!

SEEKING LARGER-SCALE CHANGE

Margaret Mead once said, "Never doubt that a small group of thoughtful, committed citizens can change the world. Indeed, it is the only thing that ever has." This is particularly true in the world of utility regulations. Many of the utility consumer protections now in place came about when ordinary citizens petitioned their PUCs to adopt rules that limit terminations in various circumstances: when there is someone seriously ill in the household, or when temperatures are very low (winter) or very high (summer), or when all of the household members are elderly. Many of the favorable payment plan rules also came about in response to petitions filed with PUCs by citizen groups.

Almost every PUC in the country allows ordinary consumers or citizen groups to petition for the adoption of new or revised rules. In most states, you don't need to be a lawyer to file such a petition, and there aren't too many formal requirements as to what the petition must contain. PUC commissioners, whether elected or appointed, are supposed to protect the interests of typical customers like you. They should take petitions from consumers seriously.

Only a handful of states offer utility consumers a broad range of protections, such as limitations on terminations of seriously ill customers, limitations on terminations during the winter, or special rules for elders. Few states have rules that require companies to offer payment plans that are truly affordable. While you may be reading this book primarily to learn how to address your particular utility problem, it's worth thinking about how you can work together with other consumers and with utility advocates to make the rules more favorable for *all* customers.

Appendix G at the back of this guide is *Consumer's Guide to Intervening in State Public Utility Proceedings.*[4] This guide provides detailed advice about how to become involved in proceedings before your PUC. We encourage you to read the Appendix G carefully if you are interested in changing your state's rules governing utility companies. Here, we are a few key points:

- First, in many states you won't need to have a lawyer represent you, although it would be a good idea to find either a legal services attorney (whose services would be free) or a consumer group that is familiar with your state's PUC to assist you.
- Second, you and other consumers are the only "experts" you will need for this type of PUC proceeding. After all, consumers know better than any "experts" the types of protections that are needed to keep families from losing their utility service.
- Third, numbers matter. If you decide that you want to seek changes to your PUC's rules, make sure to get as many other consumers and consumer groups as possible to join with you.

If you decide that you want to get more involved in proceedings at your PUC, please feel free to contact either Olivia Wein or Charlie Harak at the National Consumer Law Center.

7

A Brief Primer on Telephones and Water

TELEPHONE SERVICE

Landlines. As a general rule, each state utility commission regulates local telephone service and long-distance calls made within the state (also called "intrastate long distance"). The rules for these landline telephone services are generally similar to those for the other utilities services covered in this book. However, long-distance service for calls made to out-of-state locations are not regulated by the state utility commissions. They are determined by the contracts that consumers enter into when they sign up for long-distance service. As a result, a consumer's rights under a long-distance service contract (rights concerning the creation, interpretation, and failure to comply with those contracts) will vary depending on the specific contract law of the state in which he or she lives.

Wireless Services. Wireless services (cell phones) bring up more complex issues than those associated with landlines. In general, state utility commissions do not regulate cell phone service. In fact, federal law actually prohibits states from regulating cell phone rates. However, states can regulate the "terms and conditions" of wireless service (for example, wireless billing practices as well as procedures for billing disputes). Consumers having problems with their wireless carriers should check with their state utility commission's consumer division or telecommunication division to see if they regulate the problem at issue. To locate your state utility commission, go to Appendix C.3 at the back of this guide.

Pre-Paid Phone Cards. Pre-paid phone cards are often cheaper than traditional long-distance service, but there have been many reports of phone cards that do not work, that provide poor service, or that provide far fewer minutes than advertised. Some states require pre-paid phone card sellers to register with the state, disclose rates, provide a toll-free complaint line, and provide other types of customer service. However, the pre-paid phone card industry has proven to be very difficult to regulate successfully. Consumers choosing to use pre-paid phone cards should stick with companies that have a good reputation based on word-of-mouth recommendations from other users who have found good service and value with that particular pre-paid phone card company.

➡️ **POINTER:** When purchasing a pre-paid phone card from a new company, try purchasing a smaller amount of minutes to avoid risking too much money in case the service or value is poor.

WATER UTILITIES

Water is a unique utility because, in addition to its other uses, people consume it. This adds a layer of local, state, and federal regulation of *quality* that the other utilities are not subject to. Most water utility services in the U.S. are large, publicly owned water and sewer systems. In general, this means it is unlikely that the state utility commission regulates these utilities. Consumers served by publicly owned water utilities will need to look to their local political representatives for help with their utility problems.

As a general rule, whether the ownership of a water company is public or private determines whether it is regulated by the state utility commission. In the majority of the states, water utilities that are owned by private companies (also called investor-owned utilities or IOUs) are regulated by the state utility commission; publicly owned water companies (those owned by the local government, also called municipal utilities) are regulated by the local government. It is worth noting that state utility commissions may regulate municipal water services provided to consumers living outside of the municipality which provides protection for consumers who lack representation in the local government (such as the city council).

Water utilities that are regulated by the state utility commission have some of the same consumer protection rules as the other utilities regulated by the commission. However, these regulated water utilities generally do not have low-income affordability programs and there is no equivalent winter shut-off protection. For water service provided by municipalities, consumers should call their water company or their city council to locate the city ordinances covering service.

Submetering Issues for Tenants. Submetering occurs when a landlord or property manager uses submeters at each dwelling unit to bill tenants based on their actual water use. One emerging issue that tenants may face is the shift away from having water included in their rent and toward being billed directly for water from either their landlord or from the utility. While average water bills vary from water system to water system, water rates have been rising during the past decade. Rates are increasing for a number of reasons, including some or all of the following, depending on the area: the need to repair and replace aging water pipes and treatment facilities; increased costs for treatment of water and wastewater; scarcity of freshwater; and increased demand for water due to population growth. Rising water bills and a desire to promote conservation are driving a growing interest among apartment owners, the submetering industry, utilities, and lawmakers to shift the cost of water directly onto the tenant.

There are four basic ways a tenant can pay for water and sewer service:

1. *Rent:* payment to the landlord through rent (this is the traditional method);

2. *Submetering:* payment to the landlord or a billing agent based on actual usage as recorded by a submeter;

3. *RUBS:* payment to the landlord or billing agent based on Ratio Utility Billing System (RUBS), which is a method of billing for utility usage when individual meters cannot be installed. Bills are determined using such factors as occupant count or square footage; or

4. *Direct Utility Payment:* payment directly to the water company if the unit has its own water meter.

In the first three options, the building or property contains one "master meter." Charges are divided up and covered by all the parties either by including the overall utility costs in the tenant's rent, by using readings from the submeters or by using the RUBS formula. With submetering and RUBS, the tenant is billed separately for water by the landlord or an outside company hired to handle the billing.

Submetering relies on meters that measure a unit's water use and RUBS relies on an allocation formula that approximates water usage for a unit based on factors such as the size of the unit and the number of occupants. RUBS, in particular, poses many fairness problems for the tenant because the water bills do not reflect actual usage.[1] Where a tenant is facing a submetering or a RUBS situation, tenants should be aware of whether the bills accurately reflect the tenant's fair share of the building's water bill, whether the landlord is generating a profit from the sale of water,[2] whether the submetering is accurate, whether tenants can be evicted for failure to pay a submetered/RUBS water bill,[3] and whether there are late fees for submetered/RUBS bills.[4] Tenants facing a submetered or RUBS rental should ask the landlord how disputes over bills are handled and whether the unit has water-saving fixtures.[5] If the landlord contracts the submetering/RUBS billing to an outside company, tenants will likely be asked to pay an extra charge for this service.[6]

Submetered and RUBS tenants could find themselves without basic protections if the municipality (in a publicly-owned water system)[7] or utility commission (in a privately-owned water system)[8] does not have protective regulations governing water submetering. Tenants facing a switch to submetering and RUBS should consider raising their concerns with their elected representatives. This may be a situation where other locally-based tenants' organizations and consumer organizations can help tenants fight the pending rules that would allow submetering/RUBS or at least regulate the practice.

8

Unregulated Deliverable Fuels

Heating Oil, Propane, Kerosene, Etc.

WHAT IS DELIVERABLE FUEL?

While almost 85% of households use natural gas or electricity for home heating, millions of households rely on "deliverable" fuels such as heating oil, propane, kerosene, liquefied petroleum gas (LPG), wood, and coal. By "deliverable," we mean fuels that are delivered to your house, generally by truck (as opposed to electric or gas lines connected to your house) and the company delivering the fuel requires a cash payment or previously approved credit arrangement. The key difference between deliverable fuels and regulated fuels (electricity and natural gas) is that consumers can often continue receiving regulated fuels even if they are somewhat behind on their bills because the regulated utility company has to go through a formal termination process that proves that you're behind on your service. Companies that provide deliverable fuels will often refuse delivery if you don't have the cash to pay immediately.

Consumers of deliverable fuels do not enjoy the benefits of the state utility commission regulations regarding deposits, terminations, reconnections, and payment plans discussed earlier in this guide. Unfortunately, deliverable fuel prices and contract terms are much like those of any other non-utility good or service. The vendors set the price for their products and, in general, can serve whomever they want.

SPECIAL RATES FOR LOW INCOME
HOME ENERGY ASSISTANCE PROGRAM (LIHEAP)
CUSTOMERS AND FUEL CO-OP MEMBERS

A number of LIHEAP programs, especially in the northeastern part of the country, have negotiated with deliverable fuel vendors for discounted prices, credits, or donations for LIHEAP customers.[1] Regardless of whether your state has negotiated discounts for LIHEAP customers, low-income consumers should contact their LIHEAP office to see if they are eligible for energy assistance and for any reduced prices or discounts.[2]

Consumers in regions with large numbers of customers using deliverable fuels may be able to join fuel co-ops which pool the purchasing power of consumers to negotiate lower prices for their members. In the Boston area, for example, Mass Energy Consumer Alliance has a heating oil buying group with over 7,000 members and has been able to purchase heating oil at prices well below retail.[3] Mass Energy also runs an emergency heating oil bank for low-income households in crisis that is funded by donations from its co-op members.

ROLE OF STATE CONSUMER PROTECTION
LAWS REGARDING UNFAIR OR
DECEPTIVE ACTS OR PRACTICES

All states have at least one generally applicable law that is aimed at preventing consumer deception and abuse in the marketplace. These laws are often referred to as unfair or deceptive acts and practices (UDAP) laws and some states have UDAP laws that specifically cover deliverable fuels.[4] For example, Maine's UDAP law specifically covers the sale of residential heating oil and requires that, for heating oil sales from October 15th through April 30th, dealers must sell fuel to anyone in their service areas who pays with cash, regardless of whether the consumer owes money for a prior delivery or is not an established customer. During the period covered by the Maine heating oil UDAP law, sellers cannot unfairly discriminate among customers regarding requests for immediate service, charge more than a $5.00 fee for small deliveries, or add a surcharge for unscheduled deliveries that is greater than the actual additional costs of the service (such as extra miles driven or overtime).[5]

Connecticut recently passed a UDAP law regarding guaranteed price plans, including fixed price contracts for the retail sale of home heating oil.

The law requires the contracts to be in writing and the terms and conditions to be adequately disclosed to the buyer. Any publicly advertised price must remain available for at least 24 hours. The dealer must ensure that the oil will in fact be delivered at the contract price or that the customer will be reimbursed for the cost of any heating oil promised under the contract that is not delivered. If the dealer violates any of these provisions, the Connecticut Department of Consumer Protection may suspend or revoke the dealer's registration. Violations of these provisions constitute an unfair trade practice, and a knowing violation is a class A misdemeanor.[6] While many states will not have laws as specific as Connecticut's, in most states it may still be illegal for a heating oil, propane, or kerosene vendor to guarantee a fixed price for the winter heating season but then refuse to deliver at that price.

Almost all state UDAP laws allow consumers to bring a lawsuit, and the state's attorney general can bring a UDAP suit against a merchant. If you are interested in suing based on a UDAP claim, you should seek out legal help from a local legal services office (if you are low-income) or a private attorney that specializes in consumer law.[7] You can also alert the state attorney general's office about a fuel vendor's unfair or deceptive acts or practices, or the state consumer protection agency if there is one. If the state attorney general hears enough complaints about a particular merchant, it may open its own investigation into the matter.

MORE CREATIVE APPROACHES TO NON-REGULATED DELIVERABLE FUELS

If you heat with home heating oil, propane, or other deliverable fuels, you may feel like you've been left out in the cold, literally and figuratively, compared to those you know who use natural gas or electricity for home heating. There are few if any legal protections that will help keep you warm when you can't afford to pay your heating bills.

Because deliverable fuels are not regulated, there are very few individual solutions that work. Low-income consumers and advocates in at least one state are working on a creative approach for those who can't afford their heating oil bills. Under a proposal being considered by the Vermont legislature, the state would create a revolving loan fund for low-income consumers who make a little too much income to be eligible for fuel assistance (LIHEAP) or who have used up their LIHEAP benefits before the winter ends. The loan fund would advance credit on behalf of families who need an emergency delivery of oil, which would allow dealers to deliver one tank of oil knowing that the state will guarantee payment even if the household ultimately can't pay. The oil dealer will still take the usual steps to collect payment, but the low-income customer would have until the beginning of the next heating season (October) to catch up on the bill for the emergency delivery. In the event that the customer never catches up, the state will make up the difference out of the revolving fund.

This model highlights the problems for families who heat with deliverable fuels: the dealers won't provide service unless someone promises to pay. Since almost no state directly regulates deliverable fuels, consumers will have to band together and advocate for creative programs like the one being considered in Vermont.

Notes

Chapter One

1. The commissions are usually referred to generically as PUCs although they have different names, including "Department of Telecommunications and Energy" (MA), "Public Regulation Commission" (NM), and "Utility Regulatory Commission" (IN). For the name of the PUC in your state, go to Appendix C.3 at the back of this handbook.
2. From the perspective of consumers, unfair practices committed by a muni are just as harmful as those committed by an IOU. In practice, however, muni customers have far fewer legal rights.
3. For a map showing the state-by-state status of restructuring, go to www.eia.doe.gov/cneaf/electricity/chg_str/restructure.pdf.
4. Some gas companies have gone through somewhat similar "restructuring": gas customers in certain states can now buy their gas directly from an unregulated gas supplier but still have the local gas company deliver the gas to the home or business and provide the related metering, billing, and customer services.

Chapter Two

1. For more information on how states regulate utility deposits, go to Appendix B.1, *Deposits, Selected Regulations* at the back of this guide.
2. To review Arkansas' deposit regulations, go to your local law library and ask for the Code of Arkansas Rules, agency 126, subagency 03, chapter 003, sections 4.01, 4.02 (2005).
3. To review Missouri's regulations on establishing credit, go to your local law library and ask for Missouri Code of State Regulations Annotated, title 4, section 240–13.030 (2005).
4. To review some examples of these states' regulations on establishing credit, go to your local law library and ask for:
   - District of Columbia Municipal Regulations, title 15, section 307.6 (2005), which says that a utility shall not require a cash deposit for new or continued service on the basis of credit bureau rating, income level, home ownership, residence location, race, color, creed, sex, age, national origin, or any other criterion except those stated in this regulation.
   - Minnesota Rules, rule 7820.4700 (2005), which says that a utility shall not require a deposit based on income, home ownership, residential location, employment tenure, nature of occupation, race, color, creed, sex, marital status, age, national origin;
   - Administrative Rules of South Dakota, rule 20:10:19:01 (2005), which says that credit policy shall be easily understandable and nondiscriminatory. Redlining

though the use of "economic character of area," "collective credit reputation," home ownership, or friendly relationship with bank as means of establishing credit is explicitly prohibited.

5. To review the Equal Credit Opportunity Act, go to your local law library and ask for: United States Code, title 15, section 1691(a).

6. For an expanded discussion of these issues, go to your local law library and ask for:
   - National Consumer Law Center's *Are Credit Scores Fair and Reliable When Assessing Risk for Utility Service Applicants* in the Summer 2003 issue of the *Energy & Utility Update* newsletter, volume XX, number 3; and
   - National Consumer Law Center, Access to Utility Service, section 3.7.4 (3d ed. 2004).

   Copies of the article may also be obtained by contacting Charlie Harak at the National Consumer Law Center.

7. To review these states' rules, go to your local law library and ask for:
   - District of Columbia Municipal Regulations, title 15, section 307.6 (2005), which says that utility companies shall not require a cash deposit for new or continued service on the basis of credit bureau rating;
   - Minnesota Rules, rule 7820.7400 (2005), which limits the credit reports to specialized data on utility payment behavior and requires consumers written permission;
   - Administrative Rules of Montana, section 38.5.1104 (2005), which prohibits the use of credit scores for determining deposits.

8. For more information on the Fair Credit Reporting Act, go to your local law library and ask for:
   - United States Code, title 15, section 1681a(a) for the definition of consumer report and section 1681a(k)(1)(A) regarding adverse actions.
   - National Consumer Law Center, Fair Credit Reporting Act, section 6.4.2.7 (5th ed. 2002 and Supp.).

9. For examples of regulations allowing consumers to pay deposits in monthly installments, go to your local law library and ask for:
   - Code of Arkansas Rules, agency 126, subagency 03, chapter 003, sections 4.01, 4.02 (2005);
   - Regulations of Connecticut State Agencies, section 16-262j-1(b)(3)(D) (2005);
   - District of Columbia Municipal Regulations, title 15, section 307.6 (2005);
   - Idaho Administrative Code, rule 31.21.01.105 (2005);
   - Code of Maine Rules, agency 65, subagency 407, chapter 81, section 5(G) (2005);
   - Nevada Administrative Code, chapter 704, section 332 (2005);
   - Oklahoma Administrative Code, title 165:35-19-10 (2005);
   - Oregon Administrative Rules, rule 860-021-0205 (2005);
   - Utah Administrative Code, rule 746-200-3 (2005);
   - Code of Vermont Rules, agency 30, subagency 000, chapter 003, section 3.202 (2005).

10. For examples of deposit regulations affecting senior citizens, go to your local law library and ask for:
    - Code of Mississippi Rules, agency 26, subagency 000, chapter 002, rule 9 (2005), which states that a utility, upon request, shall not require deposits from customers/

applicants of 60+ years of age in certain circumstances if customer has reasonable payment history;

- Nevada Administrative Code, chapter 704, section 328 (2005), which lowers deposit amounts for elders but states that elders may have to pay additional deposits in case of delinquency;

- Official Compilation of Codes, Rules & Regulations of the State of New York, title 16, section 11.12(g) (2005), which states that deposits shall not be required for customers of 62+ years of age unless service has been terminated within previous six months.

11. For examples of deposit regulations affecting low-income consumers, go to your local law library and ask for:

- Regulations of Connecticut State Agencies, section 16-262j-1(b)(2005), which states that service will not be denied to *existing* customers who cannot pay a security deposit due to financial hardship;

- Illinois Administrative Code, title 83, section 280.50 (2005), which states that a utility shall not require a deposit based upon credit scores from an applicant eligible for LIHEAP;

- Minnesota Rules, rule 7820.1750 (2005), which states that during the winter no utility shall charge deposit to a residential customer who has declared to the utility an inability to pay and is income eligible;

- Official Compilation of Codes, Rules & Regulations of the State of New York, title 16, section 11.12 (2005), which states that deposits shall not be required of customers or applicants receiving public assistance, SSI, or additional state payments.

12. For examples of regulations on deposits during winter months, go to your local law library and ask for:

- Iowa Administrative Code, rule 199-19.4(16) (2005), which states that service shall not be denied for failure to pay a deposit during the winter months.

13. For more information about unpaid bills from prior addresses, go to your local law library and ask for: National Consumer Law Center, Access to Utility Service, section 11.4.2.1 (3d ed. 2004).

14. For examples of state regulations about unpaid bills from prior addresses, go to your local law library and ask for:

- Code of Arkansas Rules, agency 126, subagency 03, chapter 003, sections 3.04, 4.01 (2005);

- Official Compilation of Codes, Rules & Regulations of the State of New York, title 166, section 11.3(a) (2005).

15. For an example of a state regulations about unpaid bills from prior tenant, go to your local law library and ask for: Florida Administrative Code Annotated, rule 25-6.105(8)(a) (2005).

16. For more information on state regulations about unpaid bills from prior owner, go to Appendix B.2, *Limitations on Grounds for Disconnections and Denying Service, Selected Regulations* at the end of this guide. Or, go to your local law library and ask for: National Consumer Law Center, Access to Utility Service, section 3.2.3.2, note 76 (3d ed. 2004 and Supp.).

17. For examples of state regulations about unpaid bills from your landlord, go to your local law library and ask for:
    - General Statutes of Connecticut, section 16-262e(a)(2) (2005);
    - Illinois Compiled Statutes, chapter 765, section 735/3 (2005);
    - Maine Revised Statutes Annotated, title 35-A, section 706(2005).
18. For an example of a state law about receivership, go to your local law library and ask for: District of Columbia Official Code, sections 42-3302 and 42-3303 (2005).
19. For an example of a state regulation about rent withholding, go to your local law library and ask for: Minnesota Statues, section 504B.215(2005).
20. For an example of a state law about bills owed by third parties, go to your local law library and ask for: Pennsylvania Consolidated Statutes, title 66, section 1407(d) (2005).
21. For an example of a state regulation about bills owed by third parties, go to your local law library and ask for: Code of Arkansas Rules, agency 126, subagency 03, chapter 003, section 3.04(2) (2005).
22. For an example of a state regulation about bills owed by a spouse or roommate, go to your local law library and ask for: Code of Maine Rules, agency 65, subagency 407, chapter 81, section 4(F), stating that a utility may require that the applicant pay an undisputed unpaid debt if the applicant was *legally responsible* for the debt (emphasis added).
23. For a more thorough discussion of this issue, go to your local law library and ask for: National Consumer Law Center, Access to Utility Service, sections 3.2 (*A Utility May Not Deny Service Based on a "Collateral" Matter*), 4.2 (*Tenant Obtaining Service in Own Name Despite Landlord's Delinquency*), 11.4 & 11.5 (*Disconnections Based on "Collateral" Matters and Third Party's Debt*) (3d ed. 2004).
24. In some cases, the companies may be engaging in illegal acts of discrimination by routinely asking applicants of a particular race or national origin to produce more rigorous proof of identity and prior residence than, for example, Caucasian applicants. If you suspect that the utility is discriminating, file a complaint with the PUC and also contact the state attorney general's office.
25. To review Wisconsin's regulation, go to your local law library and ask for: Wisconsin Administrative Code, Public Service Commission, section 113.0402 (2005).
26. To review Texas' regulation, go to your local law library and ask for: Texas Administrative Code, title 16, section 25.22 (2005).
27. To review New Jersey's regulation, go to your local law library and ask for: New Jersey Administrative Code, section 14:3-3.2 (2005). The Arkansas regulation, Code of Arkansas Rules, agency 126, subagency 03, chapter 003, section 3.04 (2005), states in part:

    (d) A utility may require proof of identity with an application for service. An applicant for service may provide any one of the following items to establish identity:
    1. A valid driver's license;
    2. Employment identification;
    3. An unexpired foreign passport;
    4. A U.S. passport;
    5. An alien registration card with photograph;

    6. A county identification card;

    7. A county welfare identification card;

    8. A student identification card; or

    9. A military identification card.

    (e) A utility may require proof of prior address with an application for service. An applicant for service may provide any one of the following items to establish prior address:

    1. A notarized lease, deed, or letter from the prior landlord;

    2. A current auto insurance policy;

    3. A bank statement;

    4. A credit card statement;

    5. Mailing envelopes addressed to the applicant at the previous address, post-marked no later than two months prior to the date of application; or

    6. A letter of credit worthiness from a utility.

For more information on the Arkansas rules, go to your local law library and ask for: Code of Arkansas Rules, agency 126, subagency 03, chapter 003, section 3.04 (2005).

28. To review the New York regulation, go to your local law library and ask for: Official Compilation of Codes, Rules & Regulations of the State of New York, title 16, section 11.3(a)(2)(v) (2005).

29. Case No. 96-M-0706, order dated Feb. 17, 1998.

30. "Tariffs" are the written documents that include the rates that companies are allowed to charge for utility service and other terms and conditions, such as the rules governing applications for service. Tariffs are generally difficult to locate, although they must be filed with the PUC.

31. For more information on "line extension" fees, go to your local law library and ask for:
- Texas Administrative Code, title 16, section 25.22 (2005) which states that an electric utility that must construct new lines to serve a new customer and can require the customer to pay for the cost of the line extension as a condition of getting new service;
- Official Compilation of Codes, Rules & Regulations of the State of New York, title 16, section 11.3(a)(4)(iii) (2005) which states that a company may deny service to an applicant who fails to pay the line extension charges calculated in accordance with the PUC's rules.

32. "Tariffs" are the written documents that include the rates that companies are allowed to charge for utility service and other terms and conditions, such as the rules governing applications for service. Tariffs are generally difficult to locate, although they must be filed with the PUC.

Chapter Three

1. For a list of LIHEAP offices in each state, see Appendix C.2 at the back of this guide.

2. For examples of these regulations, go to Appendix B.3 at the back of this guide.

3. For examples of these regulations, go to Appendix B.3, *Payment Plans, Selected Regulations* at the back of this guide.

Chapter Four

1. For more information on payment periods, got to Appendix A.3, *Termination Time Frames* at the back of this guide.

2. Some state regulations call for these shutoff notices to be written in multiple languages. To review the Texas regulation, go to your local law library and ask for: Texas Administrative Code title 16, section 25.29(k) (2006), which requires electric disconnection notices to be in English and Spanish.

3. For more information on termination periods, go to Appendix A.3, *Termination Time Frames*, at the back of this guide.

4. To review state laws and regulations on termination notice, go to your local library and ask for:

   - West's Annotated California Codes, Public Utilities section 779.1 (2006), which states that a utility must make a reasonable attempt to contact an adult residing at the subject premises by phone or personal contact at least 24 hours prior to termination. If phone or personal contact cannot be accomplished, the utility must give final notice by mail or in-person at least 48 hours before termination;
   - Minnesota Rules, rule 7820.2500 (2005), which states that service may be disconnected only in conjunction with a personal visit by a utility representative in an attempt to make personal contact with the customer at the address;
   - Nevada Administrative Code, section 704.360 (2005), which states that if customer fails to respond to first termination notice, the utility shall give a second 48-hour notice prior to terminating service;
   - Baldwin's Ohio Administrative Code, section 4901:1-18-05 (2005), which states that personal or written notice shall be given on the date of disconnection;
   - West Virginia Code of State Rules, section 150-3-4, rule 4.81 (2005), which requires personal notice 24 hours prior to termination.

5. To review the Maine rule, go to your local law library and ask for: Code of Maine Rules, agency 65, subagency 407, chapter 81, section 10 (2005).

6. For more information on termination periods, go to Appendix A.3, *Termination Time Frames*, at the back of this guide.

7. For state laws and regulations providing exceptions to termination protections, go to your local law library and ask for:

   - Code of Arkansas Rules, agency 126, subagency 03, chapter 003, sections 6.04B, 6.01D, 6.13J (2005), which states that service may be suspended without prior written notice for failure to pay under delayed payment or extension agreement;
   - West's Annotated California Codes, Public Utilities, section 779.1 (2006), which states that if a customer does not comply with an amortization agreement, the corporation shall not terminate service without giving notice at least 48 hours prior to cessation of the conditions required to avoid termination;
   - Code of Maine Rules, agency 65, subagency 407, chapter 81, section 9 (2005) which states that 3-day termination notice for breach of payment plan versus a 14-day notice in other circumstances.

8. For state laws and regulations about escrow accounts, go to your local law library and ask for:

   - West's Annotated California Codes, Public Utilities, section 394.2 (2005);

- Minnesota Rules, rule 7820.2700 (2005), which states that a customer appealing unsatisfactory decisions must submit the entire payment and designate the disputed portion to be placed in escrow;
- New Jersey Administrative Code, section 14:3-7.13 (2006).

Some states also provide for situations in which the customer and the utility cannot agree what portion of the bill is undisputed. For these regulations, go to your local law library and ask for:

- Indiana Administrative Code, title 170, rule 4-1-17 (2006), which specifies that customer shall pay on the disputed bill and amount equal to average bill for 6 months preceding dispute;
- Michigan Administrative Code, rule 460.2167 (2005), which specifies that customer shall pay lesser of 50% of disputed amount or $100.

9. To review the federal poverty levels, go to Appendix F at the back of this guide.

10. To review these protections, go to Appendix A.2, *Serious Illness and Age-Related Protections*, at the back of this guide.

11. To review sample certifications, go to Appendix D, *Serious Illness Certification*, at the back of this guide.

12. For instance, Colorado customers are only entitled to one 30-day renewal following the initial 60-day period. In addition, Colorado customers are only eligible for the serious illness protection once every 12 months. To review this regulation, go to your local law library and ask for: Code of Colorado Regulations, volume 4, section 723-3-13(f) (2005).

13. To review these protections, go to Appendix A.2, *Serious Illness and Age-Related Protections*, at the back of this guide.

14. To review this regulation, go to your local law library and ask for: Michigan Administrative Code, rule 460.2174 (2005).

15. To review this regulation, go to your local law library and ask for: Weil's Code of Hawaii Rules, section 6-60-8 (2006).

16. To review this regulation, go to your local law library and ask for: Code of Massachusetts Regulations, title 220, section 25.05 (2006).

17. To review this regulation, go to your local law library and ask for: Code of Massachusetts Regulations, title 220, section 25.03 (2006).

18. For more information on theses protections, go to Appendix A.1, *Seasonal Termination Protection Regulations*, at the back of this guide.

19. To review these regulations, go to Appendix B.3, *Payment Plans, Selected Regulations*, at the back of this guide.

20. To review state laws and regulations on payment plans, go to your local law library and ask for:

- Code of Arkansas Rules, agency 126, subagency 03, chapter 003, sections 6.04B, 6.01D, 6.13J (2005), which state that service may be suspended without prior written notice for failure to pay under delayed payment or extension agreement;
- West's Annotated California Codes, Public Utilities, section 779.1 (2006), which states that if a customer does not comply with an amortization agreement, the corporation shall not terminate service without giving notice at least 48 hours prior to cessation of the conditions required to avoid termination;

- Code of Maine Rules, agency 65, subagency 407, chapter 81, section 9 (2005), which requires a 3-day termination notice for breach of payment plan versus a 14-day notice in other circumstances.

21. For more information, go to Appendix B.2, *Limitations on Grounds for Disconnections and Denying Service, Selected Regulations*, at the back of this guide.

22. For more information on bankruptcy, go to your local law library and ask for: National Consumer Law Center, Consumer Bankruptcy Law and Practice (7th ed. 2004) and National Consumer Law Center, Consumer Bankruptcy Law and Practice, Special Guide to the 2005 Act (2005).

23. To review this case, go to your local law library and ask for: 436 U.S. 1 (1978). For more information about municipal utility service's due process requirements, go to your local law library and ask for: National Consumer Law Center, Access to Utility Service, section 12.2.3 (3d ed. 2004).

Chapter Five

1. For more information about grace periods, go to Appendix A.3, *Termination Time Frames*, at the back of this guide.

2. For an example of a regulation that allows the payment period to begin when the utility company generates the bill, go to your local law library and ask for: Alaska Administrative Code, title 3, sections 52.450, 52.500 (2006), which states that a electric utility may disconnect if payment is not received within 40 days of rendering the bill and rendered is defined as the date the bill is postmarked or the billing date on the bill as long as it is within 3 days of the postmark.

3. For more information about disputed bills, go to Chapter 4, *Restrictions on the Termination of Service*, of this guide.

4. For more information about disputed bills, go to Chapter 4, *Restrictions on the Termination of Service*, of this guide.

5. For more information about "pyramiding," go to your local law library and ask for: National Consumer Law Center, Access to Utility Service, section 6.2 (3d ed. 2004 and Supp.).

6. The Federal Trade Commission Rule prohibiting this practice is Code of Federal Regulations, title 16, section 444.4. Note that private citizens cannot sue to enforce this federal law (i.e., the law does not provide a private right of action) and some utilities are not subject to this rule, but consumers may be able to argue that the violation of the federal rule is thus a violation of their state's unfair or deceptive acts and practices laws (which often have private rights of action). If you suspect a utility is engaged in this practice, you should consult with a legal services attorney or a private attorney in your state who specializes in consumer law. For more technical information on this area of law, go to your local law library and ask for: National Consumer Law Center, Unfair and Deceptive Acts and Practices, section 2.3.2 (6th ed. 2004 and Supp.).

7. To review this regulation, go to your local law library and ask for: Code of Arkansas Rules, agency 126, subagency 03, chapter 003, section 6.12 (2005).

8. To review this regulation, go to your local law library and ask for: Official Compilation of Codes, Rules & Regulations of the State of New York, title 16, section 11.9 (2005).

9. To review this settlement go to your local law library and ask for: *Re* Consol. Edison of N.Y., Inc., 170 Pub. Util. Rep. 4th 141 (N.Y. Pub. Serv. Comm'n 1996).

Chapter Six

1. There are also PUCs for Puerto Rico, the Virgin Islands, and Guam. See Appendix C.3 at the back of this guide for information on how to contact your PUC.
2. For examples of certification letters, go to Appendix D at the end of this guide.
3. For a list of PUC websites, go to Appendix C.3 at the back of this guide.
4. This guide, published by the National Consumer Law Center, is also available at www.nclc.org/action_agenda/energy_and_utility/content/Intervention_Manual.pdf.

Chapter Seven

1. In addition to the unfairness issue, there is also no incentive to conserve water since the bill will not reflect a tenant's actual usage. Some states do not permit landlords to use RUBS. For an example of a state law that does not permit RUBS, go to your local law library and ask for: General Statutes of North Carolina, section 62-110(g)(1) (2006).
2. To review examples of state laws about landlords selling water, go to your local law library and ask for:
   - General Statutes of North Carolina, section 62-110(g) (2006);
   - Vernon's Texas Statutes and Codes Annotated, Water Code, sections 13.503(b) and 13.5031(3–5) (2005).
3. To review an example of a state law about water bills and eviction, go to your local law library and ask for: General Statutes of North Carolina, section 42-26(b) (2005), which states that a water or sewer arrearage shall not be used as a basis for termination of the lease.
4. To review different examples of state laws about water bills and late fees, go to your local law library and ask for:
   - General Statues of North Carolina, section 42-46(d) (2005), which states that late fees are prohibited on water and sewer submetering bill.
   - Vernon's Texas Statutes and Codes Annotated, Water Code, sections 13.503 and 13.5031 (2005), which states that the owner can charge late fee.
5. For an example of a city ordinance providing a dispute procedure, go to your local law library and ask for: Seattle Council Bill Number 11461, Ordinance Number 121320, codified in Title 7.25 *Third Party Billing Regulation* of the Seattle Municipal Code, which states that a tenant may file a complaint with the Office of Hearing Examiner who, in the case of a violation, can award tenant damages and a penalty of $100–200 and attorney fees if the violation was deliberate, or that the tenant can institute a civil action for similar remedies.
6. For an example of a state regulation about third party fees, go to your local law library and ask for: North Carolina Administrative Code, title 4, rule 11.R18-6(a) (2006), which puts a cap on administrative fee.
7. For an example of a municipality's regulations on submetering, go to your local law library and ask for: Seattle Council Bill Number 11461, Ordinance Number 121320, codified in Title 7.25 *Third Party Billing Regulation* of the Seattle Municipal

Code, which prohibits deceptive and fraudulent practices related to third-party billing of master-metered or unmetered utility service.

8. For an example of utility commissions' regulations on submetering, go to your local law library and ask for:
   - General Statues of North Carolina, section 62-110 (2005);
   - Vernon's Texas Statutes and Codes Annotated, Water Code, sections 13.501 through 13.506 (2005).

Chapter Eight

1. LIHEAP programs in California, Connecticut, Indiana, Maine, Maryland, Massachusetts, Minnesota, Montana, New Hampshire, New Mexico, North Carolina, South Dakota, and Vermont had negotiated special deals with deliverable fuel vendors. See *LIHEAP Negotiations with Non-regulated Fuel Vendors*, NCAT LIHEAP Clearinghouse, August 2005, *available at* www.liheap.ncat.org/pubs/880.htm.

2. For a list of LIHEAP offices by state, go to Appendix C.2 at the back of this guide.

3. If you live in the Boston area and use heating oil, Mass Energy can be reached at 617-524-3950 and their website is www.massenergy.com/index.htm.

4. For more information on UDAP laws, go to your local law library and ask for: National Consumer Law Center, Unfair and Deceptive Acts and Practices (6th ed. 2004 and Supp.).

5. To review this law, go to your local law library and ask for: Code of Maine Rules, chapter 100, section 26-239 (2005).

6. To review this law, go to your local law library and ask for: Connecticut General Statutes, sections 16a-23n, 23p, 23r (2005).

7. Contact the National Association of Consumer Advocates for a referral at www.naca.net or (202) 452-1989 or call your local bar association.

APPENDIX A

Utility Terminations
Consumer Protections and Time Frames

A.1 SEASONAL TERMINATION PROTECTION REGULATIONS

Alabama

Date-based termination protection: None

Temperature-based termination protection: 32° Fahrenheit or below

Seasonal Policy: No termination for the calendar day in which the temperature is below 32° Fahrenheit. Each utility shall adopt reasonable tariff rules governing its termination of gas and electricity when life or health may be threatened by termination, the customer requires special consideration because of age or handicap.

Alaska

Date-based termination protection: None

Temperature-based termination protection: None

Seasonal Policy: None

Arizona

Date-based termination protection: November 1 through March 31 (for gas)

Temperature-based termination protection: 32° Fahrenheit (for electric and gas)

Seasonal Policy: Electric and gas may not be suspended on a day when the National Weather Service forecasts that the temperature will be 32° or lower. Gas service may not be suspended to low-income customers during the termination moratorium period (consumers must certify that they receive income-tested benefits and enter into a payment plan).

Arkansas

Date-based termination protection: December 1 through March 31

Temperature-based termination protection: below 32° Fahrenheit or 95° Fahrenheit and above

Seasonal Policy: Electric and gas utilities may not suspend residential service on a day when the National Weather Service forecasts that a temperature of 32° Fahrenheit or lower will occur at any time during the following 24-hour period. An electric or gas utility shall not suspend residential service to an elderly or disabled customer on a day when the National Weather Service forecasts that a temperature of 95° Fahrenheit or higher will occur at any time during the following 24-hour period. The Arkansas Public Service Commission amended the state's cold weather rule in 2006 to ban winter natural gas disconnections of certain income-eligible households provided they make a minimum payment, about 50% of their bill, effective December 1 through March 31.

California
Date-based termination protection: None
Temperature-based termination protection: None
Seasonal Policy: None

Colorado
Date-based termination protection: None
Temperature-based termination protection: None
Seasonal Policy: None

Connecticut
Date-based termination protection: November 1 through April 15
Temperature-based termination protection: None
Seasonal Policy: No gas company and no municipal utility furnishing gas shall terminate or refuse to reinstate residential gas service in hardship cases where the customer uses such gas for heat and lacks the financial resources to pay his or her entire account.

Delaware
Date-based termination protection: None
Temperature-based termination protection: 32° Fahrenheit or below and 105° Fahrenheit or higher
Seasonal Policy: Under no circumstances may a covered utility terminate service for non-payment on a day when the National Weather Service reports that the 8:00 a.m. temperature measured at a location in the State of Delaware that is within fifty (50) miles of the subject dwelling unit is 32° Fahrenheit or below on the morning of the date when said service is scheduled for termination or exceeds 105° Fahrenheit on the date when said service is scheduled for termination. Where termination of service, otherwise authorized, has been deferred, notice of such fact shall be left at the subject dwelling unit on the date on which termination was to be effected, notifying the occupant that unless proper payment arrangements are made, service will be terminated thereafter on a day when the protection does not apply.

District of Columbia
Date-based termination protection: None
Temperature-based termination protection: 32° Fahrenheit or below
Seasonal Policy: Whenever the temperature is forecast to be 32° Fahrenheit or below during the next 24 hours, gas or electric utilities shall not terminate service for non-payment or

a delinquent account, failure to post a cash security deposit or guarantee of payment, or failure to comply with the terms of a deferred payment plan.

Florida

Date-based termination protection: None
Temperature-based termination protection: None
Seasonal Policy: None

Georgia

Date-based termination protection: November 15 through March 15
Temperature-based termination protection: 32° Fahrenheit or below
Seasonal Policy: A marketer shall not discontinue service to a residential consumer for an unpaid bill between November 15 and March 15 if: the consumer agrees in writing to pay the past-due balance in equal installments and agrees in writing to pay all bills by their due date for current service received after said agreement. A marketer may not terminate under any circumstances if the forecasted local low temperature for a 72-hour period beginning at 8:00 A.M. on the date of the proposed disconnection is below 32° Fahrenheit.

Hawaii

Date-based termination protection: None
Temperature-based termination protection: None
Seasonal Policy: None

Idaho

Date-based termination protection: December 1 through February 1
Temperature-based termination protection: None
Seasonal Policy: No gas or electric utility may terminate service or threaten to terminate service during the months of December through February to any residential customer who declares that he or she is unable to pay in full for utility service and whose household includes children, elderly or, infirm persons. Any residential customer who declares that he or she is unable to pay in full for utility service and whose household includes children, elderly, or infirm persons must be offered the opportunity to establish a Winter Payment Plan, which affords the customer special considerations from November 1 through February 1.

Illinois

Date-based termination protection: December 1 through March 31
Temperature-based termination protection: 32° Fahrenheit or below
Seasonal Policy: Termination of gas and electric utility service is prohibited: on any day when the National Weather Service forecast for the following 24 hours covering the area of the utility in which the residence is located includes a forecast that the temperature will be 32° Fahrenheit or below and no electric or gas public utility shall disconnect service during the period of time from December 1 through and including March 31 of the immediately succeeding calendar year, unless the utility has offered a

deferred payment plan and informed the customer of specific agencies and funds available to them for payment assistance.

Indiana

Date-based termination protection: December 1 through March 15

Temperature-based termination protection: None

Seasonal Policy: Without customer request, a utility may not, during the period from December 1 through March 15, disconnect electric residential service to any customer who either is receiving or who is eligible for and has applied for assistance.

Iowa

Date-based termination protection: November 1 through April 1

Temperature-based termination protection: 20° Fahrenheit or below

Seasonal Policy: Disconnection shall not take place from November 1 through April 1 for a resident who is a head of household and who has been certified to the public utility by the community action agency as eligible for either the low-income home energy assistance program or weatherization assistance program. A disconnection may not take place where gas is used as the only source of space heating or to control or operate the only space heating equipment at the residence on any day when the National Weather Service forecast for the following 24 hours covering the area in which the residence is located includes a forecast that the temperature will be 20° Fahrenheit or colder.

Kansas

Date-based termination protection: November 1 through March 1

Temperature-based termination protection: 35° Fahrenheit or below

Seasonal Policy: A utility shall not disconnect a customer's service between November 1 and March 31 when the local National Weather Service forecasts that the temperature will drop below 35° or will be in the mid 30s or colder within the following 48-hour period. To qualify for the benefits of the Cold Weather Rule, the customer shall: (1) inform the utility of the customer's inability to pay the bill in full; (2) provide sufficient information to allow the utility to make a payment agreement; (3) make an initial payment of 1/12 of the arrearage amount, 1/12 of the bill for current consumption, the full amount of any disconnection or reconnection fees, plus any applicable deposit, and enter into an 11-month plan for payment of the rest of the arrearage; or enter a payment plan as negotiated with the utility for the payment of the arrearage amount; and (4) apply for federal, state, local or other assistance funds for which the customer is eligible.

Kentucky

Date-based termination protection: November 1 through March 31

Temperature-based termination protection: None

Seasonal Policy: A gas or electric utility shall not terminate service for 30 days beyond the termination date if the Kentucky Cabinet for Human Resources (or its designee) certifies in writing that the customer is eligible for the cabinet's energy assistance program or household income is at or below 130% of the poverty level, and the customer presents such certificate to the utility. As a condition of the 30-day extension, the customer shall exhibit good faith in paying his indebtedness by making a present payment in accordance with his ability to do so. In addition, the customer shall agree to a repayment plan which will permit the customer to become current in the payment of his bill as soon as possible but not later than October 15.

Louisiana

Date-based termination protection: None
Temperature-based termination protection: None
Seasonal Policy: None

Maine

Date-based termination protection: November 1 through March 31
Temperature-based termination protection: None
Seasonal Policy: The Public Utilities Commission adopts the general policy that electric and gas utilities should attempt to contact all customers who are in arrears by more than $50 as indicated on bills issued from November 1 through March 31, and establish a regular or special payment arrangement with the customer. Customers who enter into a regular or special payment arrangement should be required to the extent possible to pay a reasonable portion of each utility bill when due during the winter period and to avoid an accumulation of arrearages that will be difficult to pay on a reasonable schedule during the summer months. Even if the customer refuses to comply with said payment arrangement, during the winter disconnection period, a utility may not disconnect an eligible customer unless it has received the authorization of the Consumer Assistance Division.

Maryland

Date-based termination protection: November 1 through March 15
Temperature-based termination protection: 32° Fahrenheit or below
Seasonal Policy: An electric or gas utility may not terminate gas or electric service to occupants of residential buildings for nonpayment of bills during the period November 1 through and including March 31 unless the utility first certifies to the Public Service Commission by an affidavit filed at least 24 hours before the termination, that the termination does not constitute a threat to the life or health of the residential occupants. In addition to these provisions, a utility may not terminate service to any customer within a utility's designated weather station area in which the forecasted temperature made at 6:00 a.m. is not expected to exceed 32° Fahrenheit for the next 24 hours.

Massachusetts

Date-based termination protection: November 15 through March 15
Temperature-based termination protection: None
Seasonal Policy: No company may shut off or refuse to restore utility service to the home of any customer if, between November 15 and March 15, that the customer's service provides heat or operates the heating system and that the service has not been shut off

for nonpayment before November 15 and the customer is unable to pay any overdue bill, or any portion thereof, because of financial hardship.

Michigan
Date-based termination protection: November 1 through March 31
Temperature-based termination protection: None
Seasonal Policy: The Michigan Commission passed emergency rules effective November 1, 2005 through March 31, 2006. Utilities are prohibited from disconnecting service of certain elderly or low-income customers provided the customer advises the utility of his/her circumstances and pays a monthly amount equal to 6% of the customer's estimated annual bill. Utilities also may not disconnect service to a customer who has entered into a settlement agreement provided that the customer makes designated payment amounts. The law also extends the due date for utility bills from 17 days to 22 days from the date of transmittal and places limits on deposits. Emergency policy in place for 2006.

Minnesota
Date-based termination protection: October 14 through April 15
Temperature-based termination protection: None
Seasonal Policy: No utility shall disconnect the service of any residential unit during "cold weather months," when the residential customer, or any designated third party, has declared inability to pay and is receiving any type of energy assistance, including federal assistance, or is income eligible; or, if appealed, the Public Utilities Commission has determined the residential customer is unable to pay. To declare inability, the residential customer must meet the following requirements: the residential customer expresses willingness to enter into a mutually acceptable payment schedule for the current cold weather months; and the residential customer was fully paid up or was making reasonably timely payments under a payment schedule as of the billing cycle immediately preceding the start of the current cold weather months; or the residential customer makes reasonably timely payments to the utility under a payment plan that considers the financial resources of the household.

Mississippi
Date-based termination protection: December 1 through March 31
Temperature-based termination protection: None
Seasonal Policy: For the months of December, January, February and March of each year, residential customers who are unable to pay the full amount of their utility bill because of extreme financial difficulty may qualify for mid-winter rule which prohibits disconnection of service in those cases where the customer has complied with the following: customer shall inform the utility of his or her inability to pay and agree to pay the utility in full all amounts due on bills rendered prior to November 1 and enter into a payment plan designed by the utility for future bills.

Missouri
Date-based termination protection: November 1 through March 31

Temperature-based termination protection: 32° Fahrenheit or below

Seasonal Policy: Discontinuance of gas and electric service to all residential users is prohibited: (1) on any day when the National Weather Service local forecast between 6:00 a.m. to 9:00 a.m., for the following 24 hours predicts that the temperature will drop below 32° Fahrenheit; or (2) on any day when utility personnel will not be available to reconnect utility service; or (3) from November 1 through March 31, for any registered low-income elderly or low-income disabled customer, provided that such a customer has entered into a cold weather rule payment plan. [NOTE: there is a legal challenge to this rule pending as of February 13, 2006]

Montana

Date-based termination protection: November 1 through April 1

Temperature-based termination protection: 32° Fahrenheit or below

Seasonal Policy: During the period November 1 through April 1 and on any day when the reported ambient air temperature at 8:00 a.m. is at or below freezing or if the U.S. Weather Service forecasts a snowstorm or freezing temperatures for the succeeding 24-hour period, no termination of residential service may take place if the customer establishes that he or she is unable to pay, or able to pay only installments, that he or she or a member of the household is at least 62 years old or that he or she or a member of the household is handicapped. No termination of service may take place during the period of November 1 through April 1 except with specific prior approval of the Public Service Commission.

Nebraska

Date-based termination protection: November 1 through March 31

Temperature-based termination protection: None

Seasonal Policy: No jurisdictional utility may disconnect service from November 1 to March 31 without adding to the time for payment of a bill an additional 30 days before disconnecting that service, and it shall notify the residential customer before the normal disconnection date that the residential customer has such additional 30 days until disconnection. The Public Service Commission shall have the authority to order a temporary ban on any or all disconnections for jurisdictional utilities during periods of severe weather or when circumstances exist such that disconnection could create a situation dangerous to the life or health of customers or to property.

Nevada

Date-based termination protection: None

Temperature-based termination protection: 15° Fahrenheit or below and 105° Fahrenheit or above

Seasonal Policy: The utility shall postpone the termination during a forecasted period of extreme temperature. "Forecasted period of extreme temperature" means any period of 24 hours for which the National Weather Service has issued a forecast predicting that, at some point during the period of 24 hours, the outside temperature will be: (1) 105° Fahrenheit or higher or (2) 15° Fahrenheit or lower.

New Hampshire

Date-based termination protection: None

Temperature-based termination protection: None

Seasonal Policy: An arrearage resulting from non-payment of bills for service rendered during the winter and non-winter period shall exceed the following amounts before a notice of disconnection for a primary residence can be sent: (1) for gas non-heating customers, $125; (2) for electric non-heating customers, $225; and (3) for electric, gas and steam heating customers, $450. During the winter period utilities shall seek Public Utilities Commission approval before disconnecting the service of residential customers known to be 65 years or older.

New Jersey

Date-based termination protection: November 15 through March 15

Temperature-based termination protection: None

Seasonal Policy: A regulated electric or gas utility shall not discontinue service during the period from November 15 through March 15, to those residential customers who demonstrate at the time of the intended termination that they are: (1) receiving income-tested federal or state benefits or (2) unable to pay their utility bills because of circumstances beyond their control including but not limited to unemployment, illness, medically related expenses and any other circumstances that might cause financial hardship. Customers who seek the protection must: (1) make a down payment of up to 25% of the outstanding balance; (2) enroll in a budget payment plan; (3) make good-faith payments during the protection period when possible; and (4) enroll in a weatherization program.

New Mexico

Date-based termination protection: November 15 through March 15

Temperature-based termination protection: None

Seasonal Policy: A utility shall not discontinue service to a residential customer for non-payment during the period from November 15 to March 15 until at least fifteen (15) days after the date scheduled for discontinuance of service if, prior to that date, the Human Services Department contacts the utility and certifies to the utility that the customer is eligible for utility payment assistance under the Low Income Home Energy Assistance Program or the Low Income Utility Assistance Act and that payment for the utility service provided to the customer will be made within the 15-day period following the date scheduled for discontinuance.

New York

Date-based termination protection: November 1 through April 15

Temperature-based termination protection: None

Seasonal Policy: During the period from November 1 through April 15, every utility shall observe, the following procedures: (1) a utility shall attempt to contact, by telephone or in person, the customer or an adult resident of the customer's premises at least 72 hours before the intended termination, for the purpose of ascertaining whether a resi-

68

dent is likely to suffer a serious impairment to health or safety as a result of termination; (2) no utility shall terminate heat-related service for nonpayment where the utility ascertains that a resident is likely to suffer a serious impairment to human health or safety as a result of termination; (3) for the purposes of this section, a person is likely to suffer a serious impairment to health or safety due to age, infirmity, mental incapacitation, the use of life support systems, such as dialysis machines or iron lungs, serious illness, physical disability or blindness, and any other factual circumstances which indicate severe or hazardous health situations.

North Carolina
Date-based termination protection: November 1 through March 31
Temperature-based termination protection: None
Seasonal Policy: No termination shall take place without the express approval of the Utilities Commission if the customer can establish all of the following: (1) that a member of the customer's household is either certifiably disabled or elderly (65 years of age or older), or both; (2) that the customer is unable to pay for such service in full; or (3) that the household is certified by the local social service office which administers the Energy Crisis Assistance Program or other similar programs as being eligible to receive assistance under such programs.

North Dakota
Date-based termination protection: None
Temperature-based termination protection: None
Seasonal Policy: None

Ohio
Date-based termination protection: November 1 through April 15
Temperature-based termination protection: None
Seasonal Policy: The company shall not disconnect during the period of November 1 through April 15 unless, in addition to the other requirements of this rule, the company completes each of the following: (1) makes contact with the customer; (2) informs the customer that sources of federal, state, and local government aid for payment of utility bills and for home weatherization are available; and (3) at the same time, informs the customer of the right to enter into a payment plan.

Oklahoma
Date-based termination protection: None
Temperature-based termination protection: 32° Fahrenheit or below during the day, 20° Fahrenheit or below during the night, or 101° Fahrenheit or above
Seasonal Policy: If the high temperature is actually, or predicted to be, 32° Fahrenheit or below on the day of disconnection or the nighttime low is predicted to be 20° Fahrenheit or less, the utility shall suspend its disconnection of service if the electric service is used for heating purposes. If the service is utilized for cooling and the temperature is actually, or predicted to be, 101° heat index or higher on the day of disconnection, the utility shall suspend its disconnection of service activity.

Oregon

Date-based termination protection: None
Temperature-based termination protection: None
Seasonal Policy: None

Pennsylvania

Date-based termination protection: December 1 through March 31
Temperature-based termination protection: None
Seasonal Policy: The covered utilities may not be permitted to terminate heat-related service between December 1 and March 31 except if: (1) the utility makes personal contact, at the premises if occupied and (2) at the conclusion of the notification process a reasonable agreement cannot be reached between the utility and the ratepayer, the utility shall register with the Public Utility Commission, in writing, a request for permission to terminate service, accompanied by a utility report.

Rhode Island

Date-based termination protection: November 1 through April 15
Temperature-based termination protection: None
Seasonal Policy: During the utility termination moratorium period, (12:01 A.M. on November 1 until 11:59 P.M. on April 15 of each year) no gas or electric public utility subject to these regulations shall terminate service to any residence for nonpayment of a delinquent account, except where the delinquent balance of the account exceeds $500, and where such service is not the primary source of heat, except when the delinquent balance exceeds $200. During the utility termination moratorium period, no gas or electric public utility subject to state rules and regulations shall terminate service to a residence for nonpayment of utility charges where the public utility has evidence that the person or persons whose services are scheduled to be terminated is a protected status customer.

South Carolina

Date-based termination protection: December 1 through March 31
Temperature-based termination protection: None
Seasonal Policy: A residential customer during the months of December through March will not be terminated where such customer, or a member of his household at the premises to which service is rendered, can furnish to the utility, no less than 3 days prior to termination of service or to the terminating crew at time of termination, a certificate on a form provided by the utility and signed by a licensed physician, that termination of electric service would be especially dangerous to such person's health. A certification shall expire on the 31st day from the date of execution by the physician. Such certification may be renewed no more than 3 times for an additional 30-day period each.

South Dakota

Date-based termination protection: November 1 through March 31
Temperature-based termination protection: None

Seasonal Policy: A utility may not disconnect residential service from November 1 to March 31 without adding an additional 30 days before disconnecting that service. The utility shall notify the customer before the normal disconnection date that the customer has an additional 30 days until disconnection.

Tennessee
Date-based termination protection: None
Temperature-based termination protection: None
Seasonal Policy: None

Texas
Date-based termination protection: None
Temperature-based termination protection: 32° Fahrenheit or below or during a heat advisory
Seasonal Policy: An electric utility cannot disconnect a customer anywhere in its service territory on a day when: (1) the previous day's highest temperature did not exceed 32° Fahrenheit, and the temperature is predicted to remain at or below that level for the next 24 hours, according to the nearest National Weather Service reports; or (2) the NWS issues a heat advisory for any county in the electric utility's service territory.

Utah
Date-based termination protection: November 15 through March 15
Temperature-based termination protection: None
Seasonal Policy: A residential customer must meet the following criteria to qualify for the HEAT winter termination protection program: (1) gross household income is less than 125% of the federal poverty level or the household has suffered a medical or other emergency, loss of employment, or is experiencing other circumstances which have resulted in a substantial loss of income; (2) the customer has made application to public and private energy assistance programs; (3) the customer is willing to make a good faith effort to pay these utility bills on a consistent basis; and (4) any additional information required by the department.

Vermont
Date-based termination protection: November 1 through March 31
Temperature-based termination protection: 10° Fahrenheit or below
Seasonal Policy: No gas or electric utility may disconnect service to any residential ratepayer between November 1 and March 31, if the temperature, as predicted by a current National Weather Service forecast for the Burlington, Vt. area, will drop under 10° Fahrenheit during a 48-hour period beginning between 7:00 A.M. and 10:00 A.M. on the anticipated date of disconnection. Utility service to households with any member aged 62 or older shall not be disconnected during the winter period if outdoor temperatures are forecast to fall below 32° Fahrenheit during a 48-hour period beginning between 7:00 A.M. and 10:00 A.M. on the anticipated date of disconnection.

Virginia
Date-based termination protection: None
Temperature-based termination protection: None
Seasonal Policy: None

Washington
Date-based termination protection: November 15 through March 15
Temperature-based termination protection: None
Seasonal Policy: During the winter months, between November 15 and March 15, a gas utility may not discontinue residential space heating service if the customer does all of the following: (1) notifies the utility of the inability to pay the bill and any required deposit; (2) provides self-certification of household income; (3) applies for home energy assistance from appropriate government and/or private sector organizations; (4) applies to the utility or other appropriate agencies for low-income weatherization assistance if such assistance is available for the dwelling; (5) agrees and abides by a payment plan offered by the utility.

West Virginia
Date-based termination protection: December 1 through February 28
Temperature-based termination protection: None
Seasonal Policy: Termination shall be delayed and a payment plan offered if termination would be dangerous to the health of a member of the household or if it is between December and February. Written certification from a licensed physician that termination of service would be especially dangerous must be obtained, however, the certification need not be renewed if a licensed physician can state to a reasonable degree of medical certainty that the condition is permanent.

Wisconsin
Date-based termination protection: November 1 through April 15
Temperature-based termination protection: None
Seasonal Policy: A utility may disconnect only those households whose gross quarterly incomes are above 250% of the federal income poverty guidelines and where health and safety would not be endangered because of the infirmities of age, developmental or mental disabilities or like infirmities incurred at any age or the frailties associated with being very young, if service were terminated or not restored.

Wyoming
Date-based termination protection: November 1 through April 30
Temperature-based termination protection: None
Seasonal Policy: The utility shall attempt to contact the customer personally before disconnecting gas, electric or water utility service during the cold weather period of November 1 through April 30.

A.2 SERIOUS ILLNESS AND AGE-RELATED PROTECTIONS

Note: This appendix may not contain all of the relevant provisions for your state. Please refer to Appendix E.1 for citations to each state's regulations. States periodically update or amend their regulations, be sure to check your state's regulations for the most up-to-date information.

➡ **POINTER:** Households with young children or elders may be able to take advantage of the serious illness/life-threatening condition restriction on termination even where no age-related restriction exists.

Alabama

Serious Illness: Utilities shall adopt and follow reasonable tariff rules for discontinuing service when life or health may be threatened by termination. Alabama Public Service Commission General Rule 12.
Age/Disability: None.

Alaska

Serious Illness: Electric utilities must provide the notice of intent to discontinue service at least 30 days before the scheduled termination date if the electric utility knows that a person who is seriously ill, elderly, or disabled lives in the customer's residence. Electric utilities must postpone the scheduled disconnection date for 15 days and notify the customer if a customer notifies the utility that a person who is seriously ill, elderly, disabled, or dependent on human life support systems lives in the customer's residence after the notice of intent to discontinue service is issued. Alaska Administrative Code, title 3, section 52.450.
Age/Disability: None.

Arizona

Serious Illness: Service shall not be terminated for non-payment when termination would threaten the well-being of an occupant of the residence due to medical condition, illness, age, disability, or weather. Said customers will be provided with information concerning assistance and/or may be required to enter into payment plan to avoid termination. Arizona Administrative Code, section 14-2-211.
Age/Disability: None.

Arkansas

Serious Illness: Utilities must honor a physician's certificate in prescribed form that a customer/permanent resident has a serious medical condition and stating that suspension of service would result in substantial risk of death or grave impairment. Certificate can be given by telephone by doctor, nurse, R.N., or public or private agency providing mental health care services, but must be confirmed within 7 days by a physician's writing. Code of Arkansas Rules, agency 126, subagency 03, chapter 003, section 6.17.

Age/Disability: When informed that elderly/disabled customer cannot pay a bill on time, utility shall offer delayed payment agreement, arrange for levelized billing (gas and electric); explain right to third party notice; provide names of potential sources of assistance. Heightened termination notice requirements. Code of Arkansas Rules, agency 126, subagency 03, chapter 003, section 6.18.

California

Serious Illness: Customer who provides certification from licensed physician and surgeon that service termination will be life-threatening and who is unable to pay in normal period shall be permitted to amortize over a period not to exceed 12 months. West's Annotated California Codes, Public Utilities, section 779. Master-meters: A utility may not terminate service when a public health or building officer certifies that termination would result in a significant threat to the health or safety of the occupants or the public. West's Annotated California Codes, Public Utilities, section 777.1(e).
Age/Disability: None.

Colorado

Serious Illness: Service may not be discontinued or must be restored during any period when discontinuance would aggravate an existing medical condition or create a medical emergency for the customer or a permanent resident of the customer's household; certification of licensed doctor or health practitioner required; Initial certification by phone acceptable. Utility may require written confirmation within 10 days. Certification effective for 60 days with one 30 day extension period. Customer may invoke med cert provisions only once during 12 month period. Customers who secure service under this provision may enter or renegotiate installment plan. Those who have broken installment agreement may not renegotiate and must become current by expiration of certification period. Code of Colorado Regulations, volume 4, section 723-3-13(f).
Age/Disability: None.

Connecticut

Serious Illness: Company may not terminate service if resident is or becomes seriously ill or in a life threatening situation as certified by registered physician. Certification must be renewed every 15 days if physician doesn't specify length of illness. Initial cert can be made by telephone subject to company's right to written confirmation. If service continued under this section, customer shall enter amortization agreement. Regulations of Connecticut State Agencies, section 16-3-100(e).
Age/Disability: None.

Delaware

Serious Illness: Utility may not disconnect service upon receipt of certification from licensed physician or Christian Science practitioner that a named occupant is so ill that termination would adversely affect the occupant's safety. Code of Delaware Regulations, agency 10, subagency 800, chapter 003, section 3.2.
Age/Disability: None.

District of Columbia

Serious Illness: Utility shall postpone termination of service for up to 21 days if the customer provides a physician's certificate or notice from a public health official stating that termination would be detrimental to the health/safety of a person occupying the premises, provided that the customer enters into a deferred payment plan. The postponement may be extended for additional periods of not more than 21 days by renewal of the certificate or notice. District of Columbia Municipal Regulations, title 15, section 311.1.
Age/Disability: None.

Florida

Serious Illness: Each utility shall submit a procedure for discontinuance of service when that service is medically essential. Florida Administrative Code Annotated, rule 25-6.105.
Age/Disability: None.

Georgia

Serious Illness: Utility (gas) shall postpone termination for 10 days upon receiving notice form a customer followed by notice within 10 days from a licensed physician or health official that termination of service would be especially dangerous to the health of someone living at the residence. Postponement of termination shall be for 30 days and may be extended and additional 30 days. Official Compilation Rules and Regulations of the State of Georgia, rule 515-3-2.03.
Age/Disability: None.

Hawaii

Serious Illness: None.
Age/Disability: Termination of service to elderly or disabled customers may not commence without a written report and investigation by the utility to the PUC submitted not less than 5 days before the intended termination. Elderly customers must provide proof that they are 62+ by appearing in person at the utility office or by verifying date of birth in a personal written statement. Disabled customers can qualify by certification of physical condition by either a registered physician or and appropriate state agency. Weil's Code of Hawaii Rules, section 6-60-8.

Idaho

Serious Illness: A utility shall delay disconnection an additional 30 days upon receipt of a certificate from a physician or social service agency that a medical emergency exists with an option for an additional thirty-day delay. If a customer whose service has been disconnected is eligible for a medical delay, service shall be restored within 24 hours with the limit beginning on the day of restoration. Idaho Administrative Code rule 31.21.01.308.
Age/Disability: None.

Illinois

Serious Illness: When certified by either a physician or Board of Health, termination may not occur if it would aggravate an existing medical emergency. Certification must be renewed every 30 days. Illinois Administrative Code, title 83, section 280.130.
Age/Disability: None.

Indiana

Serious Illness: Utility shall delay disconnection an additional 10 days upon receipt of a certificate from a physician or social service agency that a medical emergency exists. Indiana Administrative Code, title 170, section 4-1-16.
Age/Disability: None.

Iowa

Serious Illness: Utility shall delay disconnection an additional 30 days upon receipt of a certificate from a physician or social service agency that a medical emergency exists. Medical professional may initially notify the utility, but shall provide written cert within 5 days of initial notice. Iowa Administrative Code, rule 199-19.4(15).
Age/Disability: None.

Kansas

Serious Illness: Service may not be discontinued when it would adversely affect a serious illness. Kansas Consumer Information Rule IV.
Age/Disability: None.

Kentucky

Serious Illness: Utility shall postpone termination for 30 days upon receiving notice from a licensed physician or public health official that termination of service would be especially dangerous to the health of someone living at the residence. Postponement may be extended an additional 30 days. Kentucky Administrative Regulations Service, title 807, rule 5:006, section 14.
Age/Disability: None.

Louisiana

Serious Illness: None.
Age/Disability: None.

Maine

Serious Illness: Utility shall not terminate for 3 days when notified that a medical emergency exists. Disconnection shall be delayed 30 days when a medical emergency, as certified by a medical doctor, orally or in writing, exists. Written confirmation is required 7 days after oral notification. Certificate renewable in intervals of 30 days; customer must enter into payment plan. Code of Maine Rules, agency 65, subagency 407, chapter 81, section 10.
Age/Disability: None.

Maryland

Serious Illness: Subject to physician certification, electric or gas service, or both shall not be terminated for an initial period of up to 30 days beyond the scheduled date of service termination when the termination will aggravate an existing serious illness or prevent the use of life support equipment of nay occupant of the premises; payment plans for past due bills; certification renewable. The utility may refuse to honor the certification is it is not competed, not signed by a licensed physician, or appears to have been altered. It may also petition the Commission regarding the adequacy of a certification for any other reason, but may not terminate service until a Commission determination, or expiration of a certification that in not renewed. Code of Maryland Regulations, rule 20.31.03.01.

Age/Disability: If utility is aware that termination is to occur at residence of an elderly (65+) or disabled person, utility shall attempt to make personal contact on at least two occasions and shall inform customer of any financial assistance available to avoid termination. Code of Maryland Regulations, rule 20. 31.03.02.

Massachusetts

Serious Illness: Utilities cannot terminate or refuse to restore a customer's service if the customer or someone living in the customer's house is seriously ill. Utilities cannot terminate or refuse to restore a customer's service if there's a child under the age of 12 months and service hasn't terminated for non-payment before the child's birth. Customer can begin claim for infant protection by phoning the Dept. A registered physician/ local board of health official shall return official cert form within 7 days. Serious illness cert renewal due monthly. Code of Massachusetts Regulations, title 220, section 25.03.

Age/Disability: Utilities cannot terminate or refuse to restore a customer's service if there's a child under the age of 12 months and service hasn't terminated for non-payment before the child's birth. Customer can begin claim for infant protection by phoning the Dept. Code of Massachusetts Regulations, title 220, section 25.03. Utilities cannot discontinue service to a household where all residents are 65+. Code of Massachusetts Regulations, title 220, section 25.05.

Michigan

Serious Illness: Termination may not occur for an additional 21 days if it would aggravate an existing medical emergency or condition that has been certified. Certification may be renewed an additional 42 days. Customer may notify utility of an existing medical emergency by telephone and shall have 7 days to produce certification. Michigan Administrative Code, rule 460.2153.

Age/Disability: Elderly (65+) and low-income (150% of poverty line or recipient of means-tested benefit) customer shall not have service terminated for non-payment of bills during the winter protection period (Dec. 1–Mar. 31) if they agree and satisfy terms of payment program. Michigan Administrative Code, rule 460.2174.

Minnesota

Serious Illness: None.
Age/Disability: None.

Mississippi

Serious Illness: If customer subject to termination of service, demonstrates a medical emergency from December through March, the utility shall not terminate service without offering a levelized plan. Customers demonstrating a medical emergency

shall not have service terminated after April 1st if the customer agrees to a levelized billing plan. Mississippi Public Service Commission Rule 8.
Age/Disability: None.

Missouri

Serious Illness: Discontinuance shall be postponed for 21 days due to the medical condition of an occupant. Missouri Code of State Regulations Annotated, title 4, section 240-13.055.

Age/Disability: With respect to termination for heat-related service during cold weather months, the methods of notification and discontinuance are increased when occupants within the premises are either disabled, elderly, or eligible or receiving low-income energy assistance. Missouri Code of State Regulations Annotated, title 4, section 240-13.055.

Montana

Serious Illness: When certified by either a physician or the Board of Health, termination may not occur if it would aggravate an existing medical emergency. Certificate must be renewed every 30 days. Administrative Rules of Montana, rule 38.5.1411.
Age/Disability: None.

Nebraska

Serious Illness: Termination would be postponed upon receipt of certification by licensed physician that such termination would worsen a resident's illness or disability; a 30-day extension is available. Nebraska Administrative Code, title 70, section 1606.
Age/Disability: None.

Nevada

Serious Illness: Utility shall postpone termination for 30 days upon receiving notice from licensed physician or public health official that service termination would be especially dangerous to the health of someone living at the residence. Postponement can be extended 30 days. Nevada Administrative Code, section 704.370.

Age/Disability: Utility shall not terminate service of a residence where an elderly or disabled person resides unless it's notified some adult resident, in persons or by phone, 48 hours prior to termination. Nevada Administrative Code, section 704.390.

New Hampshire

Serious Illness: During winter regulation rules, if utility is notified by a licensed physician that a medical emergency would be caused by disconnection, or the utility receives a guarantee from a welfare office, service shall not be disconnected. New Hampshire Code of Administrative Rules Annotated, Public Utilities Commission, rule 1203.11.
Age/Disability: None.

New Jersey

Serious Illness: None.
Age/Disability: None.

New Mexico

Serious Illness: None.
Age/Disability: None.

New York

Serious Illness: No utility shall terminate or refuse to restore service for 30 days when a medical emergency, as certified by a medical doctor or local board of health, orally or in writing, exists. A demonstration of the customer's inability to pay charges for service shall be required before a certificate of medical emergency can be renewed. If the medical condition is likely to continue beyond the expiration of the an initial certification, a certificate may be renewed for 60 days or, subject to commission approval, a longer period. Customers remain liable for charges incurred while certificate is in effect. Once certificate expires, utility shall abide by notification and termination requirements. Official Compilation of Codes, Rules & Regulations of the State of New York, title 16, section 11.5.

Age/Disability: No utility shall terminate or refuse to restore service where a customer is blind, disabled, or 62 years of age or older, and all the remaining residents of the household are 62+, under 18 or blind or disabled unless it makes a diligent effort to contact by phone, or in person an adult resident at the customer's premises at least 72 hours prior to termination of service for the purpose of devising a payment plan. If a plan cannot be implemented, the utility shall delay termination for 15 days and notify and request that social services assist in devising a plan. Official Compilation of Codes, Rules & Regulations of the State of New York, title 16, section 11.5.

North Carolina

Serious Illness: None.
Age/Disability: None.

North Dakota

Serious Illness: 30 day termination stay is available if a resident is elderly, disabled, or a medical emergency would result from terminating service. North Dakota Administrative Code, section 69-09-01-18.1.

Age/Disability: 30 day termination stay is available if a resident is elderly, disabled, or a medical emergency would result from terminating service. North Dakota Administrative Code, section 69-09-01-18.1.

Ohio

Serious Illness: The company shall not disconnect service for nonpayment if the disconnection of service would be especially dangerous to health. The condition shall be certified to the company by a licensed physician, physician assistant, clinical nurse specialist, certified nurse practitioner, certified nurse-midwife, or local board of health physician. Certification shall prohibit disconnection of service for thirty days. Certification may be renewed two additional times (thirty days each) by a licensed physician, physician assistant, clinical nurse specialist, certified nurse practitioner, certified nurse-midwife, or local board of health physician by providing an additional certificate to the company. The total certification period is not to exceed ninety days per household in any twelve-month period. If a medical certificate is used to avoid disconnection, the customer shall enter into an extended payment plan prior to the end of the medical certification period or be subject to disconnection. Baldwin's Ohio Administrative Code, rule 4901:1-18-05.

Age/Disability: None.

Oklahoma

Serious Illness: A delay of at least 30 days when other circumstances would endanger the life, health, or property of the consumer shall be allowed upon verification. Oklahoma Administrative Code, section 165:35-21-10.

Age/Disability: None.

Oregon

Serious Illness: Disconnection shall be delayed upon oral or written confirmation that disconnection would significantly endanger the physical health of the customer or a member of the customer's household. Oral notification shall be confirmed within 14 days. Delay shall be valid for duration of condition but may not exceed 6 months for non-chronic conditions and 12 months for chronic ones. Customer shall enter into payment arrangement for an overdue balance and may renegotiate if a financial hardship is shown. Oregon Administrative Rules, rule 860-021-0410.

Age/Disability: None.

Pennsylvania

Serious Illness: Utility may not terminate or refuse to restore service to a premise when an occupant therein is certified by a physician to be seriously ill or affected with a medical condition that will be aggravated by a cessation of service or failure to restore service. If, prior to service termination, the utility employee is informed that an occupant is seriously ill or is affected with a medical condition which will be aggravated by a service cessation and that a medical certification will be procured, termination may not occur for at least 3 days. Certification may be renewed for 2 additional 30 day periods. Pennsylvania Code, title 52, sections 56.111, 56.112, 56.114.

Age/Disability: None.

Rhode Island

Serious Illness: Utility shall postpone termination for 21 days upon receiving notice from licensed physician or public health official that termination of service would be especially dangerous to the health of someone living at the residence. Postponement of termination may be extended after review. Code of Rhode Island Rules, agency 90, subagency 060, chapter 002.

Age/Disability: Disconnection is also restricted when services are provided to the elderly, disabled, or customers eligible under RI hardship exception. Code of Rhode Island Rules, agency 90, subagency 060, chapter 002.

South Carolina

Serious Illness: 30-day delay option for certified medical reasons during winter protection months (December-March). Code of Laws of South Carolina 1976 Annotated: Code of Regulations, rule 103-352.
Age/Disability: None.

South Dakota

Serious Illness: Utility shall delay disconnection an additional 30 days upon receipt of a certificate from a physician or social service agency that a medical emergency exists. Administrative Rules of South Dakota, rule R.20:10:20:1.
Age/Disability: None.

Tennessee

Serious Illness: Upon receiving written notification from a physician, public health official, or social service agency that a medical condition would be aggravated due to termination of service, termination shall be postponed for 30 days and the utility shall refer the customer to a social service agency. Official Compilation Rules & Regulations of the State of Tennessee, rule 1220-4-4-.19.
Age/Disability: None.

Texas

Serious Illness: If, upon physician verification, a person residing in the unit would become seriously ill or more seriously ill as a result of disconnection, disconnection shall be delayed. Texas Administrative Code, title 16, section 25.29.
Age/Disability: None.

Utah

Serious Illness: Upon receipt of a physician's written notification that a medical condition may be aggravated due to termination or that a health hazard exists, service shall be restored or termination delayed for a period indicated in the physician's certification or 1 month, whichever is less. Utah Administrative Code, rule R.746-200-6.
Age/Disability: None.

Vermont

Serious Illness: No utility shall terminate or refuse to restore service for 30 days when a medical emergency, as certified by a medical doctor or local board of health, orally or in writing, exists. If the medical condition is likely to continue beyond the expiration of the an initial certification, a certificate may be renewed for 60 days or, subject to commission approval, a longer period. Customers remain liable for charges incurred while certificate is in effect. Vermont Public Service Board Rule 3.302.
Age/Disability: Service shall not be disconnected between November 1 - March 31 when the temperature will be below 32 degrees during the following 48 hours at the time of disconnection if someone 62 years+ and resides within the residence. Vermont Public Service Board Rule 3.303.

Virginia
Serious Illness: None.
Age/Disability: None.

Washington
Serious Illness: When utility is notified of a medical emergency related to disconnection, the utility shall reconnect service at least by the next business day without requiring a deposit or a reconnection fee, or disconnection shall be delayed for an additional 5 days pending written physician certification. Written certification shall delay disconnection for 60 days and may be renewed for additional 60 days. During the delay period, the utility may require the customer to keep the account current, pay 10% of any outstanding balance and enter into a payment plan that reconciles the account within 120 days. Washington Administrative Code, rule 480-90-128.
Age/Disability: None.

West Virginia
Serious Illness: Termination shall be delayed and a payment plan offered in some circumstances if termination would be dangerous to the health and safety of a household member (medically or from December through February). Medical certification must be received 10 days after utility notification and shall be renewed every thirty days unless a physician states to a reasonable degree of medical certainty that the condition is permanent. West Virginia Code of State Rules, section 150-3-4.8.
Age/Disability: Service shall not be terminated to residential customers 65+ unless the customer refuses to enter into a payment plan. West Virginia Code of State Rules, section 150-3-4.8.

Wisconsin
Serious Illness: Disconnection shall be delayed for 21 days and utility shall negotiate special payment arrangements when a licensed physician, public health, social service, or law enforcement official certifies that a medical or protective emergency would result from disconnection. Wisconsin Administrative Code, Public Service Commission, section 113.0301.
Age/Disability: None.

Wyoming
Serious Illness: Utility must notify residence subject to termination of service that an additional 15 day delay is available if it can be documented that a resident is disabled or seriously ill. An additional 30 days' notice is required if household resident is dependent on utility for life support services. Wisconsin Administrative Code, agency 023, subagency 020, chapter 002, section 242.
Age/Disability: None.

A.3 TERMINATION TIME FRAMES

Note: This appendix may not contain all of the relevant provisions for your state. Please refer to Appendix E.1 for citations to each state's regulations.

Alabama
Payment Period: 10 days
Termination Notice Period: 5-day termination notice
Notice Void: None
Applicable Regulatory Provisions: Alabama Public Service Commission General Rule 12

Alaska
Payment Period: 40 days
Termination Notice Period: 15-day termination notice
Notice Void: None
Applicable Regulatory Provisions: Alaska Administrative Code, title 3, section 52.45

Arizona
Payment Period: 15 days
Termination Notice Period: 5-day termination notice
Notice Void: None
Applicable Regulatory Provisions: Arizona Administrative Code, section 14-2-210 and 14-2-211

Arkansas
Payment Period: 14 days (22 days if late charge is imposed)
Termination Notice Period: 5-day termination notice; 8 days if mailed
Notice Void: A utility must suspend service within 30 days after the last day to pay.
Applicable Regulatory Provisions: Code of Arkansas Rules, agency 126, subagency 03, chapter 003, sections 5.03 and 6.03

California
Payment Period: 19 days
Termination Notice Period: 10-day termination notice; 15 days if mailed
Notice Void: None
Applicable Regulatory Provisions: West's Annotated California Codes, Public Utilities, sections 779.1

Colorado
Payment Period: 10 days
Termination Notice Period: Electric: 10-day termination notice; Gas: 7-day termination notice
Notice Void: None
Applicable Regulatory Provisions: Code of Colorado Regulations, volume number 4, section 723-5-13(b)

Connecticut

Payment Period: 33 days

Termination Notice Period: 13-day termination notice

Notice Void: If service is not terminated within 120 days of notice, company shall mail another notice at least 13 days before termination.

Applicable Regulatory Provisions: Regulations of Connecticut State Agencies, sections 16-3-100(a)(5) and 16-3-100(d)

Delaware

Payment Period: 20 days

Termination Notice Period: 14-day termination notice

Notice Void: None

Applicable Regulatory Provisions: Code of Delaware Regulations, agency 10, subagency 800, chapter 003, rule 3.1

District of Columbia

Payment Period: 20 days

Termination Notice Period: 15-day termination notice

Notice Void: None

Applicable Regulatory Provisions: District of Columbia Municipal Regulations, title 15, sections 306.1, 311.3

Florida

Payment Period: 20 days

Termination Notice Period: 5-day termination notice

Notice Void: None

Applicable Regulatory Provisions: Florida Administrative Code Annotated, rules 25-6.101, 25-6.105

Georgia

Payment Period: Electric: 45 days; Gas: 20 days

Termination Notice Period: Electric: 5-day termination notice; Gas: 15-day termination notice

Notice Void: None

Applicable Regulatory Provisions: Official Compilation Rules and Regulations of the State of Georgia, rules 515-3-2.0, 515-3-2.02, 515-3-3.02(B), 515-7-6.02

Hawaii

Payment Period: 15 days

Termination Notice Period: Reasonable notice of termination

Notice Void: None

Applicable Regulatory Provisions: Weil's Code of Hawaii Rules, section 6-60-8

Idaho

Payment Period: 15 days of date of issuance

Termination Notice Period: 8-day termination notice

Notice Void: Notice requirements shall be repeated if termination does not occur 21 days after the scheduled termination date.

Applicable Regulatory Provisions: Idaho Administrative Code, rules 31.21.01.202, 31.21.01.304, 31.21.01.305

Illinois

Payment Period: 21 days (considered delinquent after 23 days)

Termination Notice Period: 5-day termination notice; 8-day termination notice if mailed.

Notice Void: Disconnection notice remains effective for two consecutive 20 day periods, provided personal contact (in-person or phone) is made.

Applicable Regulatory Provisions: Illinois Administrative Code, title 83, sections 280.90, 280.130

Indiana

Payment Period: 17 days

Termination Notice Period: 14-day termination notice

Notice Void: None

Applicable Regulatory Provisions: Indiana Administrative Code, title 170, rules 4-1-13, 4-1-16

Iowa

Payment Period: 20 days

Termination Notice Period: 12-day termination notice

Notice Void: None

Applicable Regulatory Provisions: Iowa Administrative Code, rules 199-19.4(11), 19.4(15)

Kansas

Payment Period: Payment due upon receipt. Bill is delinquent if payment is not received in time to be credited before the next billing cycle.

Termination Notice Period: 10-day termination notice

Notice Void: None

Applicable Regulatory Provisions: Kansas Consumer Information Rules II and IV

Kentucky

Payment Period: 27 days

Termination Notice Period: 10-day termination notice

Notice Void: None

Applicable Regulatory Provisions: Kentucky Administrative Regulations Service, title 807, rule 5:006, section 14

Louisiana

Payment Period: 20 days

Termination Notice Period: 5-day termination notice

Notice Void: None

Applicable Regulatory Provisions: General Order U 9-10-57

Maine

Payment Period: 25 days

Termination Notice Period: 14-day termination notice

Notice Void: Disconnection notices shall expire 10 days after the scheduled date of disconnection and shall require the utility to repeat notification procedures.

Applicable Regulatory Provisions: Code of Maine Rules, agency 65, subagency 407, chapter 81, section 9

Maryland

Payment Period: 20 days

Termination Notice Period: 14-day termination notice; 7-day termination notice (obtaining service using fraudulent means)

Notice Void: None

Applicable Regulatory Provisions: Code of Maryland Regulations, rules 20.31.02.04 and 20.31.02.05

Massachusetts

Payment Period: 45 days

Termination Notice Period: 3-day termination notice

Notice Void: None

Applicable Regulatory Provisions: Massachusetts Regulations, title 220, section 25.02

Michigan

Payment Period: 17 days

Termination Notice Period: 10-day termination notice; 30-day termination notice for single-metered residence containing 5+ families

Notice Void: Utility must send final termination notice 72 hours to 14 days before termination.

Applicable Regulatory Provisions: Michigan Administrative Code, rules 460.2116, 460.2163

Minnesota

Payment Period: Payment due by next scheduled billing date which must not be less than 25 days from current billing date.

Termination Notice Period: 5 day termination notice

Notice Void: None

Applicable Regulatory Provisions: Minnesota Rules, rules 7820.5300, 7820.2300

Mississippi

Payment Period: None

Termination Notice Period: 5-day termination notice

Notice Void: None

Applicable Regulatory Provisions: Code of Mississippi Rules, agency 26, subagency 000, chapter 02, section 8

Missouri

Payment Period: Payment due 21 days from the date of billing
Termination Notice Period: 4-day termination notice when hand-delivered; 10-days when mailed
Notice Void: None
Applicable Regulatory Provisions: Missouri Code of State Regulations Annotated, title 4, sections 240-13.020, 240-13.050

Montana

Payment Period: None specified
Termination Notice Period: 10-day initial termination notice; 10-day second termination notice if no response to first notice.
Notice Void: None
Applicable Regulatory Provisions: Administrative Rules of Montana, rule 38.5.1405

Nebraska

Payment Period: None
Termination Notice Period: 7-day termination notice; if customer is welfare recipient termination notice must be sent by certified mail
Notice Void: None
Applicable Regulatory Provisions: Revised Statutes of Nebraska, sections 70-1603, 70-1605

Nevada

Payment Period: 15 days (4-day grace period for payments made by first class mail)
Termination Notice Period: 10-day termination notice
Notice Void: None
Applicable Regulatory Provisions: Nevada Administrative Code, chapter 704, sections 339, 360

New Hampshire

Payment Period: 25 days
Termination Notice Period: 14-day termination notice
Notice Void: None
Applicable Regulatory Provisions: New Hampshire Code of Administrative Rules Annotated, Public Utilities Commission, rules 1201.08, 1203.11

New Jersey

Payment Period: 15 days
Termination Notice Period: 10-day written notice
Notice Void: None
Applicable Regulatory Provisions: New Jersey Administrative Code, sections 14:3-7.12

New Mexico
Payment Period: 20 days (35 days-delinquent)
Termination Notice Period: 15 day-termination notice; 3-day termination notice when termination due to refusal of customer to allow utility access
Notice Void: None
Applicable Regulatory Provisions: New Mexico Rules, sections 17.5.410.13, 17.5.410.29

New York
Payment Period: 3 days
Termination Notice Period: 15-day termination notice after bill is 20 days past due; Note: if utility is aware that a customer subject to service termination receives public assistance or SSI, it shall notify the assisting organization 3-5 days prior to termination.
Notice Void: None
Applicable Regulatory Provisions: Official Compilation of Codes, Rules & Regulations of the State of New York, title 16, section 11.4

North Carolina
Payment Period: 25 days
Termination Notice Period: Electric: 5-day termination notice. Gas: 10-day termination notice
Notice Void: None
Applicable Regulatory Provisions: North Carolina Administrative Code, title 4, rules 11.R.12-10, 11.R.12-8

North Dakota
Payment Period: None
Termination Notice Period: 10-day termination notice by first class mail or in person
Notice Void: None
Applicable Regulatory Provisions: North Dakota Administrative Code, rule 69-09-01-18.1

Ohio
Payment Period: 14 days
Termination Notice Period: 14-day termination notice
Notice Void: None
Applicable Regulatory Provisions: Baldwin's Ohio Administrative Code, rule 4901:1-18-05

Oklahoma
Payment Period: 20 days
Termination Notice Period: 10-day termination notice
Notice Void: Disconnection may occur the date of or 30 days after scheduled disconnection.
Applicable Regulatory Provisions: Oklahoma Administrative Code, sections 165:35-19-40, 165:35-21-20

Oregon
Payment Period: 15 days
Termination Notice Period: 15-day first termination notice; 5-day final notice
Notice Void: None
Applicable Regulatory Provisions: Oregon Administrative Rules, rules 860-021-0125, 860-021-0405

Pennsylvania
Payment Period: 20 days
Termination Notice Period: 10-day termination notice; in hazardous/emergency conditions, a utility may not interrupt/terminate without personally contacting the occupant at least 3 days prior to interruption/termination.
Notice Void: None
Applicable Regulatory Provisions: Pennsylvania Code, title 52, sections 56.21, 56.91, 56.93

Rhode Island
Payment Period: 30 days
Termination Notice Period: Electric: 10-day termination notice; Gas: 5-day termination notice
Notice Void: None
Applicable Regulatory Provisions: Code of Rhode Island Rules, agency 90, subagency 060, section 002

South Carolina
Payment Period: 25 days
Termination Notice Period: 10-day termination notice (5-day termination notice for termination due to delinquent payment plan)
Notice Void: None
Applicable Regulatory Provisions: Code of Laws of South Carolina 1976 Annotated: Code of Regulations, rules 103-339, 103-352

South Dakota
Payment Period: 20 days
Termination Notice Period: 10-day termination notice certified mail)
Notice Void: None
Applicable Regulatory Provisions: Administrative Rules of South Dakota, rule R.20:10:20:03

Tennessee
Payment Period: None
Termination Notice Period: 7-day termination notice
Notice Void: None
Applicable Regulatory Provisions: Official Compilation Rules & Regulations of the State of Tennessee, rules 1220-4-4-.19

89

Texas

Payment Period: 16 days
Termination Notice Period: 10-day termination notice
Notice Void: None
Applicable Regulatory Provisions: Texas Administrative Code, title 16, sections 25.28 and 25.29

Utah

Payment Period: 20 days
Termination Notice Period: None
Notice Void: None
Applicable Regulatory Provisions: Utah Administrative Code, rules R746-200-4

Vermont

Payment Period: 30 days
Termination Notice Period: Notice of delinquency and disconnection shall be no more than 40 days after delinquency, but notice shall not be more than 20 days or less than 14 days prior to the first date of disconnection.
Notice Void: Notice shall not be more than 20 days prior to the first date of disconnection.
Applicable Regulatory Provisions: Code of Vermont Rules, agency 30, subagency 000, chapter 03, section 3.301

Virginia

Payment Period: 20 days
Termination Notice Period: 10-day termination notice
Notice Void: None
Applicable Regulatory Provisions: Virginia Administrative Code, title 20, sections 5-10-10, 56-247.1

Washington

Payment Period: None
Termination Notice Period: 8-day termination notice
Notice Void: Disconnection not occurring within 10 days of scheduled date voids the initial notice and requires notice requirements to be repeated.
Applicable Regulatory Provisions: Washington Administrative Code, rule 480-90-128

West Virginia

Payment Period: Service may be terminated 30 days after due date.
Termination Notice Period: 10-day termination notice; 5-days for violation of payment plan
Notice Void: Notice void if service not terminated within 30 days.
Applicable Regulatory Provisions: West Virginia Code of State Rules, section 150-3-4.8

Wisconsin

Payment Period: 20 days

Termination Notice Period: 10-day termination notice

Notice Void: If service is not disconnected within 10 days after disconnection date, notice procedures shall be repeated.

Applicable Regulatory Provisions: Wisconsin Administrative Code, Public Service Commission, sections 113.0301

Wyoming

Payment Period: None

Termination Notice Period: 7-day termination notice

Notice Void: None

Applicable Regulatory Provisions: Weil's Code of Wyoming Rules, agency 023, subagency 020, chapter 2, section 242

APPENDIX B

Selected Utility Regulations

B.1 DEPOSITS, SELECTED REGULATIONS

NOTE: These are *summaries* prepared by the authors, not the word-for-word text of the regulations. For complete text, consult the state PUC's web site.

Alabama
Alabama Public Service Commission General Rule 8—Deposits
Utilities may require deposits from customers before beginning or continuing service if they judge the deposit is necessary. The amount of the deposit shall not exceed the amount of an estimated bill for two (2) billing periods or for billing in advance the amount of the estimated bill for one (1) billing period plus two (2) months estimated toll. Interest shall accrue at a rate of 7% per annum and shall be credited on the December bill.

Utilities may require deposits after giving five (5) days written notice from customers if their account is not in good standing or their deposit was refunded or their usage increases. Telephone utilities may require an additional deposit from customers after giving written notice if there is an excessive toll and the customer is a known credit risk. Telephone utilities may use toll blocking if they do not receive a deposit or discontinue local service if they cannot use toll blocking.

Utilities shall keep records of customers' deposits and issue receipts to customers.

Utilities shall refund deposits to customers in December after twenty-four (24) months if the account is considered to be in good standing. Customers may apply for a refund earlier.

Minnesota
Minnesota Rules rule 7820.4700—When Deposit or Payment Guarantee Impermissible
A utility shall not require a deposit or a guarantee of payment based upon income, home ownership, residential location, employment tenure, nature of occupation, race, color, creed, sex, marital status, age, national origin, or any other criterion that does not bear a reasonable relationship to the assurance of payment of which is not authorized by this chapter.

No utility shall use any credit reports other than those reflecting the purchase of utility services to determine the adequacy of a customer's credit history without the permission in writing of a customer. Refusal of a customer to permit use of a credit rating or credit service other than that of a utility shall not affect the determination of the utility as to that customer's credit history.

Missouri

Missouri Code of State Regulations Annotated title 4, section 240-13.030—Deposits and Guarantees of Payment

A new or existing customer may be required to pay a deposit or provide a guarantee of payment if they have insufficient credit due to delinquent bills (past or present), diversion of services, or failure to meet the tariff's accepted credit rating. Deposits and guarantees shall not exceed one-sixth (1/6) of the estimated annual bill for new monthly customers, one-third (1/3) of the estimated annual bill for new quarterly customers, or twice the highest bill in the prior twelve (12) months for existing customers, and, when assessed during November-January, may be paid in six (6) monthly installments. All deposits shall accrue interest based on the tariff rate. Deposits, and guarantees, shall be returned or credited to the account after one year of timely payments.

Credit can be established with a record of home ownership or purchase, 1-year full time employment or adequate source of income, or references from commercial creditors.

South Dakota

Administrative Rules of South Dakota rule 20:10:19:01—Nondiscriminatory Credit Policy

Credit policy shall be easily understandable and nondiscriminatory. Redlining, through the use of "economic character of the area," "collective credit reputation," home ownership, or friendly relationships with a bank as means of establishing credit is explicitly prohibited.

B.2 LIMITATIONS ON GROUNDS FOR DISCONNECTIONS AND DENYING SERVICE, SELECTED REGULATIONS

[NOTE: These are *summaries* of sample regulations. For actual wording, check the regulations cited.]

LIMITATIONS ON GROUNDS FOR DISCONNECTION

Maine

Code of Maine Rules agency 65, subagency 407, chapter 81, rule 8—When Disconnection Cannot Occur

Disconnection shall not occur for non-payment of services other than basic utility service, for non-payment of a different account or account of another (unless it has been determined that the customer is legally responsible), or during a medical emergency pursuant to rule 65-407-81-11.

Minnesota
Minnesota Rules rule 7820.1300—Non-permissible Reasons to Disconnect Service
Service shall not be disconnected due to delinquency in payment for services rendered to a previous customer who occupied the premises unless the customer continues to occupy the premises; failure to pay for merchandise, appliances, or services not approved by the commission as an integral part of the utility service; failure to pay for a different class of service; failure to pay for a bill to correct a previous under-billing due to an inaccurate meter or billing error if the customer agrees to payment over a reasonable period of time.

Oklahoma
Oklahoma Administrative Code rule 165:35-21-2—Disconnection of Service by Utility
Service may not be connected for failure to pay for services of a type or classification other than requested by the customer; or for an unpaid bill for services outside of the utility's territory; or for non-payment of a bill more than 3 years old, if the utility cannot fully substantiate the billing history; or for an unpaid bill of a prior customer (not currently a household member); or failure to pay a disputed portion of an estimated bill.

GROUNDS FOR DENYING SERVICE
Arizona
Arizona Administrative Code section 14-2-203—Establishment of Service
Service may be denied due to a hazardous condition, providing false information, or indebtedness to the utility (unless payment arrangements and/or deposits have been made).

Wisconsin
Wisconsin Administrative Code, Public Service Commission, section 113.0301—Disconnections; Residential
Service may be denied for issues relating to non-payment of past or present charges (including delinquent bills of prior occupant or customer residing in the premises to be served), interference with service of others, providing false information in obtaining information, failure to supply credit information, or failure to allow the utility to conduct a meter reading.

B.3 PAYMENT PLANS, SELECTED REGULATIONS

[NOTE: These are *summaries* or portions of sample regulations. For actual wording, check the regulations cited.]

DEFERRED PAYMENT PLANS
Iowa
Iowa Administrative Code rule 199-19.4(10)—Payment agreements (gas utility)
(the payment plan rules applicable to electric utility service are substantially similar and can be found at Iowa Administrative Code rule 199-20.4(11))

a. Availability of a first payment agreement. When a residential customer cannot pay in full a delinquent bill for utility service or has an outstanding debt to the utility for residential utility service and is not in default of a payment agreement with the utility, a utility shall offer the customer an opportunity to enter into a reasonable payment agreement.

b. Reasonableness. Whether a payment agreement is reasonable will be determined by considering the current household income, ability to pay, payment history including prior defaults on similar agreements, the size of the bill, the amount of time and the reasons why the bill has been outstanding, and any special circumstances creating extreme hardships within the household. The utility may require the person to confirm financial difficulty with an acknowledgment from the department of human services or another agency.

c. Terms of payment agreements.

(1) First payment agreement. The utility shall offer customers who have received a disconnection notice or have been disconnected 120 days or less and who are not in default of a payment agreement the option of spreading payments evenly over at least 12 months by paying specific amounts at scheduled times. The utility shall offer customers who have been disconnected more than 120 days and who are not in default of a payment agreement the option of spreading payments evenly over at least 6 months by paying specific amounts at scheduled times.

1. The agreement shall also include provision for payment of the current account. The agreement negotiations and periodic payment terms shall comply with tariff provisions which are consistent with these rules. The utility may also require the customer to enter into a level payment plan to pay the current bill.

2. When the customer makes the agreement in person, a signed copy of the agreement shall be provided to the customer.

3. The utility may offer the customer the option of making the agreement over the telephone or through electronic transmission. When the customer makes the agreement over the telephone or through electronic transmission, the utility shall render to the customer a written document reflecting the terms and conditions of the agreement within three days of the date the parties entered into the oral agreement or electronic agreement. The document will be considered rendered to the customer when addressed to the customer's last-known address and deposited in the U.S. mail with postage prepaid. If delivery is by other than U.S. mail, the document shall be considered rendered to the customer when delivered to the last-known address of the person responsible for payment for the service. The document shall state that unless the customer notifies the utility within ten days from the date the document is rendered, it will be deemed that the customer accepts the terms as reflected in the written document.

4. Each customer entering into a first payment agreement shall be granted at least one late payment that is made four days or less beyond the due date for payment and the first payment agreement shall remain in effect.

(2) Second payment agreement. The utility shall offer a second payment agreement to a customer who is in default of a first payment agreement if the customer has made at least two consecutive full payments under the first payment agreement. The second payment agreement shall be for the same term as or longer than the term of the first payment agreement. The customer shall be required to pay for current service in addition to the monthly payments under the second payment agreement and may be required to make the first payment up-front as a condition of entering into the second payment agreement. The utility may also require the customer to enter into a level payment plan to pay the current bill. The utility may offer additional payment agreements to the customer.

d. Refusal by utility. A customer may offer the utility a proposed payment agreement. If the utility and the customer do not reach an agreement, the utility may refuse the offer orally, but the utility must render a written refusal of the customer's final offer, stating the reason for the refusal, within three days of the oral notification. The written refusal shall be considered rendered to the customer when addressed to the customer's last-known address and deposited in the U.S. mail with postage prepaid. If delivery is by other than U.S. mail, the written refusal shall be considered rendered to the customer when handed to the customer or when delivered to the last-known address of the person responsible for the payment for the service.

A customer may ask the board for assistance in working out a reasonable payment agreement. The request for assistance must be made to the board within ten days after the rendering of the written refusal. During the review of this request, the utility shall not disconnect the service.

Illinois

Illinois Administrative Code title 83, section 280.110—Deferred Payment Agreements

a. Residential customers who are indebted to a utility for past due utility service shall have the opportunity to make arrangements with the utility to retire the debt by periodic payments referred to hereinafter as a deferred payment agreement unless this customer has failed to make payment under such a plan during the past twelve months. . . .

b. The terms and conditions of a reasonable deferred payment agreement and the utility's decision whether or not to offer an applicant for service a deferred payment agreement shall be determined by the utility after consideration of the following factors, based upon information available from current utility records or provided by the customer or applicant:

1. size of the past due account; and
2. customer or applicant's ability to pay; and
3. customer or applicant's payment history; and
4. reason for the outstanding indebtedness; and
5. any other relevant factors relating to the circumstances of the customer or applicant's service.

c. An applicant for residential service or a residential customer shall pay a maximum of 1/4 of the amount past due and owing at the time of entering into the deferred payment agreement . . . . The utility shall allow a minimum of two months (or, in the case of a gas or electric utility, four months) from the date of said agreement and a maximum of twelve months for payment to be made under a deferred payment agreement. A gas or electric customer may be permitted to enter into a deferred payment agreement which extends over less than four months, if he so chooses. Late payments charges may be assessed against the amount owing which is the subject of a deferred payment agreement.

d. A deferred payment agreement shall be in writing, with a copy provided to the applicant or customer, and shall conform to the following requirements:
1. the applicant or customer shall be required to pay all future bills for utility service by the due date; and
2. the applicant or customer shall retire his/her debt according to the terms of the deferred payment agreement.

. . . .

f. Renegotiation
If the gas or electric customer's economic or financial circumstances change during the effective period of a deferred payment agreement, and not more than 14 days has elapsed since the customer defaulted on the deferred payment agreement, the company shall be obliged, if the customer so requests, to renegotiate the terms and conditions of the deferred payment agreement, taking into consideration the changed economic and financial circumstances substantiated by the customer. The reinstatement of a previously defaulted deferred payment agreement pursuant to the provisions of this Section set forth below shall not prevent the renegotiation of a deferred payment agreement. However, the utility shall be obliged to renegotiate any deferred payment agreement more than one time or to extend the payment period beyond the maximum of twelve months available at the time the company and the customer entered into the original deferred payment agreement.

g. Reinstatement
1. If a gas or electric customer defaults on a deferred payment agreement but has not yet had service discontinued by the gas or electric utility, the utility shall permit such customer to be reinstated on the deferred payment agreement if the customer pays in full the amounts which should have been paid up to that date pursuant to the original payment agreement (including any amounts for current usage which have become past due). A utility shall be obliged to permit such reinstatement only once during the course of a deferred payment agreement.
2. If an applicant or customer shall default upon any payment due under the deferred payment agreement, the utility shall have the right to discontinue service pursuant to section 280.130 herein, subject to the renegotiation and reinstatement provisions contained in this Section.

Mississippi
Mississippi PSC Gen. Rule 8(E)—Mid-Winter Utility Service Cutoffs For Electric And Gas Residential Customers
For the months of December, January, February and March of each year, residential customers who are unable to pay the full amount of their utility bill because of extreme fi-

nancial difficulty may qualify for mid-winter rule which prohibits disconnection of service in those cases where the customer has complied with the following:

1. The customer shall inform the utility of the customer's inability to pay the utility bill in full due to extreme financial difficulty and shall, prior to the cutoff time provided in the notice of cutoff (if such notice has been given), deliver to the local office of the utility a copy of the most recent bill along with a signed statement by the customer clearly identifying the service location involved and certifying the existence of the extreme financial difficulty claimed.

2. Upon receipt of the above, the utility shall be prohibited from disconnecting the customer's service during the months of December, January, February and March if the customer agrees to the following extended payment plan:

   a. First, the customer shall pay the utility in full all amounts due utility on bills rendered to customer prior to November 11th.

   b. Second, the utility shall determine the monthly amount the customer would pay for utility service under the utility's level payment plan as provided for in the utility's filed tariff or by adding the amounts charged to that customer for utility service for the previous twelve (12) months and dividing the sum by twelve (12). If the customer has not received service from the utility for a sufficient period of time to determine a level payment amount for that specific customer, the utility will use a level payment amount for an average residential customer in the same geographical location.

   c. Third, the customer shall enter into a special payment plan, the first payment of which will be due upon execution of the plan, under which the customer shall pay the utility a sum equal to 133% of the levelized billing amount for the customer until such time as all amounts due the utility for previous utility service have been paid and the customer is current in his utility bill. Thereafter, at the option of the utility, the customer may be required to participate in the utility's level payment plan and shall pay the utility each month, the levelized billing amount applicable to that particular customer.

3. Should the customer enter into an agreement with the utility as set forth above and fail to abide by the terms of that agreement, the utility shall have the right to terminate service to the customer after giving at least five (5) days written notice to the customer. Provided, however, a customer's service shall not be terminated under circumstances during the months of December, January, February or March if the customer has provided the utility with a written statement signed by a licensed physician certifying that the discontinuance of domestic heating service to the customer would create a medical emergency for the customer or any member of the customer's household.

4. Any customer claiming the benefit of the "medical emergency" exception to this rule shall not have service terminated following the expiration of the mid-winter period if, by April 1st following the mid-winter period the customer agrees to pay, and does pay, to the utility a sum equal to 133% of the levelized billing amount provided for above from and after April 1st and until such time as all amounts due the utility for previous utility service have been paid and the customer is current in his utility bill.

LEVELIZED BILLING

Alaska

Alaska Administrative Code title 3, section 52.440—Levelized Billing

A utility shall offer a levelized billing option to its residential electric heating customers and may offer the option to all customers based upon the customer's actual consumption history for the most recent twelve (12) months or other representative period. Levelized billing shall be adjusted annually, or more frequently, according to usage, and any over-charge shall be immediately refunded or credited to the customer's account. A utility may not refuse enrollment in levelized billing to a customer whose current bill at the time of enrollment is past due or delinquent if the customer enters into a deferred payment agreement, as described in Alaska Administrative Code title 3, section 52.445.

PREFERRED PAYMENT DATE PROGRAM

Arkansas

Code of Arkansas Rules rule 126-03-003, section 5.09—Extended Due-Date Policy

Utilities must offer an extended due-date policy to: persons receiving Aid to Families with Dependent Children (AFDC) or Aid to the Aged, Blind and Disabled (AABD); persons receiving Supplemental Security Income; or persons whose primary source of income is Social Security or Department of Veterans Affairs disability or retirement benefits. The utility may require verification of these income sources. A qualifying customer's utility bill payment due date will be changed to coincide with or follow the customer's receipt of that income. When a customer applies for an extended due date, utilities shall explain the policy and give the explanation in writing.

Customers who qualify and who pay by the new date will not be considered late, but a late payment charge may be imposed on participants who do not pay by the extended due date. Utilities may remove an extended due date for failure to pay bills by the close of business on the due date two times in a row or any three times in the last twelve (12) months, and customers shall be notified in writing when the extended due date has been removed.

Illinois

Illinois Administrative Code title 83, section 280.90—Preferred Payment Date

Customers whose primary income is received ten (10) days following their billing due date shall be eligible for the preferred payment date program. Income that qualifies for the preferred payment date program: Aid to the Aged, Blind, and Disabled (AADB), SSI, VA benefits, unemployment compensation, general assistance, and supplemental security income.

BUDGET PAYMENT PLANS

Colorado

Code of Colorado Regulations volume number 4, section 723-3-13(e)(5)(b)—Alternative Payment Arrangement

A customer may choose in the alternative a "budget billing" arrangement, under which the amount owed shall be added to the preceding year's total billing and modified for rate increases or cost adjustments, with the total being billed in eleven (11) equal monthly payments followed by a settlement billing in the twelfth month.

Illinois
Illinois Administrative Code title 83, section 280.120—Budget Payment Plan
When the character of an applicant's or customer's consumption of service causes or is likely to cause a substantial fluctuation among his/her bills over an annual period, the utility shall offer to the applicant or customer a budget payment plan which equalizes his/her payments into monthly installments.

B.4 LANDLORD-TENANT PROCEDURES, SELECTED REGULATIONS

[NOTE: These are *summaries* or portions of sample regulations. For actual wording, check the regulations cited.]

District of Columbia
District of Columbia Municipal Regulations title 15, section 401.1—Tenants' Rights
A gas or electric utility shall not terminate service to any master-metered apartment building on the basis of non-payment by the owner unless that utility provides an opportunity for the tenants to assume prospective financial responsibility for the utility services in their own names, either individually or collectively, without any liability for the amount due while service was billed directly to the owner.

District of Columbia Municipal Regulations title 15, section 402.1—Notice of Tenants' Rights and Options
At least twenty-one (21) days prior to terminating service, a utility company shall send each tenant whose name is made known to the utility company a Notice of Tenants' Rights and Options. The notice shall contain the following:
   (a) A description of the options available to tenants for the provision of utility service:
      (1) Individual metering;
      (2) Collective payment by a tenant's association;
      (3) Individual payment based on a fair and equitable allocation of the total bill; and
      (4) The appointment of a receiver;
   (b) The telephone number and address of the utility;
   (c) The date, time and place for a meeting between the tenants and a field representative from the utility to discuss the available alternatives;
   (d) The statement that the tenant has the right to deduct all future payments made by the tenant for utility services from rent owed as provided by section 3 of D.C. Law 3-94; and
   (e) A Preliminary Election Card to indicate the each tenant's preferred option.

District of Columbia Municipal Regulations title 15, section 405—Notice of Option Selected

Section 405.1. After the utility has received all of the tenants' Preliminary Election Postcards or after the expiration of the ten (10) day waiting period (whichever comes first), the utility shall advise all tenants of the option selected by the majority of the tenants for payment of utility service to the building.

Section 405.4. If the utility company does not find the selected option to be practicable, it shall state its reasons in the notice and advise the tenants of their right to appeal.

District of Columbia Municipal Regulations title 15, section 406—Tenant Payment of Bill

Section 406.1. Tenants who elect to have their units individually metered at their own expense and tenants who elect to receive service in their own name pursuant to the utility's fair and equitable share proposal shall pay their utility costs directly to the utility company.

District of Columbia Municipal Regulations title 15, section 410—Notice of Utility Charge Paid by Tenant

The utility must submit to the owner a monthly listing of utility charges made by tenants who have elected to receive service in their own name. The tenant is authorized to reduce his or her rent payment to the owner by an amount equal to the utility charge.

Maine

Code of Maine Rules rule 65-407-81-9(I)—Disconnection Notice

Tenants shall be given individual notice if the landlord's account, from which they receive service, is subject to disconnection. Notice shall also be posted in a common area of multi-unit dwellings. Tenants shall be given the opportunity receive service in the tenants name and/or assume responsibility for payment. When a master meter serves a residence, the utility shall be required to make reasonable arrangements for individual metering.

APPENDIX C

Utility Contact Information

C.1 WEATHERIZATION ASSISTANCE PROGRAM

This list and additional information about weatherization assistance programs is also available at www.eere.energy.gov/weatherization

Alabama
Alabama Department of Economic and
 Community Affairs
Community and Economic Development
 Division
401 Adams Avenue
P.O. Box 5690
Montgomery, AL 36103-5690
Phone: 334-242-5292
Fax: 334-353-4203

Alaska
Alaska Housing Finance Corporation
Rural Research & Development
 Department
P.O. Box 101020
Anchorage, AK 99510-1020
Phone: 907-338-6100
Fax: 907-338-1747

Arizona
Arizona Department of Commerce
Energy Office
1700 W. Washington
Suite 220
Phoenix, AZ 85007
Phone: 602-771-1100
Fax: 602-771-1203

Arkansas
Arkansas Department of Human Services
P.O. Box 1437, Slot# S-330
Little Rock, AR 72203-1437
Phone: 501-682-8715
Fax: 501-682-6736

California
Department of Community Services and
 Development
700 North 10th Street
Sacramento, CA 95814-0338
Phone: 1-866-860-9249
Fax: 916-341-4203

Colorado
Governor's Office of Energy Management
 and Conservation
225 E. 16th Avenue, Suite 650
Denver, CO 80203
Phone: 303-866-2384
Fax: 303-894-2388

Connecticut
Connecticut Department of Social Services
25 Sigourney Street, 10th Floor
Hartford, CT 06106-5033
Phone: 1-800-842-1508

Delaware
Delaware Office of Community Service
Division of State Service Centers
1401 North Dupont Highway
New Castle, DE 19720
Phone: 302-577-4960
Fax: 302-577-4975

District of Columbia
District of Columbia Energy Office
2000 14th Street, NW, Suite 300 East
Washington, DC 20009
Phone: 202-673-6700
Fax: 202-673-6725

Florida
Department of Community Affairs
2555 Shumard Oak Boulevard
Tallahassee, FL 32399-2100
Phone: 850-488-2475
Fax: 850-488-2488

Georgia
Division of Energy Resources
Georgia Environmental Facilities
   Authority
100 Peachtree Street, NW
Suite 2090
Atlanta, GA 30303
Phone: 404-962-3000
Fax: 404-962-3050

Hawaii
Department of Labor and Industrial
   Relations
Office of Community Services
830 Punchbowl Street, Room 420
Honolulu, HI 96813
Phone: 808-586-8675
Fax: 808-586-8685

Idaho
Idaho Department of Health and Welfare
Contracts and External Resource
   Management
823 Parkcentre Way
Nampa, ID 83651

Illinois
Office of Energy Assistance
Department of Public Aid
400 North Fifth Street
Springfield, IL 62702
Phone: 217-785-2533
Fax: 217-524-5904

Indiana
Family and Social Services Administration
Division of Children and Family
402 West Washington Street
P.O. Box 6116
Indianapolis, IN 46206-6116
Phone: 317-232-7045
Fax: 317-232-7079

Iowa
Department of Human Rights
Division of Community Action Agencies
Lucas State Office Building
321 East 12th Street
Des Moines, IA 50319
Phone: 515-242-5655
Fax: 515-242-6119

Kansas
Kansas Development Finance Authority
555 South Kansas Avenue
Topeka, KS 66603
Phone: 785-296-5865
Fax: 785-296-8985

Kentucky
Department of Community Based
   Services
275 East Main Street, 3W-B
Frankfort, KY 40621
Phone: 502-564-3703
Fax: 502-564-0328

Louisiana
Louisiana Housing Finance Agency
2415 Quail Drive
Baton Rouge, LA 70808
Phone: 225-763-8700
Fax: 225-763-8710

Maine
Energy and Housing Services
Maine State Housing Authority
353 Water Street
Augusta, ME 04330-4633
Phone: 207-626-4651
Fax: 207-624-5780

Maryland
Maryland Department of Housing and
  Community Development
100 Community Place
Crownsville, MD 21032-2023
Phone: 410-514-7000
Fax: 410-514-7191

Massachusetts
Department of Housing and Community
  Development
Energy Programs
100 Cambridge Street, Suite 300
Boston, MA 02114
Phone: 617-727-7004
Fax: 617-727-4259

Michigan
Michigan Family Independence Agency
235 South Grand Avenue
P.O. Box 30037
Lansing, MI 48909
Phone: 517-241-4871
Fax: 517-335-5042

Minnesota
Department of Commerce
85 7th Place East, Suite 500
St. Paul, MN 55101-2198
Phone: 651-297-2545
Fax: 651-297-7891

Mississippi
Mississippi Department of Human Services
Division of Community Services
750 North State Street
Jackson, MS 39202
Phone: 601-359-4500
Fax: 601-359-4370

Missouri
Department of Natural Resources
1659 East Elm Street
P.O. Box 176
Jefferson City, MO 65102-0176
Phone: 573-751-3443
Fax: 573-526-2124

Montana
Department of Public Health and Human
  Services
P.O. Box 4210
Helena, MT 59601
Phone: 406-444-1788
Fax: 406-447-4287

Nebraska
Nebraska Energy Office
P.O. Box 95085
Lincoln, NE 68509-5085
Phone: 402-471-2867
Fax: 402-471-3064

Nevada
Nevada Department of Business and
  Industry
Housing Division
1802 North Carson Street, Suite 154
Carson City, NV 89701
Phone: 775-687-4258
Fax: 775-687-4040

New Hampshire
New Hampshire Office of Energy and
  Planning
57 Regional Drive
Concord, NH 03301
Phone: 603-271-2155
Fax: 603-271-2615

New Jersey
New Jersey Department of Community
  Affairs
P.O. Box 811
101 South Broad Street
Trenton, NJ 08625-0806
Phone: 609-633-6303
Fax: 609-292-9798

New Mexico
New Mexico Mortgage Finance Authority
344 4th Street, SW
Albuquerque, NM 87102
Phone: 505-843-6880
Fax: 505-243-3289

New York
New York State Division of Housing and
   Community Renewal
Hampton Plaza
38-40 State Street
Albany, NY 12207
Phone: 518-474-5700
Fax: 518-474-9907

North Carolina
NC Department of Health and Human
   Services
Office of Economic Opportunity
2013 Mail Service Center
Raleigh, NC 27699-2013
Phone: 919-715-5850
Fax: 919-715-5855

North Dakota
ND Department of Commerce
Division of Community Services
Century Center
1600 East Century Ave.
Bismarck, ND 58503
Phone: 701-328-4140
Fax: 701-328-5395

Ohio
Ohio Department of Development
77 South High Street, 26th Floor
P.O. Box 1001
Columbus, OH 43216-1001
Phone: 614-466-6797
Fax: 614-466-1864

Oklahoma
Oklahoma Department of Commerce
Office of Community Development
P.O. Box 26980
Oklahoma City, OK 73126-0980
Phone: 405-815-6552
Fax: 405-815-5344

Oregon
Oregon Housing and Community
   Services
123 NE 3rd St., Suite 470
Portland, OR 97232
Phone: 503-963-2283
Fax: 503-230-8863

Pennsylvania
Pennsylvania Department of Community
   and Economic Development
Office of Community Services
Commonwealth Keystone Building, 4th
   Floor
Harrisburg, PA 17120
Phone: 717-787-1984
Fax: 717-214-5399

Rhode Island
Rhode Island State Energy Office
Dept. of Admin./Central Services
   Division
One Capitol Hill
Providence, RI 02908-5890
Phone: 401-222-3370
Fax: 401-222-1260

South Carolina
Office of the Governor
Office of Economic Opportunity
1205 Pendleton Street
Columbia, SC 29201
Phone: 803-734-0662
Fax: 803-734-0356

South Dakota
Department of Social Services
Office of Energy Assistance
206 West Missouri Avenue
Pierre, SD 57501-4517
Phone: 605-773-3668
Fax: 605-773-6657

Tennessee
Department of Human Services
Citizens Plaza Building, 14th Floor
400 Deaderick Street
Nashville, TN 37248-9500
Phone: 615-313-4700
Fax: 615-532-9956

Texas
Texas Department of Housing and
  Community Affairs
P.O. Box 13941
Austin, TX 78711-3941
Phone: 512-475-3800
Fax: 512-475-3935

Utah
Utah Division of Housing & Community
  Development
324 South State Street, Suite 500
Salt Lake City, UT 84111-2321
Phone: 801-538-8668
Fax: 801-538-8888

Vermont
Vermont Office of Economic Opportunity
Agency of Human Services
103 South Main Street
Waterbury, VT 05671-1801
Phone: 802-241-2450
Fax: 802-241-1225

Virginia
Virginia Department of Housing and
Weatherization Assistance
Community Development
501 North Second Street
Richmond, VA 23219-1321
Phone: 804-371-7100
Fax: 804-371-7091

Washington
Washington Department of Community,
  Trade, and Economic Development
P.O. Box 42525
Olympia, WA 98504-2525
Phone: 360-725-2908
Fax: 360-586-5880

West Virginia
Office of Economic Opportunity
Weatherization
950 Kanawha Boulevard, East
Charleston, WV 25301
Phone: 304-558-8860
Fax: 304-558-4210

Wisconsin
Wisconsin Department of Administration
Division of Energy
101 East Wilson Street, 6th Floor
Madison, WI 53702
Phone: 608-267-3680
Fax: 608-267-6688

Wyoming
Wyoming Department of Family Services
2300 Capitol Avenue, 3rd Floor
Cheyenne, WY 82002-0490
Phone: 307-777-7561
Fax: 307-777-7747

C.2 2005 STATE LIHEAP DIRECTORS

Note: Households seeking more information about LIHEAP in their state should contact the National Energy Assistance Referral (NEAR) project. NEAR is a free service for persons who want information on where to apply for LIHEAP help. NEAR can be contacted by e-mail at energyassistance@ncat.org (please include your city, county, and state along with your e-mail message) or by using NEAR's toll-free phone number, 1-866-674-6327 (or 1-866-NRG-NEAR). A number of State LIHEAP offices also have toll-free numbers (listed in the directory below).

Alabama
Mr. Gareth D. Whitehead
Energy Section Supervisor
Alabama Department of Economic and
    Community Affairs
Community Services Division
P.O. Box 5690
Montgomery, Alabama 36103-5690
Tel: (334) 242-5365
Fax: (334) 353-4311
E-mail: WillieW@ADECA.state.al.us

Alaska
Ms. Mary Riggen-Ver
Heating Energy Assistance Program
    Coordinator
Department of Health and Social Services
Division of Public Assistance
400 W. Willoughby Ave., Room 301
Juneau, Alaska 99801-1700
Tel: (907) 465-3058
Fax: (907) 465-3319
E-mail: Mary_Riggen-Ver@health.state.ak.us
Website: www.hss.state.ak.us/dpa/
    programs/hap
Public Inquiries: 1-800-470-3058

Arizona
Ms. Mary Ellen Kane
LIHEAP Coordinator
Community Services Administration
Arizona Department of Economic
    Security
1789 W. Jefferson, Site Code 086Z
P.O. Box 6123
Phoenix, Arizona 85007

Tel: (602) 542-6600
Fax: (602) 364-1756
E-mail: mekane@azdes.gov
Website: www.de.state.az.us/links/
    csa_web/index.asp
Public Inquiries: 1-800-582-5706

Arkansas
Ms. Cathy Rowe
Manager, Home Energy Assistance
    Program
Office of Community Services
Department of Health and Human
    Services
P.O. Box 1437/Slot S1330
Little Rock, Arkansas 72203-1437
Tel: (501) 682-8726
Fax: (501) 682-6736
E-mail: cathy.rowe@arkansas.gov
Website: www.state.ar.us/dhs/dco/ocs/
    index.htm#haap
Public Inquiries: 1-800-432-0043

California
Ms. Wendy Wohl
Acting Executive Director
Department of Community Services and
    Development
700 North 10th Street, Room 258
Sacramento, California 95814
Tel: (916) 341-4301
Fax: (916) 327-3153
E-mail: wwohl@csd.ca.gov
Website: www.csd.ca.gov/LIHEAP.html
Public Inquiries: 1-866-675-6623

Colorado
Mr. Glenn Cooper
Director, LIHEAP
Office of Self Sufficiency
Department of Human Services
1575 Sherman Street, 3rd Floor
Denver, Colorado 80203
Tel: (303) 866-5972
Fax: (303) 866-5488
E-mail: Glenn.cooper@state.co.us
Website: www.cdhs.state.co.us/oss/
   FAP/LEAP/
Public Inquiries: 1-800-782-0721 or 303-
   866-5970

Connecticut
Ms. Carlene Taylor
Program Supervisor
Energy Services Unit
Dept. of Social Services
25 Sigourney Street, 10th Floor
Hartford, Connecticut 06106
Tel: (860) 424-5889
Fax: (860) 424-4952
E-mail: carlene.taylor@po.state.ct.us
Website: For Energy Assistance:
   www.ct.gov/dss/cwp/view.asp?a=2353
   &q=305194
For Dept. of Social Services:
   www.ct.gov/dss/site/default.asp
Public Inquiries: 1-800-842-1132

Delaware
Ms. Leslie Lee
Management Analyst
Department of Health and Social Services
Division of State Service Centers
1901 N. Dupont Hwy.
New Castle, Delaware 19720
Tel: (302) 255-9681
Fax: (302) 255-4463
E-mail: leslie.lee@state.de.us
New Castle County: 654-9295
Kent County: 674-1782
Sussex County: 856-6310

Website: www.state.de.us/dhss/dssc/
   liheap.html
Public Inquiries: 1-800-464-HELP (4357)

District of Columbia
Mr. Keith Anderson
Chief, Energy Assistance Division
District of Columbia Energy Assistance
   Office
Reeves Center, Suite 300
2000 14th St. N.W.
Washington, D.C. 20001
Tel: (202) 673-6701
Fax: (202) 673-6725
E-mail: keith.anderson@dc.gov
Website: www.dceo.dc.gov/dceo/cwp/
   view,a,3,q,601877.asp
Public Inquiries: 202-673-6750 or 6700

Florida
Ms. Hilda Frazier
Planner, Community Services Block Grant
Department of Community Affairs
Division of Housing and Community
   Development
Community Assistance Section
2555 Shumard Oak Boulevard
Tallahassee, Florida 32399-2100
Tel: (850) 488-7541
Fax: (850) 488-2488
E-mail: hilda.frazier@dca.state.fl.us
Website: www.dca.state.fl.us/fhcd/liheap/
   index.cfm
Public Inquiries: 1-850-488-7541

Georgia
Ms. Lynn Sims
Unit Chief
Community Services Section
Division of Family and Children Services
Department of Human Resources
Two Peachtree Street, N.W.
Suite 21-253
Atlanta, Georgia 30303-3180
Tel: (404) 463-7259

109

Fax: (404) 463-8046
E-mail: lynsims@dhr.state.ga.us
Website: http://dhr.georgia.gov/portal/
site/DHR/
Public Inquiries: 1-800-869-1150

Hawaii
Ms. Patricia Williams
LIHEAP Coordinator
Department of Human Services
Benefit, Employment and Support
Services Division (LIHEAP)
820 Mililani Street, Suite 606
Honolulu, Hawaii 96813
Tel: (808) 586-5734
Fax: (808) 586-5744
E-mail: pwilliams@dhs.hawaii.gov
Public Inquiries: 1-808-586-5740

Idaho
Ms. Bev Berends
LIHEAP Director
Idaho Department of Health and Welfare
823 Parkcenter Way
Nampa, Idaho 83657
Tel: (208) 442-9991
Fax: (208) 465-8431
E-mail: berendsb@idhw.state.id.us
Website: www.healthandwelfare.idaho.gov

Illinois
Mr. Charles Jackson
Program Director
Office of Energy Assistance
Department of Healthcare & Family
Services
401 S. Clinton, 7th Floor
Chicago, Illinois 62701
Tel: (312)793-1717
Fax: (312)793-3127

Mr. Alie Kabba
LIHEAP Manager
401 S. Clinton, 4th Floor
Tel: (312) 793-2369
Fax: (312) 793-1985
E-mail: akabba@idpa.state.il.us

Website: www.liheapillinois.com
Weatherization Website:
www.illinoisweatherization.com
Public Inquiries: 1-800-252-8643
Springfield Illinois Office
Tel: (217)785-6135
Fax: (217)-524-5904

Indiana
Mr. Tom Scott
Programs Specialist
Division of Children & Families
Indiana Family and Social Services
Administration
P.O. Box 6116
Indianapolis, Indiana 46206-6116
Tel: (317) 232-7015
Fax: (317) 232-7079
E-mail: TJScott@fssa.state.in.us
Website: www.IN.gov/fssa/families/
housing/eas.html
Public Inquiries: 1-800-622-4973

Iowa
Mr. Jerry McKim
Chief, Bureau of Energy Assistance
Division of Community Action Agencies
Department of Human Rights
Lucas State Office Building
Des Moines, Iowa 50319
Tel: (515) 281-0859
Fax: (515) 242-6119
E-mail: jerry.mckim@iowa.gov
Website: www.dcaa.iowa.gov/
bureau_EA/index.html
Public Inquiries: 1-515-281-4204

Kansas
Mr. Lewis A. Kimsey
State Refugee Coordinator/SCORR
President
Kansas Refugee Program
Social & Rehabilitation Services
915 SW Harrison, 681-W, DSOB
Topeka, Kansas 66612-1505
Tel: (785) 296-0147

110

Fax: (785) 296-0146
E-mail: lak@srskansas.org
Website: www.srskansas.org/ISD/ees/
    lieap.htm
Public Inquiries: 1-800-432-0043

Kentucky
Mr. Jason Moseley
Director
Department for Community Based
    Services
Division of Policy Development
Human Resources Building
275 East Main Street, 3W-B
Frankfort, Kentucky 40621
Tel: (502) 564-7536
Fax: (502) 564-0328
E-mail: jasonc.mosely@mail.state.ky.us
Website: chfs.ky.gov/dcbs/dfs/
    LIHEAP.htm
Public Inquiries: 1-800-456-3452

Louisiana
Ms. Yvette L. Javius
Program Manager
Energy Assistance Department
Louisiana Housing Finance Agency
2415 Quail Drive
Baton Rouge, Louisiana 70808
Tel: (225) 763-8700, Ext. 236
Fax: (225) 763-8752
E-mail: yjavius@lhfa.state.la.us
Website: www.lhfa.state.la.us/programs/
    energy_assistance/ea-index.php
Public Inquiries: 1-225-763-8700

Maine
Ms. Jo-Ann Choate
LIHEAP Coordinator
Energy and Housing Services
Maine State Housing Authority
353 Water Street
Augusta, Maine 04330
Tel: (207) 624-5708
Fax: (207) 624-5780

E-mail: jchoate@mainehousing.org
Website: www.bundlemeup.org/
    grants.htm
Public Inquiries: 1-800-452-4668

Maryland
Ms. Mary Lou Kueffer
Director, Office of Home Energy Programs
Department of Human Resources
311 West Saratoga Street
Baltimore, Maryland 21202
Tel: (410) 767-7062
Fax: (410) 333-0079
E-mail: mkueffer@www.dhr.state.md.us
Website: www.dhr.state.md.us/meap
Public Inquiries: 1-800-352-1446

Massachusetts
Ms. Theresa Brewer
Director
DHCD/Community Services Unit
100 Cambridge Street, Suite 300
Boston, MA 02114-2524
Tel: 1-617-573-1438
Fax: 1-617-573-1460
E-mail: theresa.brewer@state.ma.us
Website: www.mass.gov/dhcd/
    components/cs/1PrgApps/LIHEAP/
    default.HTM
Winter Heating Helpline Website:
    www.state.ma.us/winterheating
Public Inquiries: 1-800-632-8175

Michigan
Mr. Donald Mussen
Director, Income Support Programs
Department of Human Services
235 S. Grand Avenue, Suite 1306
Lansing, Michigan 48909
Tel: (517) 335-4323
Fax: (517) 335-7771
E-mail: mussend@michigan.gov
Website: www.michigan.gov/fia
Public Inquiries: 1-800-292-5650

111

Minnesota
Mr. John Harvanko, Director
Energy Assistance Programs
Energy Division
Minnesota Department of Commerce
85 7th Place East, Suite 500
St. Paul, Minnesota 55101-2198
Tel: (651) 284-3275
Fax: (651) 284-3277
E-mail: john.harvanko@state.mn.us
Website: www.state.mn.us/portal/mn/
    jsp/home.do?agency=Commerce
Public Inquiries: 1-800-657-3710

Mississippi
Ms. Tina Ruffin, Deputy Director
Mr. Ron Anderson, Branch Director
Division of Community Services
Mississippi Dept. of Human Services
750 N. State Street
Jackson, Mississippi 39202-4772
Tel: (601) 359-4768
Fax: (601) 359-4370
E-mail: truffin@mdhs.state.us
Website: www.mdhs.state.ms.us/
    cs_info.html

Missouri
Ms. Jeanna Machon
Assistant Deputy Director
Division of Family Services
Department of Social Services
P.O. Box 2320
Jefferson City, Missouri 65102
Tel: (573) 526-4836
Fax: (573) 526-5592
E-mail: jeanna.l.machon@dss.mo.gov
Website: www.dss.mo.gov/fsd/liheap.htm
Public Inquiries: 1-800-392-1261

Montana
Mr. Jim Nolan
Chief
Intergovernmental Human Services Bureau
Department of Public Health and Human
    Services

1400 Carter Drive
Helena, Montana 59620
Tel: (406) 447-4260
Fax: (406) 447-4287
E-mail: jnolan@mt.us
Website: www.dphhs.mt.gov/
    programsservices/energyassistance/
    index.shtml
Public Inquiries: 1-800-332-2272

Nebraska
Mr. Mike Kelly
Program and Planning Specialist
Office of Economic and Family Support
Department of Health and Human
    Services
301 Centennial Mall South, 4th Floor
P.O. Box 95026
Lincoln, Nebraska 68509
Tel: (402) 471-9262
Fax: (402) 471-9597
E-mail: mike.kelly@hhss.ne.gov
Website: www.hhs.state.ne.us/fia/
    energy.htm
Public Inquiries: 1-800-430-3244

Nevada
Ms. Linda Mercer
LIHEAP Program Manager
Nevada Department of Human Resources
Welfare Division
1470 East College Parkway
Carson City, Nevada 89706
Tel: (775) 684-0730
Fax: (775) 684-0740
E-mail: lmercer@welfare.state.nv.us
Website: http://welfare.state.nv.us/ess/
    eap.htm
Public Inquiries: 1-866-846-2009

New Hampshire
Celeste Lovett
Fuel Assistance Program Manager
Office of Energy and Planning
57 Regional Drive, Suite 3
Concord NH 03301-8519

Tel: (603) 271-8317
Fax: (603) 271-2615
E-mail: celeste.lovett@nh.gov
Website: http://nh.gov/oep/programs.htm

New Jersey
Mr. Joe Walsh
Coordinator
Home Energy Assistance Program
DHS, Division of Family Development
6 Quakerbridge Plaza, CN 716
Trenton, New Jersey 08625
Tel: (609) 588-2077
Fax: (609) 588-3369
E-mail: jwalsh1@dhs.state.nj.us
Website: www.state.nj.us/humanservices/
   dfd/liheap.html
Public Inquiries: 1-609-588-2152
HOTLINE: 1-800-510-3102

New Mexico
Ms. Loretta Williams
LIHEAP Program Manager
Income Support Division
Human Services Department
Work and Family Support Bureau
P. O. Box 26507
Albuquerque, New Mexico 87125-6507
Tel: (505) 841-2693
Fax: (505) 841-2691
E-mail: Loretta.Williams@state.nm.us
Website: www.state.nm.us/hsd/liheap.html
Public Inquiries: 1-800-648-7167

New York
Ms. Phyllis Morris
Director
Division of Temporary Assistance
New York State Office of Temporary and
   Disability Assistance
40 North Pearl Street
Albany, New York 12243-0001
Tel: (518) 408-3003
Fax: (518) 474-9347
E-mail: NYSHEAP@dfa.state.ny.us

Website: www.otda.state.ny.us/otda/
   heap/default.htm
Public Inquiries: 1-518-474-9516

North Carolina
Ms. Jane Schwartz
Chief, Economic Services Section
Division of Health and Human Services
Department of Health and Human
   Services
325 North Salisbury Street
Raleigh, North Carolina 27603-5905
Tel: (919) 733-7831
Fax: (919) 733-0645
E-mail: Jane.Schwartz@ncmail.net
Website: www.dhhs.state.nc.us/dss/energy/
   index.htm
Public Inquiries: 1-800-662-7030

North Dakota
Mr. Ron Knutson
Director of Energy Assistance
Department of Human Services
State Capitol Building, Judicial Wing
600 E. Boulevard, Dept. 325
Bismarck, North Dakota 58505-0250
Tel: (701) 328-4882
Fax: (701) 328-1060
E-mail: soknur@state.nd.us
Website: www.nd.gov/humanservices/
   services/financialhelp/energyassist.html
Public Inquiries: 1-701-328-2065

Ohio
Mr. Nick Sunday
Chief, Office of Community Service
Ohio Department of Development
77 South High, 25th Floor
Columbus, Ohio 43215
Tel: (614) 644-6846
Fax: (614) 728-6832
E-mail: nsunday@odod.state.oh.us
Website: www.odod.state.oh.us/cdd/ocs/
   heap.htm
Public Inquiries: 1-800-282-0880
TDD: 1-800-686-1557

Oklahoma

Mr. Melvin Phillips
Program Supervisor
Division of Family Support Services
Department of Human Services
P.O. Box 25352
Oklahoma City, Oklahoma 73125
Tel: (405) 521-4488
Fax: (405) 521-4158
E-mail: Melvin.Phillips@okdhs.org
Website: www.okdhs.org/fssd/
    ProgramInformation.htm#
    Low-Income
Public Inquiries: 1-866-411-1877

Oregon

Mr. John Overman
LIEAP Program Manager
Oregon Department of Housing and
    Community Services
725 Summer Street, NE, Suite B
P.O. Box 14508
Salem, Oregon 97309-0409
Tel: (503) 986-2094
Fax: (503) 986-2006
E-mail: john.overman@state.or.us
Website: http://egov.oregon.gov/OHCS/
    SOS_LowIncomeEnergyAssistance.shtml
Public Inquiries: 1-800-453-5511

Pennsylvania

Ms. Donna Roe
Acting Director
Division of Federal Programs
Department of Public Welfare
P.O. Box 2675
Harrisburg, Pennsylvania 17105
Tel: (717) 772-7906
Fax: (717) 772-6451
E-mail: LIHEAPMAIL@state.pa.us
Website: www.dpw.state.pa.us/LowInc/
    HeatAssistance/003670277.htm
Public Inquiries: 1-866-857-7095
TDD: 1-800-451-5886

Rhode Island

Mr. Matteo Guglielmetti
Program Manager
Dept. of Administration, Division of
    Central Services, State Energy Office
One Capitol Hill
Providence, Rhode Island 02908-5850
Tel: (401) 222-6920 Ext. 112
Fax: (401) 222-1260
E-mail: matteog@gw.doa.state.ri.us
Website: www.riseo.state.ri.us/programs/
    liheap.html
Public Inquiries: 1-401-222-3003

South Carolina

Mr. Paul Younginer
Program Manager for Energy
Division of Economic Opportunity
Suite 342
1205 Pendleton Street
Columbia, South Carolina 29201
Tel: (803) 734-9861
Fax: (803) 734-0356
E-mail: pyounginer@oepp.sc.gov
Website: www.govoepp.state.sc.us/
    oeoprogs.htm

South Dakota

Mr. Wayne Schaefbauer
Program Administrator
Office of Energy Assistance
Department of Social Services
206 W. Missouri Avenue
Pierre, South Dakota 57501-4517
Tel: (605) 773-4131 or 3668
Fax: (605) 773-6657
E-mail: wayne.schaefbauer@state.sd.us
Website: www.state.sd.us/social/ENERGY
Public Inquiries: 1-800-233-8503

Tennessee

Ms. Regina Surber
Director, Community Services
Department of Human Services
Citizens Plaza Building
400 Deaderick Street
Nashville, Tennessee 37248

Tel: (615) 313-4762
Fax: (615) 532-9956
E-mail: regina.surber@state.tn.us
Website: www.state.tn.us/humanserv/
    commsrv.htm#home
Public Inquiries: 1-615-313-4759

Texas
Mr. Marco Cruz
Program Manager
Energy Assistance Section
Texas Department of Housing and
    Community Affairs
P.O. Box 13941
Austin, Texas 78711-3941
Tel: (512) 475-3860
Fax: (512) 475-3935
E-mail: mcruz@tdhca.state.tx.us
Website: www.tdhca.state.tx.us/ea.htm
Public Inquiries: 1-877-399-8939

Utah
Mr. Sherman Roquiero
Program Manager
HEAT & SNAPS
Department of Community & Culture
324 South State, Suite 500
Salt Lake City, Utah 84111
Tel: (801) 538-8644
Fax: (801) 538-8678
E-mail: shermr@utah.gov
Website: http://community.utah.gov/
    housing_and_community_development/
    SEAL/HEAT_program/index.html
Public Inquiries: 1-877-488-3233

Vermont
Ms. Pam Dalley
Fuel Assistance Program Chief
Office of Home Heating Fuel Assistance
Department of Children and Families
103 South Main Street
Waterbury, Vermont 05676
Tel: (802) 241-2994
Fax: (802) 241-4327
E-mail: pamd@path.state.vt.us or
    pamd@wpgate1.ahs.state.vt.us

Website: www.dsw.state.vt.us/districts/
    fuel/index.htm or www.vt.gov
Public Inquiries: 1-800-479-6151 or 1-
    802-241-1165

Virginia
Ms. Andrea Gregg
Program Manager
Energy Assistance Unit
7 North 8th Street
Richmond, VA 23219
Phone: (804) 726-7368
Fax: (804) 726-7358
E-mail: andrea.gregg@dss.virginia.gov
Website: www.dss.virginia.gov/benefit/
    ea/index.html
Public Inquiries: 1-800-230-6977

Washington
Mr. Bruce Yasutake
LIHEAP Coordinator
Department of Community
Trade and Economic Development
906 Columbia Street, S.W.
P.O. Box 42525
Olympia, Washington 98504-8350
Tel: (360) 725-2866
Fax: (360) 586-0489
E-mail: brucey@cted.wa.gov
Website: www.liheapwa.org
Public Inquiries: 1-360-725-2905

West Virginia
Mr. Dan Hartwell
Program Director
Division of Family Assistance
West Virginia Department of Health and
    Human Resources
350 Capitol Street, Room B-18
Charleston, West Virginia 25301-3704
Tel: (304) 558-8290
Fax: (304) 558-2059
E-mail: danhartwell@wvdhhr.org
Website: www.wvdhhr.org/bcf/family_
    assistance/utility.asp
Public Inquiries: 1-800-642-8589

Wisconsin
Mr. Gary Gorlen
Director, Energy Assistance Bureau
Department of Administration
Division of Energy
101 E. Wilson, 6th Floor
P.O. Box 7868
Madison, Wisconsin 53707-7868
Tel: (608) 266-8234
Fax: (608) 264-6688
E-mail: gary.gorlen@wisconsin.gov
Website: www.homeenergyplus.wi.gov
Public Inquiries: 1-866-432-8947

Wyoming
Mr. Jeffrey Dockter
Economic Assistance Manager
Department of Family Services
Room #388 Hathaway Building
2300 Capitol Avenue
Cheyenne, Wyoming 82002-0490
Tel: (307) 777-6346
Fax: (307) 777-7747
E-mail: jdockt@state.wy.us
Website: http://dfsweb.state.wy.us/fieldop/
   briefing5a.htm
Public Inquiries: 1-800-246-4221

C.3 STATE UTILITY COMMISSIONS

State utility commissions regulate consumer service and rates for gas, electricity, and a variety of other services within your state. These services include rates for telephone calls and moving household goods. In some states, the utility commissions regulate water and transportation rates. Rates for utilities and services provided between states are regulated by the Federal government.

Many utility commissions handle consumer complaints. Sometimes, if a number of complaints are received about the same utility matter, they will conduct investigations.

For more detailed and up-to-date information about each commission (including the names of the current commissioners), visit the websites listed below for each state.

Alabama
President
Public Service Commission
P.O. Box 304260
Montgomery, AL 36130-4260
Toll free in AL: 1-800-392-8050
   (Consumer Services office)
Fax: 334-242-0727 (Consumer Services
   office)
Website: www.psc.state.al.us

Alaska
Chair
Regulatory Commission of Alaska
701 West 8th Ave.
Suite 300
Anchorage, AK 99501
907-276-6222
Toll free in AK: 1-800-390-2782

TDD: 907-276-4533
Fax: 907-276-0160
E-mail: rca-mail@state.ak.us
Website: www.state.ak.us/rca

Arizona
Chairman
Arizona Corporation Commission
1200 West Washington St.
Phoenix, AZ 85007
602-542-3625
Toll free in AZ: 1-800-222-7000
TDD: 602-542-2105
Fax: 602-542-3669
General Number for Utilities: 602-542-
   4251
E-mail: jhatch@azcc.gov
Website: www.azcc.gov

Arkansas
Chairman
Public Service Commission
P.O. Box 400
Little Rock, AR 72203-0400
501-682-1453
Toll free in AR: 1-800-482-1164
    (complaints)
Fax: 501-683-3670
Website: www.state.ar.us/psc

California
President
Public Utilities Commission
505 Van Ness Ave.
Room 5218
San Francisco, CA 94102
415-703-2782
Toll free in CA: 1-800-649-7570
    (complaints)
TDD: 415-703-2032
Fax: 415-703-2532
Website: www.cpuc.ca.gov

Colorado
Chairman
Public Utilities Commission
1580 Logan St., Room 201
Denver, CO 80203
303-894-2000
Toll free in CO: 1-800-888-0170
TDD: 303-894-2512
Fax: 303-894-2065
E-mail: PUCConsumer.Complaints@
    dora.state.co.us
Website: www.dora.state.co.us/puc

Connecticut
Chairman
Department of Public Utility Control
10 Franklin Square
New Britain, CT 06051
860-827-1553
Toll free in CT: 1-800-382-4586
TDD: 860-827-2837
Fax: 860-827-2613
Website: www.state.ct.us/dpuc

Director
Connecticut Dept of Social Services
Elderly Services
25 Sigourney St.
Hartford, CT 06106
860-424-5277
Toll free in CT: 1-800-443-9946
Fax: 860-424-5301
E-mail: pamela.giannini@po.state.ct.us
Website: www.ct.gov/dss

Delaware
Commissioner
Public Service Commission
Cannon Bldg. #100
861 Silver Lake Blvd.
Dover, DE 19904
302-739-4247
Toll free in DE: 1-800-282-8574
TDD: 302-739-4247
Fax: 302-739-4849
Website: www.state.de.us/delpsc

District of Columbia
Chairperson
Public Service Commission of D.C.
1333 H St., NW
Suite 200, West Tower
Washington, DC 20005
202-626-5120 (Consumer Services
    Division)
Fax: 202-393-1389
Website: www.dcpsc.org

Florida
Chairman
Public Service Commission
2540 Shumard Oak Blvd.
Tallahassee, FL 32399-0850
850-413-6100
Toll free in FL: 1-800-342-3552
TDD/TTY: 1-800-955-8771
Fax: 850-487-1716
Toll free Fax: 1-800-511-0809
E-mail: contact@psc.state.fl.us
Website: www.floridapsc.com

117

Georgia
Chairperson
Public Service Commission
244 Washington Street, SW
Atlanta, GA 30334
404-656-4501
Toll free in GA: 1-800-282-5813
Fax: 404-656-2341
E-mail: gapsc@psc.state.ga.us
Website: www.psc.state.ga.us

Hawaii
Chairman
Public Utilities Commission
465 South King St.
Room 103
Honolulu, HI 96813
808-586-2020
Fax: 808-586-2066
E-mail: Hawaii.PUC@hawaii.gov
Website: www.hawaii.gov/budget/puc/

Idaho
President
Public Utilities Commission
P.O. Box 83720
Boise, ID 83720-0074
208-334-0300
Toll free in ID: 1-800-432-0369
TDD/TTY: 1-800-223-3131
Fax: 208-334-3762
E-mail: secretary@puc.Idaho.gov
Website: www.puc.Idaho.gov

Illinois
Chairman
Illinois Commerce Commission
527 East Capitol Ave.
Springfield, IL 62701
217-782-7295
Toll free in IL: 1-800-524-0795
TDD/TTY: 1-800-858-9277
Fax: 217-782-1042
Website: www.icc.illinois.gov

Indiana
Indiana Utility Regulatory Commission
Consumer Affairs Division
302 West Washington St.
Suite E-306
Indianapolis, IN 46204
317-232-2712
Toll free in IN: 1-800-851-4268
TDD: 317-232-8556
Fax: 317-233-2410
E-mail: jjohnson@urc.state.in.us
Website: www.IN.gov/iurc

Iowa
Chairperson
Iowa Utilities Board
350 Maple St.
Des Moines, IA 50319-0069
515-281-5979
Toll free in IA: 1-877-565-4450
Fax: 515-281-5329
Website: www.state.ia.us/iub

Kansas
Chairman
Kansas Corporation Commission
1500 SW Arrowhead Rd.
Topeka, KS 66604-4027
785-271-3140
Toll free in KS: 1-800-662-0027
Fax: 785-271-3111
E-mail: public.affairs@kcc.state.ks.us
Website: www.kcc.state.ks.us

Kentucky
Chairman
Public Service Commission
211 Sower Blvd.
P.O. Box 615
Frankfort, KY 40602
502-564-3940
Toll free in KY: 1-800-772-4636
    (complaints only)
TDD/TTY: 1-800-648-6056
Fax: 502-564-3460
Website: www.psc.ky.gov

Louisiana
Commissioner
Public Service Commission
Galvez Building, 12th Floor
602 North Fifth Street
P.O. Box 91154
Baton Rouge, LA 70821-9154
225-342-4404
Toll free in LA: 1-800-256-2397
Fax: 225-342-2831
Website: www.lpsc.org

Maine
Chairman
Public Utilities Commission
242 State St., State House Station 18
Augusta, ME 04333
207-287-3831
Toll free in ME: 1-800-452-4699
TTY toll free relay: 1-800-437-1220
Fax: 207-287-1039
E-mail: maine.puc@maine.gov
Website: www.state.me.us/mpuc

Maryland
Chairman
Public Service Commission
6 St. Paul St.
16th Floor
Baltimore, MD 21202-6806
410-767-8000
Toll free in MD: 1-800-492-0474
TDD toll free in MD: 1-800-735-2258
Fax: 410-333-6495
E-mail: mpsc@psc.state.md.us
Website: www.psc.state.md.us/psc

Massachusetts
Chairman
Department of Telecommunications and
    Energy
1 South Station
12th Floor
Boston, MA 02110
617-305-3500
TDD toll free: 1-800-323-3298

Fax: 617-345-9101
Website: www.magnet.state.ma.us/dpu

Michigan
Chairperson
Public Service Commission
6545 Mercantile Way, Suite 7
P.O. Box 30221
Lansing, MI 48909
517-241-6180
Toll free in MI: 1-800-292-9555
Fax: 517-241-6181
Website: www.michigan.gov/mpsc

Minnesota
Chairman
Public Utilities Commission
121 7th Place East, Suite 350
St. Paul, MN 55101-2147
651-296-0406
Toll free: 1-800-657-3782
TDD: 651-297-1200
Fax: 651-297-7073
E-mail: consumer.puc@state.mn.us
Website: www.puc.state.mn.us

Mississippi
Chairman
Public Service Commission
Northern District
P.O. Box 1174
Jackson, MS 39215
601-961-5430
Toll free in MS: 1-800-356-6428
TTY 573-522-9061
Fax: 601-961-5476
Website: www.psc.state.ms.us

Missouri
Chairman
Public Service Commission
P.O. Box 360
Jefferson City, MO 65102
573-751-9300
Toll free in MO: 1-800-392-4211
TDD toll free in MO:
    1-800-RELAY-MO (735-2966)

Fax: 573-526-7341
Website: www.psc.mo.gov

Montana
Chairman
Public Service Commission
1701 Prospect Ave.
P.O. Box 202601
Helena, MT 59620-2601
406-444-6199
Toll free in MT: 1-800-646-6150
TDD: 406-444-6199
Fax: 406-444-7618
Website: www.psc.mt.gov

Nebraska
Chairman
Public Service Commission
P.O. Box 94927
Lincoln, NE 68509-4927
402-471-3101
Toll free in NB: 1-800-526-0017
TDD: 402-471-0213
Fax: 402-471-0254
E-mail: cheryl.elton@psc.ne.gov
Website: www.psc.state.ne.us

Nevada
Chairman
Public Utilities Commission
1150 East William St.
Carson City, NV 89701
775-687-6001
702-486-2600 (Las Vegas office)
Toll free in NV: 1-800-992-0900
Fax: 775-687-6110
Website: www.puc.state.nv.us

New Hampshire
Chairman
Public Utilities Commission
21 South Fruit Street
Suite 10
Concord, NH 03301
603-271-2431
Toll free in NH: 1-800-852-3793
TDD toll free in NH: 1-800-735-2964

Fax: 603-271-3878
Website: www.puc.nh.gov

New Jersey
President
Board of Public Utilities
Two Gateway Center
Newark, NJ 07102
973-648-2026
Toll free in NJ: 1-800-624-0241
Fax: 973-648-2836
Website: www.bpu.state.nj.us

New Mexico
Director
New Mexico Public Regulation
    Commission
Consumer Relations Division
P.O. Box 1269
Santa Fe, NM 87504-1269
505-827-4593
505-827-4660
Local complaint: 505-827-6940
Toll free in NM: 1-800-663-9782
TDD: 505-827-6911
Fax: 505-827-6973
E-mail: BarbaraA.Rae@state.nm.us
Website: www.nmprc.state.nm.us/
    consumers/crdutility.htm

New York
Public Service Commission
Office of Consumer Services
3 Empire State Plaza
Albany, NY 12223-1350
518-474-1540
Toll free in NY: 1-800-342-3377
    (complaints—gas, electric, telephone)
Toll free: 1-877-661-9223 (Business
    Advocates)
E-mail: sandra_sloane@dps.state.ny.us
Website: www.dps.state.ny.us or
    www.askpsc.com

North Carolina
North Carolina Utilities Commission
    Public Staff

Consumer Services
4326 Mail Service Center
Raleigh, NC 27699-4326
919-733-9277
Fax: 919-733-4744
E-mail: consumer.services@ncmail.net
Website: www.ncuc.commerce.state.nc.us

North Dakota
North Dakota Public Service Commission
600 E. Boulevard Ave., Dept 408
12th Floor
Bismarck, ND 58505-0480
701-328-2400
TDD in ND: 1-800-366-6888
Fax: 701-328-2410
E-mail: ndpsc@state.nd.us
Website: www.psc.state.nd.us

Ohio
Chairman
Public Utilities Commission of Ohio
180 East Broad St.
Columbus, OH 43215-3793
614-466-3292
Toll free in OH: 1-800-686-7826
TDD Toll free in OH: 1-800-686-1570
Fax: 614-752-8351
Website: www.puco.ohio.gov

Oklahoma
Chairman
Oklahoma Corporation Commission
P.O. Box 52000-2000
Oklahoma City, OK 73152-2000
405-521-2211
Toll free in OK: 1-800-522-8154
TDD: 405-521-3513
Fax: 405-521-2087
Website: www.occ.state.ok.us

Oregon
Chairman
Public Utility Commission
550 Capitol St., NE, Suite 215
Salem, OR 97301-2551
503-378-6611

Toll free in OR: 1-800-522-2404
   (consumer services only)
Toll Free in OR: 1-800-553-9600
TTY: 503-648-3458
Fax: 503-378-5505
Website: www.puc.state.or.us

Pennsylvania
Chairman
Public Utility Commission
P.O. Box 3265
Harrisburg, PA 17105
717-783-7349
Toll free in PA: 1-800-782-1110
Fax: 717-787-5813
Website: puc.paonline.com

Puerto Rico
Chairman
Public Service Commission
Hato Rey Station
P.O. Box 190870
San Juan, PR 00919
787-756-1919
Fax: 787-758-3418

Rhode Island
Chairman
Public Utilities Commission
89 Jefferson Blvd.
Warwick, RI 02888
401-941-4500
Toll free in RI: 1-800-341-1000
TDD: 401-277-3500
Fax: 401-222-2626
Website: www.ripuc.org

South Carolina
Chairman
Public Service Commission
PO Drawer 11649
Columbia, SC 29211
803-896-5100
TDD toll free in SC: 1-800-735-2905
Fax: 803-896-5199
Website: www.psc.sc.gov

South Dakota
Director
Public Utilities Commission
Consumer Affairs
500 East Capitol Ave.
Pierre, SD 57501-5070
605-773-3201
Toll free: 1-800-332-1782 (consumer affairs only)
Fax: 605-773-3809
Website: www.state.sd.us/puc/puc.htm

Tennessee
Chairman
Tennessee Regulatory Authority
460 James Robertson Pkwy.
Nashville, TN 37243-0505
615-741-3668
Toll free: 1-800-342-8359
Fax: 615-741-5015
Website: www.state.tn.us/tra

Texas
Chairman
Public Utility Commission
1701 North Congress Ave.
P.O. Box 13326
Austin, TX 78711-3326
512-936-7000
Toll free: 1-888-PUC-TIPS (782-8477)
TDD/TTY Toll free: 1-800-735-2989
Fax: 512-936-7003
E-mail: customer@puc.state.tx.us
Website: www.puc.state.tx.us

Utah
Chairman
Public Service Commission
160 East 300 South
Salt Lake City, UT 84111
801-530-6716
Toll free in UT: 1-800-874-0904
TDD: 801-530-6716
Fax: 801-530-6796
E-mail: sfmecham@state.ut.us
Website: www.psc.state.ut.us

Vermont
Chairman
Vermont Public Service Board
112 State St.
Montpelier, VT 05620-2701
802-828-2358
Fax: 802-828-3351
E-mail: clerk@psb.state.vt.us
Website: www.state.vt.us/psb

Virgin Islands
Commissioner
Public Services Commission
Post Office Box 40
Charlotte Amalie
St. Thomas, VI 00804
340-776-1291
Fax: 340-774-4971

Virginia
Chairman
State Corporation Commission
P.O. Box 1197
Richmond, VA 23218
804-371-9141 (general information)
Toll free in VA: 1-800-552-7945
TDD: 804-371-9206
Fax: 804-371-9211
Website: www.scc.virginia.gov

Washington
Chairman
Utilities and Transportation Commission
1300 S. Evergreen Park Dr., SW
Olympia, WA 98504
360-664-1173
Toll free in WA: 1-800-562-6150
TTY: 360-586-8203
Fax: 360-586-1150
Website: www.wutc.wa.gov

122

West Virginia
Chairman
Public Service Commission
201 Brooks St.
Charleston, WV 25301
304-340-0482
Toll free in WV: 1-800-344-5113
TDD: 304-340-0300
Fax: 304-340-0325
Website: www.psc.state.wv.us

Wisconsin
Consumer Affairs Program Director
Public Service Commission of Wisconsin
Consumer Affairs Unit
610 North Whitney Way (53705)
P.O. Box 7854
Madison, WI 53707-7854
608-266-2001
Toll free for WI: 1-800-225-7729
TDD: 608-267-1479
Fax: 608-266-3957
E-mail: lawrej@psc.state.wi.us
Website: http://psc.wi.gov

Wyoming
Chairman
Public Service Commission
2515 Warren Ave., Suite 300
Cheyenne, WY 82002
307-777-7427
Toll free in WY: 1-888-570-9905
TTY: 307-777-7427
Fax: 307-777-5700
E-mail: surtn@state.wy.us
Website: http://psc.state.wy.us

123

APPENDIX D

Serious Illness Certification

D.1 SAMPLE SERIOUS ILLNESS CERTIFICATION AND SAMPLE RESPONSE TO UTILITY THAT REFUSES TO GRANT SERIOUS ILLNESS PROTECTION

Sample Serious Illness Letter[1]

[Physician's Name, Address, Phone Number, License Number]

Re: [Patient Name, Utility Account Number]

To Whom It May Concern:

[Patient] resides at [Address] and is my patient [or: is under my care]. [Patient] is being treated for [name and describe condition], a serious illness.
   -and-

Depending on your state's serious illness rules, you may need to add:
Disconnection of utility service would result in a significant threat to [patient's] health.
   -or-
Disconnection of utility service would result in grave impairment.
   -or-
Disconnection of utility service would result in substantial risk of death.
   -or-
Disconnection of utility service would aggravate an existing medical emergency.
   -or-
Disconnection of utility service would prevent the use of life support equipment by the person named above.

_____
Physician's signature and date

[Representative]
[Utility Company Name and Address]

Re: Serious Illness Certificate for [Client Name; Utility Account Number;]

Dear Mr. Representative:

My client, [name], recently submitted a letter to the Company from her doctor stating that she is seriously ill and under a doctor's care.[2] I understand from our conversation that the Company is refusing to protect her account under the serious illness rules based on its determination that the letter does not include sufficient medical detail about my client's condition [or that her illness is not sufficiently serious to justify protecting her account].

Please note that [insert citation to your state's serious illness regulation] does not provide for discretion on the part of the utility. Once a serious illness certificate conforming with the requirements set forth in [insert citation] have been met, the utility must comply with the regulation and desist in its disconnection efforts.

If you fail to immediately protect this account, I, acting on behalf of my client, will pursue all legal options available.

Sincerely,
[Attorney/Advocate]

D.2 PHYSICIAN CERTIFICATION OF SERIOUS ILLNESS OR LIFE SUPPORT

PHYSICIAN CERTIFICATION OF
SERIOUS ILLNESS OR LIFE SUPPORT

This is to certify that _____ is a resident of:

Street Address: _____

City, State, Zip: _____

Telephone Number: _____

Relationship to Customer: _____

Account Number: _____

THIS SECTION IS TO BE COMPLETED
BY A LICENSED PHYSICIAN ONLY

I hereby certify that termination of electric and/or gas service will either (check applicable box or boxes):

☐ aggravate an existing serious illness* or

☐ prevent the use of life support equipment by the person named above.**

(Please print)

Physician's Name _____

License No. _____

Title _____

Address _____

_____

Office Number _____ **Fax Number** _____

E-Mail Address (optional) _____

Physician's signature _____ **Date** _____

This medical certificate is only valid for a period not to exceed 30 days.

*"Serious illness" means an illness certifiable by a licensed physician to be such that termination of service during the period of time covered by the certificate would be especially dangerous to the health of the person certified to be seriously ill.

**"Life-support equipment" means any electric or gas energy-using device certified by a licensed physician as being essential to prevent, or to provide relief from, a serious illness or to sustain the life of the customer or an occupant of the premises.

Form SC-1   Orig.102204

Notes

1. This sample is only intended as a general guideline. Before relying on it, check to make sure it complies with your state's serious illness regulations. You may also be able to obtain a blank serious illness certificate directly from your utility.

2. *If necessary pursuant to your state's regulations, insert:* "and that termination of the utility service would [aggravate an existing medical condition; result in substantial risk of death; result in grave impairment; result in a significant threat to [patient's] health; result in a medical emergency; prevent the use of life support equipment by the person named above.]"

APPENDIX **E**

State Utility Regulations

ALABAMA

The Alabama Public Service Commission's regulations are codified in five separate sections: General Rules, Special Electric Rules, Gas Rules, Telephone Rules, and Water Rules. The General Rules govern deposits, termination and termination protections for gas, electric, water and telephone utilities. The regulations can be found at www.psc.state.al.us/Administrative/administrative_division.htm.

ALASKA

The Alaska Public Utilities Commission's regulations governing telecommunications service are codified at Alaska Administrative Code, title 3, sections 52.200 through 52.340 (2004). Regulations governing electric service are within Alaska Administrative Code, title 3, sections 52.400 through 500 (2004). Access to the regulations can be found at www.state.ak.us/rca/Regulations.

ARIZONA

The Arizona Corporate Commission's regulations governing electric service can found within Arizona Administrative Code, sections 14-2-201 through 14-2-213 (2004); gas, Arizona Administrative Code, sections 14-2-301 through 14-2-314 (2004); water, Arizona Administrative Code, sections 14-2-401 through 14-2-411 (2004); telephone, Arizona Administrative Code, sections 14-2-501 through 14-2-510 (2004); sewer, Arizona Administrative Code, sections 14-2-601 through 14-2-610 (2004). Access to the regulations can be found at www.azsos.gov/public_services/Table_of_Contents.htm.

ARKANSAS

Regulations relating to electric, gas and water are located in Code of Arkansas Rules, agency 126, subagency 03, chapter 003, sections 1 through 8 (2004). Regulations relating to telecommunications are located in Code of Arkansas Rules, agency 126, subagency 03, chapter 014, sections 1 through 16 (2004). Website: http://170.94.29.3/rules_select2.asp.

CALIFORNIA

The law governing electric is found in West's Annotated California Codes, Public Utilities, sections 392, 394.2, 394.4, 394.5 and 761.5 (2004); the law governing master metering is found in West's Annotated California Codes, Public Utilities, sections 739.5, 777 and 777.1 (2004); provisions applicable to electric, gas, heat & water are found in West's Annotated California Codes, Public Utilities, sections 761.5, 779, 779.1, 779.2, 779.5, 780, 781 and 785 (2004); and provisions applicable to telephone service are found in West's Annotated California Codes, Public Utilities, sections 779.2, 786, 788, 2889.5, 2896 and 2898 (2004). Website: www.cpuc.ca.gov/static/documents/codelawspolicies.htm.

COLORADO
The regulations governing telephone, electric, gas, and water are located in Code of Colorado Regulations, volume number 4, sections 723-2-1.1 through 723-2-27.11, 723-3-1 through 723-3-34, 723-4-1 through 723-4-32, and 723-5 rules 5001 through 5410 (2004), respectively. Website: www.dora.state.co.us/puc/rulesandregulations.htm.

CONNECTICUT
Regulations relating to electric, gas, water and sewage are located in Regulations of Connecticut State Agencies, sections 16-3-100 through 16-3-102 (2004). Regulations relating to telephone are located in Connecticut State Agencies, section 16-3-101 (2004). Regulations relating to estimated billing are located in Connecticut State Agencies, section 16-3-102 (2004). Regulations relating to security deposits are located in Connecticut State Agencies, section 16-262j-1 (2004). Website: www.state.ct.us/dpuc/administ.htm.

DELAWARE
The regulations relating to telecommunications are located in Code of Delaware Regulations, agency 10, subagency 800, chapter 020, rules 1 through 5 (2004). Regulations relating to electric are located in Code of Delaware Regulations, agency 10, subagency 800, chapter 007, rules 1 through 42 (2004). Regulations relating to water are located in Code of Delaware Regulations, agency 10, subagency 800, chapter 004, rules 1.1 through 6.8.2 (2004). Regulations relating to termination of electric and gas service during the heating season are located in Code of Delaware Regulations, agency 10, subagency 800, chapter 003, 1.1 through 7.2 (2004). Website: www.state.de.us/delpsc/legal.shtml.

DISTRICT OF COLUMBIA
District of Columbia Municipal Regulations, title 15, sections 300 through 399, 400 through 499 (2004), available at www.dcpsc.org/commorders/dcmr15/dcmr15.shtm. *See also* D.C.'s "Consumer Bill of Rights," available at www.dcpsc.org/pdf_files/commorders/consumerbill/consbillofrights.pdf. The D.C. Commission's website is: www.dcpsc.org. "BOR," below, refers to sections of the "Consumer Bill of Rights."

FLORIDA
The Florida Public Service Commission's regulations governing electric service can be found within the customer relation subsection of the Florida Administrative Code Annotated, rules 25-6.093 through 25-6.109 (2004); gas, Florida Administrative Code Annotated, rules 25-7.079 through 25-7.091 (2004); water and wastewater, Florida Administrative Code Annotated, rules 25-30.310 through 25-30.360. The customer relations regulations governing telephone service can be found within Florida Administrative Code Annotated, rules 25-4.107 through 25-4.119 (2004). Access to the regulations can be found at www.psc.state.fl.us/rules.

GEORGIA

The Georgia Public Service Commission's general rules governing electric, gas, and telephone service can be found within Official Compilation Rules and Regulations of the State of Georgia, rules 515-3-1-.01 through 515-3-4-.12 (2004). Electric and gas disconnection of service rules can be found in Official Compilation Rules and Regulations of the State of Georgia, rules 515-3-2-.01 through 515-3-3-.03 (2004) and Official Compilation Rules and Regulations of the State of Georgia, rules 515-3-3-.01 through 515-3-3-.10 (2004) respectively. Additional rules governing gas and electric service billing procedures can be found within Official Compilation Rules and Regulations of the State of Georgia, rules 515-7-1-.01 through 515-7-12-.01 (2004). Specific regulations governing telephone service can be found within Official Compilation Rules and Regulations of the State of Georgia, rules 515-12-1.01 through 515-12-1-.34. Access to regulations can be found at http://rules.sos.state.ga.us/cgi-bin/page.cgi?d=1 (PDF Format).

HAWAII

The regulations regarding gas and electric service are located in Weil's Code of Hawaii Rules, sections 6-601-1 through 6-60-10 (2004), and the regulations regarding telecommunications are located in Weil's Code of Hawaii Rules, sections 6-80-1 through 6-80-137 (2004). Reference should also be made to Public Utility Commission General Order No. 7 (Oct. 27, 1972) (Electric), Public Utility Commission General Order No. 8 (Dec. 20, 1972) (Telephone), and Public Utility Commission General Order No. 9 (Gas), available at www.hawaii.gov/budget/puc/statutes.htm.

IDAHO

The Idaho Public Utilities Commission's regulations governing utility service can be found within Idaho Administrative Code, rules 31.01.001 through 31.01.401 (2004). The general rules governing electric, gas, and water customer relations can be found within Idaho Administrative Code, rules 31.21.01.000 through 31.21.01.701 (2004). The regulations governing telephone customer relations can be found within Idaho Administrative Code, rules 31.41.01.000 through 31.41.01.703 (2004). The regulations can found at: www.puc.state.id.us/laws/laws.htm.

ILLINOIS

The Illinois Commerce Commission's general regulations governing electric, gas, water, and sewer service can be found within Illinois Administrative Code, title 83, section 280.10 through 280.200 (2004). The regulations governing telephone services can be found within Illinois Administrative Code, title 83, sections 735.10 through 735.230 (2004). The regulations can be found at www.ilga.gov/commission/jcar/admincode/083/083parts.html.

INDIANA

The Indiana Utility Regulatory Commission's regulations governing electric service can be found within Indiana Administrative Code, title 170, rules 4-1-1 through 4-1-30 (2004); gas, Indiana Administrative Code, title 170, rules 5-1-1 through 5-1-30 (2004); water, Indiana Administrative Code, title 170, rules 6-1-1 through 6-1-28 (2004); telecommunications, Indiana Administrative Code, title 170, rules 7-1.3-1 through 7-1.3-12 (2004). The regulations can be found at www.in.gov/legislative/iac/title170.html.

IOWA

The Iowa Utilities Division's regulations governing gas service can be found within Iowa Administrative Code, rules 199-19.1 through 199-19.16 (2004). Specific regulation governing electric, water, and telephone service can be found within Iowa Administrative Code, rules 199-20, 199-21, and 199-22 respectively. General regulations governing complaint procedures can be found within Iowa Administrative Code, rules 199-6.1 through 199-6.8 (2004). The regulations (in PDF form) can be found at www.legis .state.ia.us/Rules/Current/iac/gnac/gnac761/gna762.pdf.

KANSAS

The Kansas Corporation Commission regulates electric, gas, water, and telephone service providers under their consumer information rules. Access to the regulations, in PDF format, can be found at www.kcc.state.ks.us/index.htm or www.kslegislature.org/legsrv-kars/ index.do.

KENTUCKY

The Kentucky Public Service Commission's general regulations governing electric, gas, telephone, and water service can be found within Kentucky Administrative Regulations Service, title 807, rule 5:006, sections 1 through 27 (2004). The regulations can be found at http://lrc.ky.gov/kar/titles.htm.

LOUISIANA

The Louisiana Public Service Commission's regulations governing electric, gas, water, sewage, and telephone service are codified and amended in a series of general orders. Although not summarized below, additional regulations can be found within West's Louisiana Revised Statutes Annotated, sections 45:845 through 45:859 (2004). The Public Service Commission's website can be found at www.lpsc.org.

MAINE

The Maine Public Utility Commission's general regulations governing electric, gas, telephone, and water service can be found within Code of Maine Rules, agency 65, subagency 407, chapter 81, sections 1 through 17 (2004) and Code of Maine Rules, agency 65, subagency 407, chapter 870, sections 1 through 4 (2004). Although not summarized, additional regulations governing telephone service can be found within Code of Maine Rules, agency 65, subagency 407, chapter 290, section 1 through 20 (2004), and the telephone anti-cramming regulations can be found within Code of Maine Rules, agency 65, subagency 407, chapter 297, sections 1 through 7 (2004). The regulations can be found at www.state.me.us/mpuc/doing_business/rules/mpuc_laws_rules.html.

MARYLAND

The Maryland Public Service Commission's general regulations governing electric and gas service can be found within Code of Maryland Regulations, rules 20.25.01.01 through 20.25.01.07 (2004). The regulations governing telephone service can be found within Code of Maryland Regulations, rules 20.45.01.01 through 20.45.01.03 (2004). Although not summarized, specific regulations governing electric can be found within Code of Maryland Regulations, rules 20.50.01.01 through 20.50.01.03 (2004); gas, Code of Maryland Regulations, rules 20.55.01.01 through 20.55.01.04 (2004); water, Code of Maryland

Regulations, rules 20.70.01.01 through 20.70.01.03 (2004); sewage, Code of Maryland Regulations, rules 20.75.01.01 through 20.75.01.03 (2004). The regulations can be found at www.dsd.state.md.us/comar/subtitle_chapters/20_Chapters.htm.

MASSACHUSETTS

The Massachusetts Department of Telecommunications and Energy's regulations governing electric, gas, and water service billing, termination and protection from termination are codified at Code of Massachusetts Regulations, title 220, sections 25.01 through 25.06 (2004). Code of Massachusetts Regulations, title 220, section 27.00 (2004) prohibits utilities from requiring deposits before starting or continuing service. Code of Massachusetts Regulations, title 220, sections 29.01 through 29.13 (2004) outlines the refund procedure for tenants whose landlords violate the regulations governing metering. The regulations can be found at www.mass.gov/dte/cmr/cmr220-001-004.htm.

MICHIGAN

The Michigan Public Service Commission's general regulations governing electric and gas service can be found within Michigan Administrative Code, rules 460.2101 through 460.2105 (2004). Specific regulations governing electric and gas service, although not summarized here, can be found within Michigan Administrative Code, rules 460.3101 through 460.3103 (2004) and Michigan Administrative Code, rules 460.20101 through 460.20104 (2004) respectively. The regulations can be found at www.cis.state.mi.us/mpsc/orders/rules.

MINNESOTA

The Minnesota Public Utility Commission's general regulations governing electric and natural gas service can be found within Minnesota Rules, rules 7820.0200 through 7820.0600 (2003). The regulations governing telecommunications service can be found within Minnesota Rules, rules 7810.0100 through 7810.0300 (2004). The regulations can found at www.revisor.leg.state.mn.us/arule/a670.html.

MISSISSIPPI

The Mississippi Public Service Commission general rules governing electric, gas, telecommunications, water, and sewer service can be found within their General Rules 1 through 15 and at Code of Mississippi Rules, agency 26, subagency 000, chapter 02, sections 1 through 15. Access to the regulations can be found at www.psc.state.ms.us/regs/contents.html.

MISSOURI

The Missouri Public Service Commission's general regulation governing electric, gas, and water can be found within Missouri Code of State Regulations Annotated, title 4, sections 240-13.010 through 240-13.070 (2004); the regulation governing telecommunications can be found in Missouri Code of State Regulations Annotated, title 4, sections 240-33.010 through 240-22.160 (2004). Many of the substantive issues within the telecommunications regulations are substantially similar to those dealing with gas, electric, and water and are indicated accordingly. The regulations can found at www.psc.mo.gov/rules.asp.

MONTANA

The Montana Department of Public Service's general regulations governing electric, gas, and water can be found within Administrative Rules of Montana, rules 38.5.901 through 38.5.904 (2004); privately owned water utilities can be found within Administrative Rules of Montana, rules 38.5.2501 through 38.5.2514 (2004); telecommunications service standards can be found within Administrative Rules of Montana, rules 38.5.3333 through 38.5.3371 (2004). The regulations can be found at http://arm.sos.state.mt.us/ 38/38-425.htm.

NEBRASKA

The Nebraska Public Service Commission's regulations governing denial and discontinuance of electric, natural gas, and water services are within Revised Statutes of Nebraska, sections 70-1601 through 70-1615 (2003). The regulation governing telecommunications are within Nebraska Administrative Code, title 291, chapter 5, sections 002.01 through 002.51 (2004). Regulations governing unauthorized changes in telecommunications service (slamming) and unauthorized charges (cramming) are within Nebraska Administrative Code, title 291, chapter 5, sections 004.01 through 004.12B2 (2004). Additional regulations governing telecommunication's slamming practices, although not summarized herein, can be found within Revised Statutes of Nebraska, sections 86-201 through 86-211 (2004). The regulations can be found at www.psc.state.ne.us/home/ NPSC/rules/rules.htm.

NEVADA

The majority of the Nevada Public Utility Commission's regulations governing consumer electric and gas services can be found in Nevada Administrative Code, chapter 704, sections 302 through 390 (2004). Although the majority of regulations concerning consumer telephone services can be found in Nevada Administrative Code, chapter 704, sections 395 through 421 (2004), many of the substantive issues within the regulations are substantially similar to those dealing with gas and electric and are indicated accordingly. The regulations can be found at http://leg.state.nv.us/NAC/CHAPTERS.HTML.

NEW HAMPSHIRE

The New Hampshire Public Utility Commission's general regulations governing electric, gas, sewer, telephone, and water can be found in New Hampshire Code of Administrative Rules Annotated, Public Utilities Commission, rules 1201 through 1204 (2004). Regulations dealing with each specific utility can be found in New Hampshire Code of Administrative Rules Annotated, Public Utilities Commission, rules 301 through 310 (2004) (Electric); New Hampshire Code of Administrative Rules Annotated, Public Utilities Commission, rules 401 through 411 (2004) (Telephone); New Hampshire Code of Administrative Rules Annotated, Public Utilities Commission, rules 501 through 513 (2004) (Gas); New Hampshire Code of Administrative Rules Annotated, Public Utilities Commission, rules 601 through 610 (2004) (water). The regulations can found at www.puc.state.nh.us/Regulatory/rules.htm.

NEW JERSEY

The New Jersey Board of Public Utilities' regulations governing all utilities are codified within New Jersey Administrative Code, sections 14:3-1.1 through 14:3-13.5 (2004), and contains the basic rules regarding applications for service, payments, deposits, termination of service, resolution of disputes, and related topics. In some cases, it may be important to consult New Jersey Administrative Code, sections 14:5-1.1 through 14:5-7.13 (2004) for rules specific to electric service (regarding electric meters); New Jersey Administrative Code, sections 14:6-1.1 through 14:6-6.4 (2004) for rules specific to gas service (regarding meters), or New Jersey Administrative Code, sections 14:10-1.1 through 14:10-11.9 (2004) for rules specific to telephone service. Access (on a limited basis) to the regulations can be found at www.state.nj.us/bpu/home/rulePage.shtml.

NEW MEXICO

The New Mexico Public Utility Commission's regulations governing electric and gas service can be found at Code of New Mexico Rules, sections 17.5.410.01 through 17.5.410.43 (2003). The majority of regulations governing telecommunications services can be found in Code of New Mexico Rules, sections 17.11.16.1 through 17.11.16.29 (2003). The regulation governing unauthorized charges and/or changes in telephone service provider (cramming & slamming) can be found at Code of New Mexico Rules, sections 17.11.8.1 through 17.11.8.15 (2003). The regulations can be found at www.nmcpr.state.nm.us/nmac/_title17/title17.htm.

NEW YORK

The New York Public Service Commission's regulation governing electric, gas, and steam can be found within Official Compilation of Codes, Rules & Regulations of the State of New York, title 16, sections 11.1 through 11.32 (2004); Official Compilation of Codes, Rules & Regulations of the State of New York, title 16, sections 14.1 through 14.20 (2004) contains the regulations governing water utilities; Official Compilation of Codes, Rules & Regulations of the State of New York, title 16, sections 609.1 through 609.17 (2004) contains the general regulations governing telephone utilities. The regulations can be found at www.dps.state.ny.us/brochures.html.

NORTH CAROLINA

The North Carolina Department of Commerce Utilities Commission's general regulations governing electric, gas, water, and telecommunications service providers can be found within North Carolina Administrative Code, title 4, chapter 11 (2004). Although not summarized here, North Carolina Administrative Code, title 4, rule 11.R6-1 through 11.R6-94 (2004) contains specific regulations governing natural gas providers, North Carolina Administrative Code, title 4, rules 11.R7-1 through 11.R7-38 (2004) contains specific regulations governing water services, and North Carolina Administrative Code, title 4, rules 11.R8-1 through 11.R8-63 (2004) contains specific regulations governing electrical service. North Carolina Administrative Code, title 4, rule 11.R20-1 (2004) contains specific regulations governing unauthorized changes in telephone service provider (slamming) and unauthorized telephone service charges (cramming). The regulations can be found at http://ncrules.state.nc.us/ncadministrativ_/default.htm.

NORTH DAKOTA

The North Dakota Public Service Commission Public Utility Division's Standards of Service Regulations governing natural gas can be found at North Dakota Administrative Code, rules 69-09-01-01 through 69-09-01-30 (2004); Electric, North Dakota Administrative

Code, rules 69-09-02-01 through 69-09-02-39 (2004); Telephone, North Dakota Administrative Code, rules 69-09-05-01 through 69-09-05-13 (2004). The regulations can be found at www.legis.nd.gov/information/acdata/html/69-09.html.

OHIO

Baldwin's Ohio Administrative Code, rules 4901:1-5-01 through 4901:1-5-36 contains the rules regarding telephone service. Baldwin's Ohio Administrative Code, rules 4901:1-17-01 through 4901:1-17-09 (2004) and rules 4901:1-18-01 through 4901:1-18-13 contain the general rules regarding utility service. In some cases it may be important to consult Baldwin's Ohio Administrative Code, rules 4901:1-10-01 through 4901:1-10-33 for specific rules regarding electric utility service, and Baldwin's Ohio Administrative Code, rules 4901:1-15-01 through 4901:1-15-36 regarding water and sewer service. The regulations can be found at www.puco.ohio.gov/puco/docketing/DocketingInformation .cfm?doc_id=888.

OKLAHOMA

The Oklahoma Corporate Commission's Regulations governing electric utilities can be found within Oklahoma Administrative Code, sections 165:35-1-1 through 165:35-1-5 (2000). Natural Gas regulations can be found in Oklahoma Administrative Code, sections 165:45-1-1 through 165:45-1-6 (2000). Telecommunications regulations can be found in Oklahoma Administrative Code, sections 165:55-1-1 through 165:55-1-16 (2000). Water regulations can be found in Oklahoma Administrative Code, sections 165:65-1-1 through 165:65-1-8 (2000). The regulations can be found at www.sos.state .ok.us/oar/oar_welcome.htm.

OREGON

The Oregon Public Utility Commission's general regulations regarding gas, electric, and telecommunications service can be found in Oregon Administrative Rules, rules 860-021-0001 through 860-021-0000 through 860-021-0037 (2004); water regulations can be found in Oregon Administrative Rules, rules 860-036-0001 through 860-036-0097 (2004). In some cases it may be important to consult Oregon Administrative Rules, rules 860-034-0010 through 860-034-0750 (2004) for the rules specific to small telecommunications utilities. The regulations can be found at http://arcweb.sos.state.or.us/banners/ rules.htm.

PENNSYLVANIA

The Pennsylvania Public Utility Commission's general regulations governing electric, gas, steam-heat, waste-water, and water service can be found within Pennsylvania Code, title 52, sections 56.1 through 56.231 (2004). The regulations governing telecommunication service can be found within Pennsylvania Code, title 52, sections 64.1 through 64.213 (2004). The regulations can be found at www.pacode.com/secure/data/052/052toc.html.

RHODE ISLAND

The Rhode Island Public Utilities Commission's regulations governing telephone utilities can be found within Code of Rhode Island Rules, agency 90, subagency 030, section 001 (2004). Regulations governing termination of electric, gas, and water service can be found within Code of Rhode Island Rules, agency 90, subagency 060, section 002

(2004). Standards of service for electric are governed under Code of Rhode Island Rules, agency 90, subagency 070, section 005 (2004); gas, Code of Rhode Island Rules, agency 90, subagency 070, section 008; water Code of Rhode Island Rules, agency 90, subagency 070, section 014. The regulations (without citations) can be found at www.ripuc.ri.gov/rulesregs/divrules.html.

SOUTH CAROLINA

The South Carolina Public Service Commission's regulations governing electric utilities can be found within Code of Laws of South Carolina 1976 Annotated: Code of Regulations, rules 103-300 through 103-392 (2003). The regulations governing gas utilities can be found within Code of Laws of South Carolina 1976 Annotated: Code of Regulations, rules 103-400 through 103-494 (2003). The regulations governing sewage service can be found within Code of Laws of South Carolina 1976 Annotated: Code of Regulations, rules 103-500 through 103-582 (2003). The regulations governing telecommunications service can be found within Code of Laws of South Carolina 1976 Annotated: Code of Regulations, rules 103-600 through 103-684 (2003), and the regulations governing water service can be found within Code of Laws of South Carolina 1976 Annotated: Code of Regulations, rules 103-700 through 103-782 (2003). The regulations can found at www.scstatehouse.net/coderegs/c103.htm.

SOUTH DAKOTA

The South Dakota Public Utilities Commission's regulations governing electric and gas utility service can be found within Administrative Rules of South Dakota, rules 20:10:15:01 through 20:10:20:11 (2004). The regulations governing telecommunications service can be found within Administrative Rules of South Dakota, rules 20:10:05:01 through 20:10:05:05 (2004). Regulations governing unauthorized changes in telecommunications providers (slamming) and unauthorized charges (cramming) can be found within Administrative Rules of South Dakota, rules 20:10:34:02.01 through 20:10:34:11 (2004). The regulations can be found at http://legis.state.sd.us/rules/index.aspx.

TENNESSEE

The regulations governing electric utility service can be found within the Official Compilation Rules & Regulations of the State of Tennessee, rules 1220-4-4-.03 through 1220-4-4-.54 (2004). The regulations governing gas service can be found within Official Compilation Rules & Regulations of the State of Tennessee, rules 1220-4-5-.01 through 1220-4-5-.48 (2004). The regulations governing water service can be found within Official Compilation Rules & Regulations of the State of Tennessee, rules 1220-4-3-.03 through 1220-4-3-.43 (2004). The regulations governing telecommunications service can be found within Official Compilation Rules & Regulations of the State of Tennessee, rules 1220-4-2-.03 through 1220-4-2-.58 (2004). The regulations can be found at www.state.tn.us/sos/rules/1220/1220-04/1220-04.htm.

TEXAS

The majority of regulations governing consumer electric services can be found in Texas Administrative Code, title 16, sections 25.24 through 25.30 (2004). The majority of regulations concerning consumer telephone services can be found in Texas Administrative

Code, title 16, sections 26.23 through 26.34 (2004), and Sewer and Water regulations can be found within in Texas Administrative Code, title 30, sections 291.81 through 291.88. The regulations can be found at www.sos.state.tx.us/tac/index.shtml.

UTAH

The Utah Public Service Commission's general regulations governing electric, gas, water, and sewer services can be found within Utah Administrative Code, rules R746-200-1 through R746-200-9 (2004), with specific regulations governing electric service within Utah Administrative Code, rules R746-310-1 through R746-310-10 (2004) and gas service within Utah Administrative Code, rules R746-320-1 through R746-320-9 (2004). Telecommunication service rules can be found within Utah Administrative Code, rules R746-240-1 through R746-240-8 (2004). The regulations can be found at www.psc.utah.gov/rules.html.

VERMONT

Vermont's Public Service Board (PSB) rules governing the deposit requirements for receiving or continuing general utility service (electric, gas, water, telephone, and cable television) can be found within Code of Vermont Rules, agency 30, subagency 000, chapter 03, sections 3.200 through 3.205. The general regulations governing the disconnection of general services can be found within Code of Vermont Rules, agency 30, subagency 000, chapter 03, sections 3.300 through 3.307. Specific regulations governing gas and water service can be found within General Order Number 29 and General Order Number 43, respectively. The regulations, although not available on traditional legal-research databases, can be found at www.state.vt.us/psb/rules/rules.stm.

VIRGINIA

The general regulations governing electric and gas service utilities can be found within Virginia Administrative Code, title 20, sections 5-10-10 through 5-10-20 (2004) and within West's Annotated Code of Virginia, sections 56-246 through 56-253 (2004). The regulations can be found at http://legis.state.va.us/Laws/AdminCode.htm.

WASHINGTON

The Washington Utilities and Transportation Commission's regulations governing gas service can be found within Washington Administrative Code, rules 480-90-103 through 480-90-199 (2004); electric, Washington Administrative Code, rules 480-100-103 through 480-100-199 (2004); water, Washington Administrative Code, rules 480-110-205 through 480-110-325 (2004); telecommunications, Washington Administrative Code, rules 480-120-011 through 480-120-999 (2004). The regulations can found at http://apps.leg.wa.gov/wac/.

WEST VIRGINIA

The West Virginia Public Service Commission's regulations governing electric service provider's customer relations can be found within West Virginia Code of State Rules, sections 150-3-4.1 through 150-3-4.18.6 (2004); gas, West Virginia Code of State Rules, sections 150-4-4.1 through 150-4-4.16.7 (2004); sewer, West Virginia Code of State Rules, sections 150-5-4.1 through 150-5-4.12.g (2004); telecommunications, West Virginia Code of State Rules, sections 150-6-2.1 through 150-6-2.9 (2004); water, West

Virginia Code of State Rules, sections 150-7-4.1 through 150-7-4.15 (2004). The regulations can be found at www.wvsos.com/csr/.

WISCONSIN

The Wisconsin Public Service Commission's regulations governing electric service can be found within Wisconsin Administrative Code, Public Service Commission, sections 113.01 through 113.012 (2004); gas, Wisconsin Administrative Code, Public Service Commission, sections 134.01 through 134.31 (2004); telecommunications, Wisconsin Administrative Code, Public Service Commission, sections 165.01 through 165.10 (2004); water, Wisconsin Administrative Code, Public Service Commission, sections 185.11 through 185.88. The regulations can be found at www.legis.state.wi.us/rsb/code/psc/psc.html.

WYOMING

The Wyoming Public Service Commission's general regulations governing electric, gas, and water service can be found within Weil's Code of Wyoming Rules, agency 023, subagency 020, chapter 2, sections 201 through 251 (2004); Electric Weil's Code of Wyoming Rules, agency 023, subagency 020, chapter 3, sections 301 through 324 (2004); gas, Weil's Code of Wyoming Rules, agency 023, subagency 020, chapter 4, sections 401 through 419 (2004); water, Weil's Code of Wyoming Rules, agency 023, subagency 020, chapter 6, sections 601 through 615 (2004). The rules and regulations can be found at http://soswy.state.wy.us/Rule_Search_Main.asp.

APPENDIX F

Federal Poverty Guidelines

2006 Poverty Guidelines for the 48 Contiguous States and the District of Columbia

Persons in family unit	Poverty guideline
1	$9,800
2	13,200
3	16,600
4	20,000
5	23,400
6	26,800
7	30,200
8	33,600

For family units with more than 8 persons, add $3,400 for each additional person.

2006 Poverty Guidelines for Alaska

Persons in family unit	Poverty guideline
1	$12,250
2	16,500
3	20,750
4	25,000
5	29,250
6	33,500
7	37,750
8	42,000

For family units with more than 8 persons, add $4,250 for each additional person.

2006 Poverty Guidelines for Hawaii

Persons in family unit	Poverty guideline
1	$11,270
2	15,180
3	19,090
4	23,000
5	26,910
6	30,820
7	34,730
8	38,640

For family units with more than 8 persons, add $3,910 for each additional person.

Source: *Federal Register*, volume 71, page 3848 (Jan. 24, 2006).

APPENDIX G

Consumer's Guide to Intervening in State Public Utility Proceedings

A CONSUMER'S GUIDE TO INTERVENING IN STATE PUBLIC UTILITY PROCEEDINGS

INTRODUCTION	**145**
A. Overview	145
B. Nature of Utility Regulation	146
C. Changing Structure of the Utility Industry	147
I. WHAT YOU NEED TO PARTICIPATE IN UTILITY PROCEEDINGS	**148**
A. Framework for Decision-making: Determining when to Participate	148
B. Examples of How Consumers Can Participate	149
C. Formally Participating as an Intervenor	150
II. THE WONDERFUL WORLD OF UTILITY PROCEEDINGS: THE PROCESS	**154**
A. Introduction	154
B. Types of Proceedings	156
C. Procedural Rules	158
D. Chronology of a Case	158
III. THINKING OUTSIDE THE BOX—AND OUTSIDE THE "PROCEEDING"	**162**
A. Community Organizing	163
B. Media	163
C. The Legislature	164

IV. RESOURCES   **165**

    A. Sample Pleadings   165

    B. Useful Treatises and Handbooks   166

    C. Groups That Intervene in Utility Proceedings   166

Attachment A: Sample Petition (Motion) to Intervene   168

Attachment B: Sample Notice of Appearance in Jurisdiction Not Requiring   171
                    Formal "Petition to Intervene"

Attachment C: Sample Discovery Regarding Arrearages and Terminations   172

Notes to Appendix G   177

INTRODUCTION

A. *Overview.*

The well-being of low-income households can be profoundly affected by the decisions that their Public Utility Commission (PUC) makes regarding rate hike requests, billing and termination regulations, utility-funded energy efficiency and payment assistance programs, and how utilities are structured. Commissions can set rates higher or lower, within a band of reasonableness; order companies to implement low-income payment assistance programs; prohibit terminations to low-income households during the winter or during extreme temperatures; and require companies to invest in cost-effective energy efficiency programs. Yet, in some states, these proceedings rarely include effective, direct participation of low-income ratepayers or the community-based organizations that deliver fuel assistance and weatherization services to low-income households.

Clearly, participation before PUCs requires time and financial resources, and a working knowledge of the legal rules and political dynamics that drive PUC decision-making. However, the potential benefits of involvement before the PUC cannot be overstated. Through effective participation, advocates can win enhanced energy and economic security for low-income households through more affordable utility service, more efficient energy usage, and regulatory protections against harsh service termination or credit and collection policies. Considering the range of services regulated by the PUC (electricity, natural gas, local phone service, and in some cases water) low-income advocates need to be familiar with commission proceedings to identify when and how they should become involved.

Community-based organizations that deliver the Low Income Home Energy Assistance Program (LIHEAP) and Weatherization Assistance Program (WAP) are especially well-situated to credibly advocate for state-level utility programs and policies that benefit low-income ratepayers. These organizations understand the energy and utility needs of the poor, as well as the practical aspects of program design and delivery. They employ staff who work directly with low-income people, year in and year out, and who can be convincing speakers at public hearings. They have the ability to mobilize large numbers of low-income consumers to support policies that help the poor.

The purpose of this manual is to enhance the abilities of these organizations, their members, clients and others to effectively advocate before regulators for reliable and affordable utility service for low-income customers. It is intended to serve as a practical guide for how to get involved in those utility proceedings with a focus on issues of particular importance to low-income ratepayers. These issues include the following:

- Adoption of affordable rate structures;
- Implementation of payment assistance and arrearage management programs;
- Implementation of energy efficiency programs and services; and
- Adoption of effective regulatory consumer protections regarding termination, restoration of service, late payment fees, security deposits, and establishment of workable payment plans for low-income customers experiencing payment troubles.

These issues are of vital importance to low-income households. Access to affordable utility service is a necessity of life. Without electricity and gas, families cannot cook their meals or warm or cool their homes, and health and safety may be threatened. House-holds at or below the federally-determined poverty level must often spend over 20% of annual income for residential energy, whereas households at the median income level spend about 3%. Each year, over 1 million low-income households suffer loss of heat be-cause of inability to pay utility or fuel bills or for a needed heating system repair. For the low-income elderly, high energy costs coupled with particular susceptibility to weather-related illnesses can create a life-threatening challenge, especially during periods of ex-treme heat or cold. Consumers also face health and safety risks if they lose their telephone or water service. These are all basic, vital necessities in the modern world.

Despite the importance of these issues and the disproportionate financial burden that falls on the poor to retain access to basic utility service, proceedings regarding the rates, rules, and regulations that govern the delivery of service are usually dominated by utility companies, their lawyers and consultants. While Attorneys General or state Ratepayer Advocates[1] are charged with representing the public in these proceedings, these entities often must pay attention to the broad needs of all classes of ratepayers rather than the particular interests of low-income utility customers. (To choose one notable example, Ratepayer Advocates often do not support and sometimes actively oppose low-income discount rates or energy efficiency programs, arguing that these programs can raise rates for customers who are not low-income.) Absent direct participation of low-income indi-viduals and advocates, PUCs make important decisions without having heard the unique needs of the poor.

Many low-income advocates and direct service agencies view PUC proceedings as impor-tant, but they may also view them as forums where complex rules and a firmly established core of "insiders" prohibit their participation. As this manual describes, participation re-quires time and other resources. However, it is possible to participate on a number of dif-ferent levels and achieve outcomes that can profoundly benefit low-income households for years to come. Viewed from another perspective, when PUCs make decisions without hearing from low-income consumers or their advocates, those decisions will almost cer-tainly increase the hardship these households face.

This Manual contains additional information on the nature of utility regulation and the changing structure of the utility industry. In addition, the reader will find in-depth discussion of what they need to participate in PUC proceedings, the people involved in the proceedings, the PUC process and types of proceedings that are conducted, and how advocates can work outside of a proceeding to obtain desired results. There are also ap-pendices that provide state PUC contact information and samples of petitions to inter-vene and information requests.

B. *Nature of Utility Regulation*

Each state and the District of Columbia has a regulatory utility commission. These com-missions go by various names in different states. For the purposes of this manual, we will refer to the state commissions that have regulatory authority over electricity, natural gas, and other utilities as "Public Utilities Commissions," "Commissions," or "PUCs." Each state has a PUC, in most cases consisting of commissioners who are appointed by the state's governor. However, as indicated in Appendix C of this guide, several states elect their commissioners. While each state's commission structure and operation is governed by its own state laws and is therefore somewhat unique, there is relative uniformity in many PUC processes, as this manual explains. Each PUC has a set of commissioners at the top, who oversee technical and legal staff; each operates according to rules governing practice and decision-making; and each conducts proceedings where information is presented and decisions are rendered following fairly similar procedures.

Some Common Names for Utility Commissions

—Public Utility Commission
—Public Service Commission
—Corporation Commission
—Regulatory Commission
—Commerce Commission

See Appendix C of this guide for more information on your state utility commission.

As the utility industry was developing around the turn of the 20th century, most regulators and elected officials discerned efficiencies from the monopoly delivery of utility service. It was widely agreed that having one company operating a set of gas or electric lines and related facilities in any geographic area would result in lower prices than if several companies tried to build duplicate, competing systems. At the same time, many policymakers saw a great need to protect the public against the risks of that monopolies pose: higher prices and lower service quality. Starting around 1910, states created PUCs for the purpose of protecting the public from the abuses of monopoly while providing utility companies with a fair return on their investments.

Specific PUC decisions are often based on the "standards of review" (decisional rules) and precedents unique to each state. More broadly, however, Commissions make decisions within a broad set of rules set by legislators that are fairly similar state to state. Legislators set PUC operating budgets, determine the structure of the commission, and sometimes set funding levels for programs to provide low-income energy efficiency and bill payment assistance. Thus, there is always a legislative role in PUC decision-making and regulation. As discussed later in this manual, consumers who wish to intervene in utility proceedings should also pay close heed to the potential impact and influence of state legislatures on utility issues that affect low-income households.

There is also the overlay of federal agencies, laws, and regulations that may come into play when dealing with some utility issues. However, the focus on this manual is on how to intervene in a state commission proceeding, where most of the low-income consumer utility services and protections are regulated.

C. *Changing Structure of the Utility Industry.*

The structure of the electric and natural gas utility industries are today fundamentally different than they were ten years ago. Deregulation or "restructuring" of these industries has placed new emphasis on the theory that market forces and competition can more efficiently and effectively provide low prices and consumer benefit than traditional regulation of monopoly production and delivery of energy services. However, experience with utility restructuring to date has been that of increasing price volatility and general price increases. Utility restructuring puts consumers at risk because regulators simply assume that competition will inherently protect the interests of consumers. Nothing could be further from the truth, especially when it comes to the interests of low-income consumers. Indeed, for utilities focused on the bottom line, programs and policies that have protected low-income consumers have ended up on the chopping block (e.g., loss of local customer service centers, reduced willingness to work out payment plans, pressure to remove the prohibitions on unregulated utilities' ability to disconnect service). The implementation of "competition" has also elevated the need for low-income advocates to be vigilant about redlining.

Low-income customers have not been well-insulated from the adverse impacts of restructuring, despite efforts in many states to adopt new affordability programs and demand greater investment in low-income energy efficiency. The structure of the industry has undergone irreversible change, but the programs and policies needed to adequately protect low-income ratepayers have lagged behind. The need for increased advocacy before PUCs to protect low-income households has never been greater.

I. WHAT YOU NEED TO PARTICIPATE IN UTILITY PROCEEDINGS

A. *Framework for Decision-making: Determining when to Participate*
Each year, hundreds of matters come before PUCs. Among these, how can advocates facing very real time and financial constraints determine when best to get involved? While there is no clear-cut answer to this question, and an organization's particular goals and circumstances will ultimately dictate whether resources should be devoted to PUC proceedings, the purpose of this section is to provide a set of evaluative criteria to aid in decision-making regarding when to get involved, and, in some cases, how to maximize effectiveness once the determination to get involved has been made. Section B, below, deals with the types of resources that are necessary to participate effectively. The evaluative criteria discussed here pertain primarily to the types of benefits that may be gained through successful participation, and the likelihood that a successful outcome may be achieved. They are intended to help advocates decide when to get involved and to examine the issues discussed below.

Potential for Benefits to Low-income Clients
Perhaps the primary question to ask in determining when to get involved for the PUC is, "What is at stake for low-income households?" Does the proceeding in question offer the potential for more affordable rates, more efficient use of energy resources, or meaningful regulatory consumer protection? What is the magnitude of the benefits that may be gained through successful participation in this proceeding? In order to determine the potential for low-income customer benefits, advocates must become familiar with the types of proceedings that come before public utility commissions (See Section II, below.). Utility rate cases and fuel charge or cost of fuel proceedings are examples of cases that have direct bearing on the cost of utility service. Rate cases are also forums where advocates may raise issues regarding payment assistance and energy efficiency programs.

From a more defensive perspective, there are times when advocates may need to determine the potential for a proceeding to result in the loss of previous payment assistance for energy efficiency gains, or a deterioration of consumer protections. Participation in PUC proceedings is often necessary to preserve previous gains.

Likelihood of Success

Advocates operating with limited resources must make realistic assessments regarding whether their participation in PUC proceeding will result in the achievement of organizational goals. Such an assessment must entail taking stock of available financial, time, and human resources, as well as the political context in which a preceding will take place.

Organization-Building Capacity

Advocates should assess the extent to which participation in a PUC proceeding will achieve organizational goals such as expansion of membership base, building advocacy capacity within the organization, enhancing organizational visibility, or building ties with existing or prospective allies.

Precedential Value

There are times when a limited victory in a PUC proceeding with a very narrow scope may serve to set a precedent in future proceedings were greater benefits are at stake. For example, winning a low income energy efficiency program in a proceeding pertaining to a single electric utility may ultimately result in similar programs being ordered for each of the regulated electric utility companies and a particular state.

Geographic Value

Some PUC proceedings pertain to a single utility company that operates within a defined service territory. Other proceedings have bearing on policies and programs that are implemented across service territory lines and may therefore carry a potential for greater low-income benefits.

Longevity

Finally, advocates may wish to assess the extent to which potential low-income benefits gained through a successful PUC intervention will last. For example, a one-time success in lowering a quarterly fuel charge may have less lasting value than obtaining a PUC determination regarding the ways in which a company procures wholesale electricity or natural gas and passes the costs for those resources on to consumers.

B. *Examples of How Consumers Can Participate*

There are a number of types of proceedings in which low-income consumers and advocates may want to participate in some capacity: as a full party (often called "an intervenor"); by speaking at public hearings; by filing written comments; or other means. This section will briefly provide examples of how consumers most often participate in utility proceedings and the resources needed to have an impact on the proceeding.[2]

Adjudicatory proceedings: Frequently, consumers want to intervene in rate hike cases, which are considered "adjudicatory proceedings." This means that the commission formally "adjudicates" (decides) the case based upon the testimony of witnesses who are sworn under oath and who are subject to cross-examination by other parties, as well as upon written documents formally accepted as evidence in the case. Rate hike cases address a very broad range of issues: how much the company will collect in overall revenues; how the rate increase is "allocated" to (divided up among) the residential, commercial, and industrial classes of customers; how much profit the company is allowed to make. Most commissions will allow consumers who become "intervenors" to raise a host of program and policy issues. For example, low-income intervenors can propose that a company offer a low-income discount; or change the way it operates an existing energy efficiency program; or conduct better outreach towards those who may be eligible for fuel assistance payments and discount rates.

Commissions conduct adjudicatory proceedings not only in rate hike cases, but in most cases involving mergers; approvals of new power plants; issuance of bonds; miscellaneous cases involving the cost of gas or fuel; new fees or charges for specific services; or a specific utility company's safety and maintenance operations. The resources needed to intervene in adjudicatory proceedings are discussed in section B.

Rulemaking proceedings: Commissions also reach many of their important decisions in "**rulemaking proceedings**." Rulemaking proceedings generally address rules, policies, practices, or procedures that apply to an entire regulated industry (e.g., the gas, electric or local telephone industries). For example, most commissions adopted their rules governing the initiation of new service, deposits, payment plans, and terminations in rulemaking proceedings. Commissions also may adopt accounting or rules that apply to a class of companies in a rulemaking proceeding. Many states have restructured their electric and gas industries.[3] Commissions in those states have adopted new rules governing a range of restructuring issues in rulemaking proceedings. These proceedings usually require less resources than intervening in rate cases. (Rulemaking proceedings are discussed more fully in section II.)

Informal proceedings: Commissions also take all kinds of actions outside of formal adjudicatory or rulemaking proceedings. For example, a competitive electric supplier might write a letter to the commission seeking approval to change the practices used to switch customers from the local distribution company to a competitive supplier. The commission might then provide an answer without conducting any formal proceeding. Or low-income consumers might request a meeting with the commission to discuss whether the commission's staff should require companies to offer longer payment plans to low-income customers, and the commission might agree to do so. These examples highlight the importance of keeping track of what types of decisions the commission is making through highly informal practices, as well as the importance of making sure you are one of the parties or groups whose views are being heard as the commission informally establishes new policies.

C. *Formally Participating as an Intervenor*
The adjudicatory proceedings are the most resource intensive form of commission participation, so this section spells out what it takes to "intervene". In order to intervene effectively in an adjudicatory proceeding, intervenors need:
- Time
- Money
- Legal resources
- Expertise

Time

Adjudicatory hearings can consume huge amounts of time. The cases often take several months, sometimes more than a year, from start to finish. This does not mean that consumers will be spending a lot of time on a case or proceeding each and every week from beginning to end. In fact, there may be stretches of time when consumers simply wait for the next step in the process: the commencement of hearings or the release of some interim decision. But consumer intervenors must be prepared to monitor and stay involved in a case that, in some instances, will go on for years.

The actual number of hours intervenors will need to commit to a case will vary, depending on the nature of the case (e.g., a full-blown rate case versus an investigation of a company's energy efficiency programs, discount rates, or construction plans), but it is unusual to spend less than 50 hours on any one adjudicatory proceeding (although less rare in rulemaking proceedings), and not rare to spend 100 to 200 hours on an adjudicatory proceeding. Again, this time will usually be spread over several months. However, there are certain portions of a case where consumer intervenors may need to spend 20 or more hours per work in order to accomplish their goals.

At the outset of a case, intervenors need to spend time reviewing the company's filing; gathering information to support their own case; lining up resources (legal assistance, expert witnesses, etc.), and developing a strategy. In most cases, there will then be a "discovery" phase that can be very time-consuming: writing questions about the company's case and reviewing the answers the company provides. The amount of time needed to participate in hearings will depend quite heavily on the number of witnesses and number of hearing days scheduled, as well as on the range of issues of interest to the consumer intervenors. For example, it is possible that a commission will hold 10 or 20 days of hearings in a rate case, but that a consumer group will only attend a small handful of those hearings because the bulk of the hearing days involve issues of little interest. At the back end of the case, intervenors file "briefs," written arguments that attempt to convince the commission to rule a particular way on each issue in the case. Writing a brief generally takes several days of work, sometimes a full week or more.

Money

Utility companies tend to spend hundreds of thousands of dollars on their hearings before commissions, mostly on lawyers fees, expert witness fees, and production of documents. Consumers will rarely have significant money to devote to a utility proceeding, but it is important to plan in advance for any expenditures that will have to be incurred.

At a minimum, consumer intervenors will have to cover out-of-pocket copying and postage costs. These can range from quite minimal to hundreds of dollars and more. For example, if there are many parties in the case (in some cases, there are dozens of intervenors), simply serving each party with a copy of everything the consumer group files (the initial petition to intervene, "discovery,"[4] written testimony, and briefs) can quickly become expensive. Some commissions may require you to deliver some documents by messenger service or overnight delivery, further increasing out-of-pocket expenses.

Consumer intervenors may also need to pay various people who help present their case. For example, consumers may decide to retain a lawyer to represent them.[5] (See the discussion of "Legal resources" immediately below.) Consumer intervenors may need the services of administrative staff to help with all of the copying, filing, and organizing of documents and may want to hire one or more expert witnesses. (See the discussion of "Expertise" below.) Any of these costs (legal, administrative, expert) can vary quite significantly, and it is not possible to provide even a broad range of estimates as to what a particular case might cost. However, if a consumer group plans to retain a lawyer or expert witnesses, the group should plan on spending several thousand dollars in almost any type of proceeding (unless those services can be obtained free or at greatly reduced rates, as discussed in "Legal resources" and "Expertise," below).

Consumer intervenors should always explore ways of getting the resources needed without spending money, or at least limiting those costs. Many states have an "Office of Consumer Counsel," "Consumer Advocate," "Ratepayer Advocate" (or other similar name) that intervenes in most utility proceedings. In some states, the Office of the Attorney General fulfills this role. A consumer group may be able to convince the Consumer Counsel to pursue its issues, maybe even to sponsor an expert witness who will address its concerns. For example, a consumer group may be aware that a particular company is engaging in unfair or overly aggressive collection tactics, or that a telephone company is targeting certain high-pressure and deceptive sales practices toward minority communities. By meeting with the Consumer Counsel and sharing this information, the consumer group may find that it has an ally, one who already has lawyers on staff and a budget to sponsor expert witnesses. If this option is not available, a consumer group can still consider working with other consumer groups or intervenors who have a similar interest and who may be able to share in the costs of the intervention.[6]

Many of the consumers or consumer groups that participate in utility cases do so without spending much money. By collaborating with other parties, picking issues carefully, and limiting their involvement only to the most essential portions of a case, many consumer groups have had a very useful impact in hearings involving a range of issues. The lack of money should not hold consumers back from intervening in a utility case that will have a significant impact on them.

Legal resources

Before deciding to intervene in a case, it is important for consumer intervenors to decide whether they will get a lawyer to represent them. The obvious drawback is that lawyers are expensive. Therefore, consumers should start by thinking about ways that to get a lawyer's help without paying expensive legal fees. As mentioned in the discussion of "Money," above, consumer groups should find out whether there is an Office of Consumer Counsel (or similar entity) in their state, and whether the Consumer Counsel is willing to raise issues of concern to the consumer group. (However, the Consumer Counsel will not literally represent the group and will not be bound by any suggestions the group may make.) Consumer intervenors can also review prior cases the commission has heard to see if there are other parties who have similar interests. It is quite common in utility cases for consumer groups to band together, given the overwhelming resources that a company can bring to bear in any proceeding. Many states have groups that have intervened a number of times in utility cases. By joining forces, a consumer group that is new to the process will be able to draw on the experience of people who are familiar with the commission's rules and who have already learned the ropes of intervening in a proceeding.

If a consumer group has enough money to hire a lawyer, the group should be cautious about who it hires. Try to find a lawyer who is familiar with the commission's rules of practice and who has represented consumers before—this will tend to save money and get the group more effective representation. If possible, speak to more than one lawyer to get different estimates about how much a case might cost, but don't expect a lawyer to guarantee you a set price. They almost always bill by the hour. Also ask the lawyer questions about how he or she would conduct the case. Ask questions about witnesses the lawyer thinks will be necessary; how long he or she expects the case to take (both elapsed time, from start to finish, and number of billable hours); and some notion of the chances of success on the issues the consumer group wants to raise.

Expertise

Utility cases can raise some very technical and rarified issues. Even when a consumer intervenor is addressing less technical issues (for example, urging the commission to adopt low-income discount rates), there may still be a need to get expert advice or to have an expert witness testify. Just as with lawyers, consumer groups may be able to get expert help from the Office of Consumer Counsel or from some other party that has similar interests. For example, a consumer group might convince the Consumer Counsel that a particular company is running its low-income energy efficiency programs quite poorly, both wasting ratepayers' money and not meeting the needs of low-income customers. The Consumer Counsel might decide that this issue is important enough to put on a witness who will propose a better program design for the company's energy efficiency programs. Or, more likely, the Consumer Counsel may direct his or her staff to file extensive discovery requests about the operation of the energy efficiency program and then cross-examine the company's witnesses on this issue. Again, the Consumer Counsel will not literally be representing the consumer group, but the group may gain a great deal of useful information for its own case and for writing its brief.

Sometimes, consumer intervenors have sufficient resources to employ expert witnesses. As with employing a lawyer, consumer intervenors should be very careful about how you go about choosing an expert. Like lawyers, they can be very expensive. Unlike lawyers, they are not obliged to aggressively represent their client's interests. A good and honest expert will form his or her own views of the issues after reviewing the company's filing and at least some (if not most) of the discovery responses. It is entirely possible that the expert will say some things in his or her testimony that the consumer group does not entirely agree with! Therefore, it is very important to read prior testimony the witness has filed on similar issues, if possible, and crucial to speak to the expert at some length before deciding to use him or her as a witness.

There are some ways to get expert assistance either for free or very inexpensively. Sometimes, professors or other staff associated with universities or non-profit organizations are very interested in the same issues as the consumer group and interested in getting their views before the commission. There might be someone who is very knowledgeable about low-income rates, for example, and who would be willing to testify for free or at a greatly reduced price.

There are other witnesses or experts who may be available. Low-income consumers most often address issues around discount rates; low-income energy efficiency programs;

terminations and payment plans; and customer service issues. In many states, consumer intervenors should be able to find people who work in the fuel assistance or weatherization programs or at community action programs (or similar agencies) who can provide very helpful testimony about the burdens low-income households face in paying their energy bills; about the benefits of low-income energy efficiency programs; or about company credit and collection practices. Most of these people, if they are willing to testify, will do so for free because they consider it part of their jobs. A number of medical and public health researchers and professionals have been studying the connection between high home energy expenditures and increased malnutrition and other health problems. This type of research can be helpful when advocating for discount rates and utility-sponsored low-income energy efficiency programs. Most of these professionals are willing to testify for free, if they have the time to do so.

Even if consumer intervenors do not plan or have the ability to put on an expert witness, they may need some form of expert advice to help analyze and understand the company's filing.[7] Just as with expert witnesses, consumer groups should consider ways to get expert advice without spending too much of their scarce resources. There are many people around who can help analyze and respond to a utility company's filing: the Office of Consumer Counsel or Attorney General; other intervenors who are interested in similar issues; national, regional or state groups that work on low-income energy issues;[8] academics; legal services offices; and others. Inventing the wheel from scratch can be a slow and tedious process. Copying an existing wheel design is usually a lot easier.

II. THE WONDERFUL WORLD OF UTILITY PROCEEDINGS: THE PROCESS

A. *Introduction*

If you play football, it's always good to know which goal post is yours, or you might score a touchdown for the other side. And if you plan to intervene in a utility proceeding, it's just as important to get familiar with the decision-making process, from the initial filing through to the final decision, or you might miss opportunities to score your own points.

Get familiar with the key players: One step that sometimes gets overlooked is learning something about the people involved. For example, find out how many commissioners there are; what their names are; and which ones are most likely to support your issues.[9] You should consider trying to set up a meeting with one or more commissioners to discuss your issues and concerns, although preferably not while a particular case that addresses those issues is pending before the commission.[10] Find out which staff are assigned to the case, and the roles that they play (e.g., assigned "hearing officer" or "administrative law judge;" rate analyst; consumer or complaint division staff; etc.). The commission's rules may allow you to speak more freely with staff about the case, especially staff who are considered intervenors or who do not play any role in the final decision. You should also consider making yourself known to one or more people in the commission's docket or filing office, as these people can often save you time and help you avoid mistakes by explaining some of the procedural rules that are second nature to them: how many copies to file and who to serve; deadlines; etc.

Be alert for settlement opportunities: You also need to be alert to the possibility that two or more parties are engaged in settlement discussions. Just like most court cases settle before an actual trial, many utility cases settle. It's even more common that parties reach a settlement on some of the issues raised, even if some issues go to hearings. **Make sure to be at the table if you hear that there are settlement discussions.** You won't necessarily be able to force your way into settlement discussions if other parties don't want you there, but they also will have a hard time getting a settlement that addresses your issues approved if you are not one of the parties who signs off. Many of the low-income discount rates and energy efficiency programs around the country were either initially adopted or later modified by settlements between the local utility company and low-income intervenors. In fact, low-income groups often have better success negotiating these issues directly with companies than getting favorable decisions out of their commissions.

Do Your Homework! Before getting involved in any case, make sure you have a good grasp of the following (unless you are already experienced in utility cases):

- **What type of proceeding is this?** Are you getting into an "adjudicatory" proceeding; rulemaking case; informal proceeding; etc? (See "Types of Proceedings," section B., immediately below.)
- **What is the "Standard of Review"?** Does the party filing the case (often, but not always, the utility company) have to convince the Commission that its request is "reasonable," or "in the public interest," or the "least cost approach"? The standard of review may determine, for example, how strictly the commission scrutinizes the company's case and also the weight of the opposing arguments you will have to muster to convince the commission to adopt your view.
- **What laws, regulations and prior case decisions govern your case?** Usually, there are a relatively small number of laws the legislature has passed and regulations that the commission has adopted that apply to your case. For example, if you are intervening in a cost of gas adjustment (CGA) case, find out if your legislature has passed a statute that directly addresses CGAs, or if the commission has regulations governing how a company is supposed to calculate the CGA. If you are advocating for a change to a company's low-income energy efficiency program, find out whether the company must offer these programs as a result of a state law (and then find out the particulars of that law), or whether the company adopted the energy efficiency programs as part of a settlement in its prior rate case (in which case read the prior rate case decision).

  It's also well worth the time to read the commission's most recent decisions involving the company you're up against, especially if any earlier cases addressed similar issues.

  If you haven't hired a lawyer who is already familiar with utility law in your state, the easiest way to find out which laws and regulations apply is to ask the types of people and agencies mentioned in the discussion of legal and expert resources (section I. B.): meet with someone from the Office of Consumer Counsel or Attorney General's office; or find a friendly commission staff lawyer; or seek out an experienced intervenor group that might be willing to get you up to speed.

If you want to do your homework exceptionally well, you should consider looking at laws, regulations, or utility commission decisions of other states. Sometimes, a nearby state will offer exactly the model you want your state to adopt, and you'll have an easier time convincing your commission if you can point to an existing precedent.[11] It's also worth considering whether there are any federal laws that apply, either ones that help your case or hurt it. This is particularly true in telephone cases, since Congress has passed a number of laws that apply and that often preempt state laws.

- **What issues are you going to address?** Identify your issues at the earliest possible date. Rate cases can be time-consuming and overwhelming—expect this! But also expect to win something for all of your effort. The best way to come away with a success is to define a concise and short list of your issues at the earliest possible date. And be specific—defining your goal as "beating back the rate hike" is much less likely to help your organize your efforts than deciding to "get the commission to exclude the company's advertising costs from rates" or "get the commission to adopt lower percentage increase for residential (versus commercial) customers." Defining your issues early on will provide benefits throughout the case—you'll spend a shorter amount of time writing more focused discovery that gets you the information you need; you'll line up the expert witnesses you need at an early date so they have adequate time to prepare; your cross-examination will be focused on exactly what you need to cover; and your brief will come across to the commission as targeted and forceful.[12] **Once a case starts, it can move so quickly that you won't have the luxury of being able to develop your strategy on the fly—make sure you do so at the beginning of the case!**

- **How will you deal with all of the paper?** Utility cases burn through trees faster than a summer forest fire. Initial filings often fill up a ream box or two, and discovery can fill an entire filing cabinet drawer. While some commissions are moving to electronic filing, this can create it's own problems: there's no easy electronic-equivalent of literally flipping through hundreds of pages of documents and using the incredible ability that humans have to spot the needle in the haystack. From day one, set up a filing system (both paper and electronic) that will allow you to find precisely the documents you need, recognizing that you often won't know which documents are most important until you begin preparing for hearings and cross-examination.

B. *Types of proceedings*

Commissioners handle a variety of types of proceedings. It helps to be familiar with each. While each state has its own set of rules governing utility proceedings, there are enough similarities to offer suggestions and guidance that should be helpful most of the time.[13]

- **Adjudicatory proceedings:** These are the cases that commissions formally "adjudicate" (decide) after hearing witnesses, accepting evidence, and reading briefs. The steps in an adjudicatory hearings are described in Section IV D, below. Bear in mind that in most states to participate in an adjudicatory proceeding you will have to file a "petition to intervene" and have the commission accept or approve your petition.[14] Adjudicatory hearings are run somewhat like formal civil cases in court. You will therefore need to become familiar with and follow the commission's adjudicatory hearing rules.

Commissions generally (but not always) hold adjudicatory hearings when they review rate hike requests; approve the construction of new power plants; review merger proposals; and review a specific company's operations.

■ **Rulemaking proceedings:** Commissions conduct rulemaking proceedings when they adopt rules that apply generally to an entire industry or class of companies, or that are not specific to a particular company. Common examples of rules adopted this way include: commission rules of practice and procedure; rules governing terminations, payment plans, and resolution of customer disputes; rules governing utility accounting practices; rules governing gas safety; rules governing service quality; etc.

Rulemaking often begins by the commission issuing a "Notice of Proposed Rulemaking" or "Order Instituting Rulemaking" or some other form of general notice to the public. This initial notice will specify the subject matter of the proceeding and will usually invite any interested member of the public to offer written comments. Anyone can file written comments, and there is no need to file a petition to intervene.[15] Sometimes the commission will hold public hearings at which anyone can testify, but sometimes the commission will only allow written comments. Other times, the commission will hold informal sessions at which interested parties and staff exchange ideas about what is good or bad about the proposed rules (e.g., low-income consumers support a proposal to adopt low-income discounts; companies argue this would be too expensive); or the best ways to implement policies the commission has made clear it will adopt (e.g., consumers and companies suggest better ways of conducting outreach to people eligible for existing low-income discounts); or technical issues (e.g., the ability of companies to identify customers eligible for discounts).

The good news about rulemaking proceedings is that you won't have to file a petition or follow the formal rules of procedure that apply in adjudicatory cases. It's also less likely, although still possible, that you'll need expert witnesses or a lawyer to represent you. In general, rulemaking proceedings tend to take less of your time and cost less. But rulemaking proceedings sometimes go on for years without a final conclusion. It is also a little less likely that you will know that the commission has opened a rulemaking because the adjudicatory cases (especially rate hike cases) tend to get the most publicity. If you or your group think that you want to get involved in rulemaking proceedings, speak to the chief of the docket office, "Executive Secretary" or chief administrative officer for the commission. Most commissions maintain mailing lists of people who are interested in receiving notices of newly-filed cases and rulemaking proceedings. It's very easy to get yourself on such a list, and it won't take much time to monitor the notices you'll receive.

■ **"Generic" proceedings:** Generic proceedings can be a hybrid of adjudicatory and rulemaking proceedings, and may go by other names in your state. (Some states, however, might not have anything like what is described here.) In generic proceedings, the commission may use adjudicatory-type proceedings (that is, allow for discovery and cross-examination of witnesses, filing of written briefs, etc.) but address broad issues that affect an entire industry (gas, electric or telephone) and issue a decision that has long-term effect (as opposed to rate cases, where many of the issues are decided anew in each case).

- **Informal proceedings:** Commissions do all kinds of things that affect consumers and utilities without employing any of the procedures just described. For example, the commission's general counsel may clarify some issue or policy in response to a letter from a company, from legislators, or from consumers. Unless someone learns of this letter ruling and questions it, the general counsel's letter may become the commission's *de facto* policy on that issue. Similarly, consumer division staff constantly set informal policies about when utilities may actually terminate service (for example, informally letting companies know that staff will not tolerate terminations for arrearages of less than $100, or requiring longer payment plans for low-income customers) and other issues. It is very important to understand the extent to which policies that matter to you or your group are being set informally, for two reasons. First, to the extent policies are set informally, the public tends to have little or no involvement. Utility companies are always speaking to and making requests of the commissioners and their staff, and informal policies therefore tend to reflect the utility companies' view of the world. It's important to bring some light into the back rooms of your utility commission. Second (and somewhat contradictory to the first point), it's often easier for consumers to have a successful impact on informal policymaking than in adjudicatory proceedings, because the informal proceedings require less in terms of lawyers, experts, time, and money. Consumers should always look at opportunities to advance their goals through informal proceedings.[16]

C. *Procedural rules*

Almost every commission has formal, written rules of practice and procedure.[17] These rules will address: the format of petitions to intervene and deadlines for filing; the manner in which copies of filings must be served on the commission itself and other parties; the format of written documents that are filed in cases; the conduct of hearings; etc. In some states, the rules will also address the extent to which parties may have "ex parte" contact with commissioners (meaning: one party speaking to or communicating in writing to commissioners, outside the presence of other parties); the format of any motions that are filed; the type of discovery that will be allowed (e.g., written requests that must be answered; inspection of physical premises; depositions; etc.); procedures governing oral arguments; and the process by which the commission reaches and issues its decisions.

Procedural rules vary greatly from state to state. If you are not familiar with your commission's rules, get a copy and read the rules carefully.[18] If you cannot easily locate a copy, ask the commission staff for advice.

D. *Chronology of an adjudicatory proceeding*

Initial filing and petitions to intervene: An adjudicatory case begins with some party, usually the utility company, filing an initial "petition" or "application."[19] **Make sure you get a copy of this initial filing at the earliest possible date.** Usually, you can get a copy by calling the company's attorneys (who might be in-house staff attorneys or an outside private firm). Call the commission's staff if you are having any difficulty obtaining a copy. Review the initial filing carefully to determine which issues of interest to you will be raised during the case.

The commission then orders the issuance of public notice of the filing, usually through newspaper ads and by sending notice to a mailing list the commission maintains of those interested in getting notices of cases filed. This initial notice may include: (1) the date(s) of any public hearings in the case; (2) a deadline for filing petitions to intervene, and brief explanation of what is required to do so; (3) a summary of the issues raised by the initial filing; (4) contact information for the commission and the party making the filing. Some states have less information than this, some have more. **It is very important to learn when petitions to intervene are due and to make sure you file on time.** Many states are strict about this deadline, although some states do not even require a formal petition to intervene if you show up at the initial "pre-hearing conference" (described below) and no one objects to the intervention.

In order to file a successful petition to intervene in states that require a formal petition, you will need to clearly state the interest that you or your group has in the proceeding, including a brief description of how you or your group will be affected. Each state has developed its own standards about how much, or how little, you must include in your petition. **Review your commission's intervention rules *very carefully*** and, if possible, speak to lawyers or commission staff about whether your commission freely grants interventions or whether they require petitions to meet all of the formal requirements of the rules and prior decisions.

In some states, commissions allow (or require) parties to seek "full party" (or "full intervenor") status versus "limited" status. Always ask to be granted "full" status. Parties with "limited" status may be prohibited from filing discovery or cross-examining witnesses or otherwise be limited in what they are allowed to do in the case.

"Procedural" or "prehearing" or "scheduling" conferences: Many commissions schedule a "procedural" or "prehearing" conference not too long after the initial filing is made. Many different things can happen at this early conference. The commission may set the schedule for discovery, future evidentiary hearings, and the filing of written briefs. It may rule on petitions to intervene. It may address preliminary motions that have been filed, for example, motions to define the scope of issues that can be raised. It is very helpful to attend this conference. It is your first chance to get a good sense of which parties intend to play an active role in the case. It is also your first chance to let the hearing officer and other parties know, in person, that you will be in the case and actively pursuing your issues. Also keep in mind that many cases are resolved through settlement, not through formal hearings. By attending the pre-hearing conference, you are more likely to be seen as an active party who should be included in any settlement talks.

Discovery: Parties in an adjudicatory case have the right to conduct "discovery"— that is, to "discover" information that other parties may know or possess. Discovery in utility cases most commonly takes the form of "information requests" or "interrogatories." These are written questions that one party writes and serves upon another party. The other party must then provide a written response, or produce documents that respond to the question.

In some jurisdictions, parties to a case may also conduct "depositions," although these are not done very frequently and may not be allowed in some states. Where depositions are allowed, you can ask another party (e.g., the utility company) to produce a witness who must answer questions you ask. A stenographer is present and records the questions and answers. The party requesting the deposition usually must pay the cost of having a stenographer present.

Discovery rules vary from state to state. Sometimes, there are no written discovery rules, just accepted practice as to how discovery may be conducted. Often, the hearing officer, administrative law judge, or commissioner assigned to the case will set discovery rules at the pre-hearing conference, including the date by which discovery requests may be filed and the number of days a party is allowed to respond to discovery. Because utility cases raise very technical and complicated factual issues, discovery is often quite voluminous. Parties often battle over whether the requested information can be produced in the time allowed, or whether it would cost too much to produce an answer. Consumer intervenors who are not experienced with the discovery process should keep in mind that you can always file a motion with the hearing officer requesting that a party be ordered to provide an answer (a motion to compel). You can also seek the assistance from the hearing officer to resolve other discovery disputes: if the company objects that it would cost too much to answer certain questions; claims that the requested information is privileged; etc.

Most commissions set rolling deadlines for answers to discovery, meaning that the answering party must provide an answer within a specified number of days from when the requests are made. **Under a rolling discovery deadline, it is in your interest to ask you questions at the earliest possible date.** This may allow you to file follow-up questions. For example, assume a case is filed on May 1; hearings begin on June 10; and the rolling discovery deadline is 10 days. If you get your first set of information requests out by May 10, you should expect answers by May 20. If some of those answers are not very clear, you could send out follow-up questions by May 25[20] and expect answers to your second set by early June, enough time to review those answers and prepare for hearings.

Testimony: Most utility cases have an "evidentiary" phase[21]: hearings days when witnesses take the stand, testify and introduce written or graphic exhibits. However, these witnesses submit their testimony in writing, well in advance of the actual hearings. For example, when a company makes an initial filing in a rate case, it will include all of the accounting data that supports its rate hike request as well as the written testimony of the witnesses who will testify in support of the rate case. Intervenors who plan to offer testimony also must put this testimony in writing, although it is submitted several weeks or even a few months after the company's filing.

Written testimony is submitted in advance of the evidentiary hearings. This allows you to conduct discovery of the company's witnesses. This also means that the company and any other party in the case can conduct discovery of any witnesses you plan to offer. If you plan to put on any witnesses, it is important that the witness understands this obligation to answer any discovery.

Parties are free to put on expert or non-expert witnesses. Unlike many court trials, where many of the witnesses are not experts and simply testify about things they saw, heard, or experienced, most utility case witnesses are experts—in accounting issues, or plant operations, rate design, etc. While you may think that some witnesses you want to offer are not sufficiently "expert" to testify, there are many people who can help your case and who would be allowed to testify, even if they are not experienced "expert" witnesses.[22] For example, you may be pushing the utility to modify or expand an existing energy efficiency program. The director of you local weatherization program may be able to testify to the benefits that customers will gain by reducing energy consumption, and the favorable cost-benefit ratio of the specific measures you are proposing, even if the director has never been a witness before and doesn't have a lot of advanced degrees. Or you may be in a case arguing that the company is not following the commission's rules (or what you consider to be fair practices) regarding deposits, payment plans, and collections. You may be able to find a local organizer or advocate who routinely works with customers and has documented the company's aggressive credit and collection practices through notes to his or her case file. Using witnesses like these will both help your case and avoid the cost of using traditional "expert" witnesses, most of whom charge very high fees.

Any witness you put on will be obliged to answer any discovery requests relating to his or her testimony, and to take the witness stand. Any party to the case will then be allowed to cross-examine your witness. If you plan to put on a witness, it is important to choose someone you think will come across as honest, open and credible when cross-examined. Avoid witnesses who you think will be defensive or combative on cross-examination.

All of the evidentiary hearings are transcribed by a court stenographer. If you put on a witness, you should make sure to get a copy of that day's transcript.

Briefs: At then end of the evidentiary hearings, parties will be allowed some number of days (in rare cases) or weeks (more commonly) to write their briefs. A brief is nothing more than a written argument that summarizes the relevant portions of the evidence in the case and urges the commission to take certain positions on the issues presented, based on the relevant law (including statutes, regulations, and prior commission decisions). "Briefs" are by no means always brief: they can be dozens of pages long, sometimes more than 100 pages. But compared to an evidentiary record that often includes hundreds of pages of hearing transcripts and thousands of pages of documentary evidence, your "brief" in fact serves as a summary of all of the information in the record that supports the arguments you make.

Commissions usually have some rules governing the format of briefs, and you should review those rules carefully. These rules are usually less detailed than the rules governing briefs filed in court, but it is still important to follow the rules. In addition, the hearing officer or administrative law judge may impose additional rules that will apply to the format and timing of briefs in your case. Sometimes, commissions require all parties to file their initial briefs on the same day, and allow parties then to submit reply briefs a short time later. Other times, the commission will require one party (say, the company) to file its brief first; require all other parties to file their reply briefs; and then allow the first party (the company) to file a reply to the other parties. There are advantages and disadvantages to each approach, and the practice varies not only from state to state, but from case to case within any state. Just make sure you are aware of and comply with the briefing schedule. The commission may "strike" (refuse to accept) a brief that is filed even one day late.

It is very helpful to have a general idea of what you would like to say in your brief even before you start discovery! Your goal when getting into a case is to obtain a favorable ruling from the commission on one or more issues: e.g., adopting discount rates for low-income customers; or changing the company's rules around deposits; etc. To do so, you will need to write a brief that convinces the commission that your position is supported by the facts in the case and by the relevant law. But that means you will need to have a good idea of what facts you'd like to be in the record as the record is being developed. Once you start writing your brief, the record in the case will be closed and you won't be able to add in any new facts. You should always have a clear vision as to what facts will help you write a convincing brief—while you're writing discovery; when you're thinking about witnesses you'd like to put on the stand; as you're cross-examining the company's witnesses.

The decision: Some time after briefs are filed, the commission will issue a decision. In some states, you simply do nothing and wait until the final decision comes out. In other states, the hearing officer or administrative law judge issues a proposed decision, and parties then have an opportunity to file written comments on the draft before the full commission rules. In yet other states, a single commissioner who is assigned to the case writes a draft decision which the parties can comment on at an open meeting of the full commission before a final decision is released. There are yet other variations, but the key point is to determine whether your state allows you the opportunity to comment, in writing or in person, on a draft decision before the final one is released. This is an important opportunity to make your case one more time. Make sure you avail yourself of this opportunity.

Court appeals: Utility commission decisions can be appealed to court. The decision itself (or an attachment to the decision) may explain, in highly simplified terms, how to file an appeal—naming the court in which it must be filed and the deadline for doing so (often 30 days or less from the time of the decision). Appeals by consumers are difficult to win because courts begin by assuming the commission ruled properly, unless convinced to the contrary. It is very hard to pursue a successful appeal without the assistance of a lawyer. If you are thinking about filing an appeal, contact a knowledgeable attorney immediately after receiving the decision that you wish to appeal.

III. THINKING OUTSIDE THE BOX—AND OUTSIDE THE "PROCEEDING"

Utility companies have many advantages over consumer groups in proceedings before utility commissions. They can spend large amounts of money on lawyers and experts. They have easy access to most of the relevant information, as their employees and consultants usually prepare the initial filing that starts a case. Utility commissioners frequently meet and communicate with company executives, at conferences, in hearings, and at face-to-face meetings arranged by those executives or their lawyers. Many utility commissioners have similar educational training and backgrounds as company executives; relatively fewer commissioners have a background as consumer advocates or working on consumer issues.

In order to overcome these inherent disadvantages, consumers need to think outside of the box and outside of the confines of the hearing room itself. Consumer groups will have to play to their potential strengths: being aligned with the interests of consumers; being able to mobilize community support; and being able to shine some light on the often overlooked process by which utility commissions make their decisions. The most useful tools for breaking out of the box are community organizing, using the media, and generating support among legislators and other policymakers outside of the commission.

A. *Community Organizing*

Utility companies like their proceedings to occur as quickly and quietly as possible. Whether filing for a rate increase, approval of a merger, or authority to issue bonds, the companies prefer not to have intervenors in their cases and to minimize the amount of discovery, hearing days, and public attention to the case.

Consumer groups can change the dynamic in utility proceedings by organizing their own members and the general public. Most proceedings before commissions require a truly "public hearing": one that is duly noticed in newspapers and other means; held in an accessible public meeting space; and fully open for lay people (non-lawyers) to make statements. But many public hearings see few, if any, members of the public speak. A consumer group that can mobilize even ten people to testify at a public hearing will have some impact on the case. The utility company will know that the public is watching what is going on. More importantly, the commission will be far more likely to pay attention to the issues that lawyers or other advocates for consumers raise in formal, evidentiary hearings if there is a large turnout by consumers themselves at the initial public hearing.[23]

Community organizing is extremely important when consumers are seeking rules or programs that benefit them, and not only when they are opposing utility proposals. A good example of the importance of community organizing in such proceedings is the initial adoption of basic billing and termination rules by the Massachusetts Department of Public Utilities in the early 1970s. Legal services programs, working with their low-income clients, offered:

> testimony about the experiences of low-income customer with their utility services. This came largely from attorneys in legal services offices knowledgeable in the problems of the poor. Some of the testimony was illustrated by affidavits of the customers involved, and there was some direct testimony by customers.[24]
>
> The Department adopted the billing and termination rules in response to the presentations made by low-income customers and advocates.

Community organizing plays to the strength of consumer groups. Utility companies simply cannot mobilize public support in favor of their rate hikes and other proceedings before state commissions. Instead, they rely on their lawyers and the experts that their money can buy to win their cases. Consumer groups have the ability to remind commissions that their primary obligation in to carry out the "legislature's intent to protect ratepayers from overreaching by public utilities."[25] They have the ability to make sure the voices of real consumers are heard in the hallways of power, which will lead to more commission decisions that reflect the interests of consumers rather than utility companies.

B. *Media*

Working with the media is the logical corollary of community organizing. The media have the ability to amplify the voices of consumers to a much wider audience and with much greater effect. Low-income consumers can effectively use the media, for example, by publicizing increases in utility prices and the number of people of who are facing termination.[26] This type of media coverage can be critical, for example, if consumers are petitioning for the adoption of rules limiting terminations during winter months or allowing for more generous payment plans.

Getting media attention can be difficult. A few points that may help:

- Don't overlook smaller newspapers and radio stations. These sources are often looking for news, where the biggest newspaper or radio station in the state will generally be inundated with groups looking to get their story covered.

- Put a human face on the story. The local newspaper may think that a story about hearings before your utility commission on termination rules is not very interesting, but it may be very interested in covering the story of families living without heat because they've been terminated. The story might then also mention the hearings before the commission. Similarly, the local radio station might not think much of a story about a new low-income energy efficiency program a local group is proposing—but it may cover the story if the group highlights individual families who have benefited from weatherization, or if the group ties the need for energy efficiency programs to how many people are being terminated due to high bills.

- Look for allies who the media pays attention to. The Attorney General, Office of Ratepayer Advocate, or other well-recognized organizations might be willing to help draw the media's attention to your issues to the extent your interests overlap. In some states, for example, the Attorney General's office may routinely appear on a consumer program on a TV or radio station. Particularly during the winter, the AG's office might be willing to talk about high bills, payment plans, termination rules, and other issues that bring attention to issues you are advocating.

C. *The Legislature*

Ultimately, the legislature is the source of both a utility commission's general authority to regulate utility companies[27] and of specific rights granted to consumers.[28] Consumer groups should always consider the extent to which the legislature can help in any efforts to promote the interests of consumers.

First, the primary business of legislatures is to adopt laws. Consumer groups should be alert to opportunities to advocate for the adoption of pro-consumer laws, particularly in any state that is about to adopt or revise restructuring laws. In many of the states that currently have restructuring laws, low-income consumer groups were at the table as bills were being negotiated, seeking "systems benefit charges" or other mechanisms that fund low-income energy efficiency programs, discount rates, or other consumer benefits. Many of those states adopted time-limited rate caps that will soon be expiring, which may once again create an opportunity for consumers to be a the table as legislatures wrestle with what to do once the rate caps expire. Quite apart from restructuring, legislatures are an important route for consumers to obtain any number of beneficial programs and policies, from rules governing payment plans to mandated discount rates and affordability programs.

Second, legislatures can often play a useful oversight role, whether through formal oversight hearings or less formal contacts between key legislative committees and utility commissions. For example, if key legislators let commissioners know that they are very concerned about the high level of residential arrearages and the numbers of people being terminated, the commission will be more likely to respond favorably to consumer petitions for better termination rules or utility investments in low-income energy efficiency programs. Consumer groups should consider having once-a-year or more frequent meetings with key legislators to brief them on the issues that the consumer groups consider important.[29]

IV. RESOURCES

A. *Sample pleadings*
Consumer groups will rarely have to start from scratch when filing many of the routine papers in a utility proceeding.

1. Petition to Intervene
There will almost always be a "Petition to Intervene" previously filed by another consumer group or other intervenor that can serve as a good model or starting point. Attachment A contains a sample petition (styled as a "Motion") and supporting memorandum filed by the Utility Workers Union of America (UWUA) in a Cincinnati Gas & Electric (CG&E) case. CG&E vigorously opposed this intervention, which companies sometimes do, but the motion was ultimately granted.[30] Attachment B is a sample request of the National Consumer Law Center to be placed on the service list in a California rulemaking proceeding regarding the adoption of a telecommunications consumers Bill of Rights. In some proceedings and in some jurisdictions, parties that file before a set deadline do not need to file a formal petition to intervene but instead have the right to intervene by filing a notice that sets forth the interest of the intervenor and other required facts. Attachment B is an example of such a notice.

2. Discovery
Almost every adjudicatory proceeding before a commission allows parties "discovery" rights. Discovery varies quite widely, depending on the subject matter of the proceeding and the interest of the intervenor filing the discovery requests. Therefore, it is harder to find sample discovery from a prior case that will match the needs of an intervenor in the current case, although discovery from one rate case to the next case involving the same company is often similar. Attachment C is sample discovery filed by low-income intervenors in a KeySpan rate case, seeking to build a record regarding arrearages and terminations, and the need for the company's proposed "OnTrack" arrearage forgiveness program.

3. Other pleadings
Once a consumer group gets beyond the initial stages of filing a petition to intervene and discovery, it becomes increasingly hard to find good samples. Expert testimony is usually quite specific to a particular case, although it may be helpful to find testimony in other cases on similar topics.[31] Briefs are also quite specific to a particular case. However, for any consumer group that has not intervened previously, it would be useful to review one or more briefs from prior cases to get a feel for the format and scope of these documents.

B. *Useful treatises and handbooks*

The National Consumer Law Center publishes *Access to Utility Service: Regulated, De-Regulated and Unregulated Utilities, Deliverable Fuels, and Telecommunications*. This 650 page treatise (with 500+ page supplement) addresses a broad range of low-income energy and utility topics, including restructuring, telephone service, metering issues, issues around utility payments, and various energy assistance programs.[32]

A book that is specific to Massachusetts but still may prove useful in other states is *The Right to Light (and Heat) Handbook* by Charlie Harak, available from Massachusetts Continuing Legal Education at 800-966-6253 (product #19938701720; price $6). This 100+ page handbook provides an overview of customer rights and remedies and how to intervene in commission proceedings. It is written to be used directly by consumers or advocates with little experience in utility issues.

The California Public Utilities Commission publishes a very useful *Guide to Public Participation* available at http://www.cpuc.ca.gov/PUBLISHED/REPORT/46182.htm. This Guide is very readable, reviews the various types of commission proceedings, and explains how to intervene. While it is specific to California, it provides a useful roadmap of what questions to ask when getting involved in utility cases in other states.

The National Consumer Law Center also maintains a list serve for those interested in low-income energy issues. Contact the Center's energy unit at 617-542-8010 for more information.

C. *Groups That Intervene in Utility Proceedings*

There is no need for a consumer group to reinvent the wheel of how to get more involved in utility proceedings, as there are many groups that are very experienced in doing so. It is best to find a group in your own state that has done so, but experienced groups in almost any area of the country can be helpful. Here are just a few of the consumer groups that have a great deal of experience in utility intervention:

National Consumer Law Center
77 Summer Street
Boston, MA 02110
617-542-8010
www.consumerlaw.org
Contact: Charlie Harak, John Howat or Olivia Wein

Public Utility Law Project
90 State St., Ste. 601
Albany, NY
518-449-3375
www.pulp.tc
Contact: Charlie Brennan

The Utility Reform Network
711 Van Ness Ave., Suite 350
San Francisco, CA 94102
415-929-8876

www.turn.org
Contact: Bob Finkelstein

Texas Legal Services Center
815 Brazos St. Suite 1100
Austin, TX 78701
512-477-6000
www.tlsc.org
Contact: Randy Chapman

Pennsylvania Utility Law Project
118 Locust St.
Harrisburg, PA 17101-1414
717-232-2719
www.palegalservices.org/Specialty/utility_law_project.htm
Contact: Harry Geller

Ohio Partners for Affordable Energy
Legislative Liaison
Ohio Association of Community Action Agencies
337 S. Main St.,
4th Floor, Suite 5
P.O. Box 1793
Findlay, OH 45839-1793
419-425-8860
Contact: Dave Rinebolt

ATTACHMENT A

SAMPLE PETITION (MOTION) TO INTERVENE BEFORE THE PUBLIC UTILITIES COMMISSION OF OHIO

In the Matter of the Application of the Cincinnati Gas & Electric Company for an Increase in Its Gas Rates	CASE NO. 01-1228-GA-AIR
In the Matter of the Application of the Cincinnati Gas & Electric Company for Approval of an Alternative Rate Plan for Its Gas Distribution Service	CASE NO. 01-1478-GA-ALT

MOTION TO INTERVENE, UTILITY WORKERS UNION OF AMERICA AND IUU, LOCAL 600 OF THE UWUA

In accordance with the Commission's Administrative Provisions, OAC 4901-1-1, the Utility Workers Union of America (UWUA) and IUU, Local 600 of the UWUA move that they be allowed to intervene as a full parties in the three applications of Cincinnati Gas & Electric Company cited above. UWUA and Local 600 are separately filing a Memorandum in Support of this motion.

Respectfully Submitted,

Charles Harak, Esq.
[Address]
[Phone Number]
[E-mail Address]
DATED: [Date]

BEFORE THE PUBLIC UTILITIES COMMISSION OF OHIO

In the Matter of the Application of the Cincinnati Gas & Electric Company for an Increase in Its Gas Rates	CASE NO. 01-1228-GA-AIR
In the Matter of the Application of the Cincinnati Gas & Electric Company for Approval of an Alternative Rate Plan for Its Gas Distribution Service	CASE NO. 01-1478-GA-ALT

MEMORANDUM IN SUPPORT OF MOTION TO INTERVENE, UTILITY WORKERS UNION OF AMERICA AND IUU, LOCAL 600 OF THE UWUA

In accordance with Ohio R.C. § 4903.221 and the Commission's Administrative Provisions, OAC 4901-1-1, the Utility Workers Union of America (UWUA) and IUU, Local 600 of the UWUA (Local 600) file this memorandum in support of their motion to intervene.

I. PARTIES

UWUA is a national union that represents 50,000 workers employed by gas, electric and water companies across the United States. It maintains business offices at [Address] and at [Address]. UWUA has intervened in a number of utility regulatory proceedings in Ohio, Massachusetts, New York, California, and other states.

Local 600 is based in Cincinnati and represents approximately 700 workers employed by Cincinnati Gas & Electric Company (CGE) in the areas of customer service, meter reading, billing, facilities maintenance, and gas engineering. Many members of Local 600 are also customers of CGE.

II. INTEREST OF UWUA AND LOCAL 600

UWUA and Local 600 have a real and substantial interest in the present proceeding. No other party can adequately represent their interests. OAC 4901-1-11(A)(2).

On behalf of its members who are customers, Local 600 is concerned that CGE has proposed an alternative rate plan that would allow it to collect funds from ratepayers, on a current basis, to pay for the replacement of cast iron and steel pipe mains. CGE's proposal will raise rates for all customers and should not be approved.

UWUA and Local 600 are also concerned that CGE, while proposing to raise its rates, is planning to relocate the handling of a significant portion of customer calls out of the state of Ohio. UWUA and Local 600 believe that this relocation will cause a decline in the quality of service that customers expect as well as result in a loss of jobs for Local 600 members. CGE should not be allowed to raise its rates if customer service will decline.

Cinergy One, an unregulated affiliate of Cinergy Corp (CGE's parent), has entered into an arrangement with MakeTheMove (MTM) under which Cinergy (through its distribution company subsidiaries such as CGE) will transfer to MTM calls from customers who are moving. MTM will then assist the customer with transferring cable, telephone and other services to the new address. UWUA and Local 600 believe that the arrangement with MTM has the potential to result in a cross-subsidization of MTM by distribution company customers and also to interfere with CGE's responsiveness to customers.

Finally, UWUA and Local 600 are concerned that CGE has recently closed one district office in Loveland, Ohio and is considering the closure of other offices as well, to the detriment of customers who rely on access to the company through those offices.

No other party can represent these interests. The intervention of UWUA and Local 600 will contribute to a just and expeditious resolution of the issues before the Commission, through the information and arguments that these parties will present to the Commission. UWUA and Local 600 will abide by any schedule set in these cases, and their intervention therefore will not unduly delay the proceeding or unduly prejudice any party.

III. CONCLUSION

UWUA and Local 600 ask that their motion to intervene be granted.

Respectfully Submitted,

Charles Harak, Esq.
[Address]
[Phone Number]
[E-mail Address]
DATED: [Date]

ATTACHMENT B

SAMPLE NOTICE OF APPEARANCE IN JURISDICTION NOT REQUIRING FORMAL "PETITION TO INTERVENE"

BEFORE THE PUBLIC UTILITIES COMMISSION OF THE STATE OF CALIFORNIA

Order Instituting Rulemaking on the Commission's
Own Motion to Establish Consumer Rights and
Consumer Protection Rules Applicable to All
Telecommunications Carriers
Rulemaking, #00-02-004

REQUEST OF NATIONAL CONSUMER LAW CENTER TO BE PLACED ON SERVICE LIST

In accordance with the Order Instituting Investigation (OII) in this docket (Feb. 4, 2000), the National Consumer Law Center (NCLC) requests that it be placed on the service list for this docket and be allowed to participate in all future proceedings in this docket. In connection with this request, NCLC states:

1. The National Consumer Law Center is a non-profit organization established in 1969. Its central mission is to protect low-income consumers from injustices in the marketplace. In carrying out its work, NCLC has participated in adjudicatory and rulemaking proceedings involving electric, gas and telecommunications companies before regulatory commissions across the United States. NCLC seeks to participate in this docket on behalf of low-income consumers.

2. In its February 4, 2000 OII, the Commission established that parties may be added to the service list by "submitting a written request to the Commission's Process Office, [with a] copy to the assigned ALJ," and including identifying information. OII, at 12.

3. NCLC hereby requests that it be allowed to appear in this case, that it be added to the service list in this case (under "Appearance"), and that all papers be served upon its staff attorney, Charles Harak, whose full address and other identifying information appear below.

4. NCLC will serve a copy of this Request on all parties listed on the service list, as updated through July 20, 2001.

5. NCLC will fully comply with all schedules and deadlines that apply to other parties in this docket.

WHEREFORE, NCLC asks that its request be granted.
Respectfully submitted,
[Address]
[Phone Number]
[E-mail Address]
DATED: [Date]

ATTACHMENT C

SAMPLE DISCOVERY REGARDING ARREARAGES AND TERMINATIONS

COMMONWEALTH OF MASSACHUSETTS DEPARTMENT OF TELECOMMUNICATIONS AND ENERGY

RE: BOSTON GAS COMPANY
      PERFORMANCE BASED RATE PLAN   DTE 03-40

SECOND SET OF INFORMATION REQUESTS OF MASSACHUSETTS COMMUNITY ACTION PROGRAM DIRECTORS ASSOCIATION

Please send one copy of the responses to these information requests to:

Charles Harak
[Address]

Jerrold Oppenheim
[Address]

MASSCAP 2-1:   [FOLLOW-UP T0 AG 2-1]

(a) Please explain whatever factors may have caused "total residential billing 30 to 59 days arrears" to decline from $58.5 million in 1999 to the range of $7 million to $7.7 million in 2000 and 2001.

(b) Please explain why "system conversion" prevents the Company from being able to calculate the 2002 arrears (30 to 59 days and 60+ days, AG 2-1, parts C and D). If this information is available for the portion of 2002 prior to the conversion (e.g., for the first six months of 2002), please provide the requested information for that period (e.g., the six-month period) and for the same portion (e.g., the first six months) of the years 1999, 2000 and 2001.

(c) Is the increase in residential billing from $402 million (2000) to $546 million (2001), and the subsequent decline to $398 million (2002) attributable (i) primarily to changes in the number of degree days; (ii) primarily to changes in the cost of gas adjustment or (iii) a combination of changes in degree days and the CGA? If other factors are involved, please explain.

(d) Please provide the information requested by the Attorney General in AG 2-1, parts C and D, for any and all months of 2003 for which the data is now available. If no information is available, please explain why not, including whether it will become available at a later date (specify when).

(e) For each of the years 1999 to 2002, and for portions of 2003 for which information may be available, provide the number of residential accounts that were in arrears (i) between 30 and 59 days and (ii) 60 days or more. To the extent the data is available monthly (or, failing that, quarterly), provide this information monthly (or quarterly).

(f) Please provide the information requested in the preceding section, (e), for only those residential accounts coded as receiving fuel assistance or as "financial hardship" and for customers on the company's low-income discount rates (heating and non-heating).

(g) Please provide the information requested in AG 2-1, sections A, B, C, D, E, H, I, J and K only for those residential accounts coded as receiving fuel assistance or as "financial hardship" and for those customers on the company's low-income discount rates.

(h) Please restate the answer to AG 2-1(E) so that the data for all four years are comparable: either include bad debt related to gas costs for the years 2001 and 2002, or exclude gas costs for the years 1999 and 2000.

(i) Please provide the information requested in the preceding section, (h), only for those residential accounts coded as receiving fuel assistance or as "financial hardship" and for those customers on the company's low-income discount rates.

(j) [See AG 2-1(G)]

(i) Does the company impose late charges on any residential accounts? If yes, please provide a reference to the appropriate portion of the Terms and Conditions, tariffs, or other source where these charges are listed.

(ii) Please explain the term "forfeited discounts," and whether residential customers ever forfeit any discounts.

(k) When the answer to AG2-1(H) is finally provided, please also state the number of such customers whose accounts were coded as receiving fuel assistance or as "financial hardship" accounts and the number of such customers on the company's low-income discount rates.

MASSCAP 2-2

(a) Does the Company code the accounts of residential customers that it knows are receiving fuel assistance payments?

(b) Does it provide a separate code (that is, separate than the code for fuel assistance) for the accounts of customers who have submitted a "financial hardship" form or asserted "financial hardship" status, but who are not receiving fuel assistance payments on their gas bills?

(c) To the extent that the Company's practices regarding the coding policies described in the preceding paragraphs (i) and (ii) have changed since 1999, please describe those changes.

MASSCAP 2-3

(a) Please provide the number of residential customers coded as receiving fuel assistance, for each of the years 1999 to 2003, inclusive. If the Company separately codes residential accounts as "financial hardship" (apart from those households coded as "fuel assistance"), please provide the number of these accounts as well, for the period 1999 to 2003.

(b) Please provide the number of customers on the company's low-income discount rates (heating and non-heating separately) as of year-end (or date closest to year-end) 1999, 2000, 2001 and 2002, and for the most recent date in 2003 for which data is available.

MASSCAP 2-4

(a) Please provide the (i) number of warrants the Company obtained from courts, for the purposes of entering property to terminate residential service of Massachusetts customers,

173

for each year 1999 to 2002, and for 2003 to date; (ii) the number of such warrants actually executed (i.e., premises physically entered under authority of a warrant), for the same time periods.

(b) Please provide the (i) number of warrants the Company obtained from courts, for the purposes of entering property to read residential meters in Massachusetts, for each year 1999 to 2002, and for 2003 to date; (ii) the number of such warrants actually executed (i.e., premises physically entered under authority of a warrant), for the same time periods.

MASSCAP 2-5

Please provide the number of liens on residential property obtained from courts, for the purposes of obtaining or securing payment from Massachusetts residential customers, for each year 1999 to 2002, and for 2003 to date.

MASSCAP 2-6

(a) Please provide the number of residential accounts referred for collection, for each year 1999 to 2002 and 2003 to date.

(b) If available, provide the number of such accounts, by year, that were coded as receiving fuel assistance or as "financial hardship" accounts, and that were receiving service under one of the low-income discount rates (heating or non-heating).

(c) Does the Company have an internal group or set of employees (including at any KeySpan affiliate) who perform collections work? If so, please name and/or describe the affiliate or group or employees and the types or nature of accounts that are referred to them.

MASSCAP 2-7

(a) How many days must amounts due be in arrears before an account is charged to "bad debt"? Please specify whether the number of days is calculated from the date a bill for service is first mailed, or from some other date (e.g., initial due date).

(b) If there are other criteria employed for determining "bad debt" other than the number of days overdue, please describe those criteria.

MASSCAP 2-8

For each month or quarter (if not available monthly), please provide the (i) number of new residential payment plans entered; (ii) the total number of plans in force; and (iii) the dollar amounts protected through payment plans, all for the period January 1, 1999 to the most recent date available.

MASSCAP 2-9 [Mr. [Smith], JFB-1, pp. 13-15]

Please provide any evaluations of the New York On Track program completed by KeySpan, any KeySpan affiliate, or any outside contractor. Whether or not considered an "evaluation," include any internal reports prepared by KeySpan or any KeySpan affiliate on the operation of On Track, including any quarterly, annual or other periodic reports. Also include any cost-benefit analysis of On Track and any reports on the On Track Program filed with the New York Public Service Commission.

MASSCAP 2-10

(a) When did KeySpan (or one of its affiliates) institute the New York On Track program?

(b) How many people have been enrolled, per year, for each year since the start of the program?

(c) How many employees, and of what job categories, are assigned to the New York On Track program?

(d) Please provide the average arrears of customers entering the New York On Track program, for each year (or shorter reporting period) since the program began, and the average arrears of those same customers at some milestone after the customers joined the program (e.g., at one year or 18 months after joining).

(e) For the same years or reporting periods provided in response to the preceding paragraph, (d), provide the average arrears of customers coded as receiving fuel assistance payments but who did not participate in On Track (with "average arrears" meaning the total amount of dollars in arrears for those customers, as of a particular date during the year or reporting period, divided by the number of customers coded as receiving fuel assistance).

(f) For the same years or reporting periods provided in response to the preceding paragraph, (d), provide the average arrears of all residential customers (with "average arrears" meaning the total amount of dollars in arrears for those customers, as of a particular date during the year or reporting period, divided by the number of residential customers).

MASSCAP 2-11

Did KeySpan (or any of its affiliates) obtain the approval of the New York Public Service Commission regarding its operation of the On Track program? If yes, include a copy of the relevant decision or order. [If the decision is a lengthy general rate hike decision, the Company may provide the portion or portions of the decision that mention or discuss On Track.]

MASSCAP 2-12

Please describe the operation of the proposed Massachusetts On Track program including:

(a) the title and location of the person or persons who will be in charge of the program;

(b) the titles and locations of other personnel who will be involved in operating the program;

(c) the criteria for accepting customers into the program;

(d) the number of customers that will be accepted into the program, both in the initial year and in subsequent years;

(e) any assumptions or projections the company has made regarding changes in the bill-paying behavior of customers who will be accepted into the On Track program.

MASSCAP 2-13

(a) Please describe the "education" component of the On Track program (JFB-1, p. 13, l. 21), including a description of any written or audio-visual materials provided to customers and any in-person educational sessions, in connection with the existing New York program and, if relevant, any different features of the educational component of the proposed Massachusetts program.

(b) Please describe the "counseling" component of the On Track program (JFB-1, p. 13, l. 21), including a description of who provides the counseling and the type of counseling offered (financial/budget, other), in connection with the existing New York program and, if relevant, any different features of the educational component of the proposed Massachusetts program.

(c) Please describe the "advocacy" component of the On Track program (JFB-1, p. 13, l. 21), including a description of who provides the advocacy and the type of advocacy offered (financial/budget, other), in connection with the existing New York program and, if relevant, any different features of the educational component of the proposed Massachusetts program.

MASSCAP 2-14 [See JFB-1, p. 14, l. 5]

(a) Will customers eligible for fuel assistance be excluded from the proposed Massachusetts On Track program, under the proviso that anyone "eligible for any public assistance that would cover utility arrears" is not eligible for On Track"?

(b) Does the answer to (a) depend on whether public assistance would cover the entire amount of the utility arrears, rather than being large enough to cover only a fraction of the arrears?

MASSCAP 2-15 [See JFB-1, p. 14, l. 8]

Please provide copies of any training materials or guidelines used in the New York On Track program to help determine the amounts of payments that should be sought under "an affordable payment plan."

MASSCAP 2-16

How many social workers does the Company (or any KeySpan affiliate) propose to assign to the Massachusetts On Track program, and where will they be based?

MASSCAP 2-17

Please provide the timing of the New York On Track program's arrearage forgiveness component:

(a) How frequently, or at what points during the program, are the $100 credits offered to customers?

(b) What happens to customers who fall behind on their payments under any payment plan established? Specifically, what rules or policies are followed to determine if the customer will be terminated from the program (if that ever occurs) or allowed to negotiate a new payment plan, or otherwise allowed to continue in the program despite missing one or more payments?

(c) Does the Company propose any different policies or rules regarding the timing and amount of credits to be offered in the Massachusetts program, or any different policies regarding customers who fall behind on their payments?

MASSCAP 2-18 [See JFB-1, p. 15, l. 11–13]

To the extent not provided in response to MASSCAP 2-10, please provide:

(a) the evaluations, studies or reports that show "participants paid about $190 a year more toward their energy bills;" and

(b) the data or reports showing the comparison between "customer termination actions and contacts concerning payment" before and after entering the On Track program.
DATED: May 30, 2003

NOTES TO APPENDIX G

1. There is further discussion of ratepayer advocates in I.B. The National Association of State Utility Consumer Advocates has a website that provides a directory of state ratepayer advocates. *See* www.nasuca.org.

2. Section II discusses at greater length the types of proceedings that most utility commissions use to collect information and decide cases or issues.

3. According to the Energy and Information Administration, "Status of State Electric Industry Restructuring Activity—as of February 2003," states that restructured are Arizona, Connecticut, Delaware, Illinois, Maine, Maryland, Massachusetts, Michigan, New Hampshire, New Jersey, New York, Ohio, Oregon, Pennsylvania, Rhode Island, Texas, Virginia and the District of Columbia. States that have delayed restructuring are Arkansas, Montana, Nevada, New Mexico and Oklahoma. California has partially reversed its electric restructuring.

4. "Discovery" refers to written requests sent to the company or other parties in the case seeking information you need to prepare your own case.

5. In every state, an individual will be allowed to represent himself or herself in a utility proceeding. However, in some states an organization that appears in a utility case, even a non-profit organization or consumer group, must be represented by an attorney because the commission has determined that non-lawyers are not allowed to represent the interests of groups or organizations. You can check with the legal staff of the commission to find out the commission's policies on who may "**appear**" (represent another party) in cases.

6. It is very rare for a party to be able to recover the costs of either its attorneys or expert witnesses in a utility proceeding. One state commission, the California Public Utilities Commission (CPUC), has extensive rules that allow for certain categories of intervenors, including non-profit consumer groups, to recover their costs. The commission frequently awards attorneys fees and costs to parties that substantially contribute to a final decision. Consumers participating in a California proceeding should carefully review the applicable rules and file a Notice of Intent to Seek Intervenor Compensation. Go to www.cpuc.ca.gov, then click "Laws, Rules, Procedures," then "Rules of Practice and Procedures" to locate the CPUC's rules.

7. The initial filing that a company makes in a general rate case usually fills up a ream box and includes very technical accounting and operational data. For those not experienced in reviewing a rate case filing, this can at first appear overwhelming. In fact, the issues that low-income consumers care most about are not that technical and usually require reviewing and understanding a small fraction of the company's case. Don't be deterred by the mere size of the company's filing!

8. See section IV, "Resources."

9. See Appendix C of this guide for a current list of commissioners in all fifty states.

10. Note that in most states there are absolute prohibitions or strict limitations on "ex parte" contacts, meaning contacts by just one of the parties to a case with any of the

commissioners regarding the pending case. Check the commission's rules carefully before holding any meetings about a pending case.

11. For a fifty-state summary of utility regulations governing billing, terminations and basic terms of service, see the National Consumer Law Center's treatise Access to Utility Service, described more fully in section IV. B.

12. These procedural steps are discussed in IV.D.

13. The National Association of Regulatory Utility Commissioners (NARUC) has a useful web site that links to the home page of each state utility regulatory commission that maintains a web site. See www.naruc.org/resources/state.shtml. Many (but not all) of those web sites include links to the rules of practice of that commission, and some allow on-line, electronic access to documents filed in cases before the Commission. Always review the commission's rules before getting involved in a utility case or proceeding.

14. Sample documents relating to petitioning to intervene or otherwise enter a case are included as Attachments A and B.

15. See Attachment B for the type of notice parties need to file in California rulemaking proceedings.

16. One important caveat, however, is that policies adopted informally can easily be undone. If you win a change in policy informally, this victory can be reversed due to a change in commissioners, in staff, or other reasons. If you win a victory in an adjudicatory case, that victory is far more likely to be long-lasting.

17. Some states may have rules of practice that apply generally to state agencies, not just to the commission.

18. Copies of commission rules are sometimes available on the commission's web page or elsewhere via the Internet.

19. This section addresses the chronology of an adjudicatory proceeding both because adjudicatory proceedings are more consistent state-to-state than rulemaking proceedings and because there are more formal steps in adjudicatory proceedings.

20. If you think that the company as withheld information it possesses, or if the company simply refuses to answer on time, you should file a motion to compel answers.

21. One major difference between utility cases and regular civil cases in court is that commissions also hold "public" hearings at which any member of the public can testify.

22. See discussion of "Expertise" under section I, above.

23. This is particularly true of issues like customer service—handling of customer phone calls, disclosing basic information to consumers, willingness to make payment plans, billing and termination practices, etc. In these areas, consumers are the "experts" on how the company is doing. See, for example, Revised Draft Decision of Comm. Wood, *In Re: Consumer Rights and Consumer Protection Rules Applicable to All Telecommunications Carriers*, CAPUC Docket 00-02-004 (Mar. 2, 2004)

(available at http://www.cpuc.ca.gov/PUBLISHED/COMMENT_DECISION/ 34459.htm), at 4 (referencing the "20 public participation hearings" the 300 people who made public statements; and the 2000 people who submitted mail or e-mail comments); at 148 ff. (basing the "great need for the [consumer protection] rules we adopt today" on the benefits to the public, as evidenced in the public participation hearings).

24. Cambridge Electric Light Co. v. Department of Public Utilities, 295 N.E.2d 876, 879 (1973). This decision describes the crucial role that low-income consumers and their legal services advocates played in adoption of these rules. In overruling a challenge by the utility companies to adoption of the pro-consumer rules, the court relied heavily on the record developed by low-income consumers and their advocates about the essential nature of utility service and the harshness of the companies' previously unregulated deposit and collection practices.

25. Fitchburg Gas & Electric Light Co. v. Dept' of Telecommunications & Energy, 801 N.E.2d 200, 228 (2004).

26. See, for example, Todd Grady, "Heating bills squeeze budgets—Area utility costs are second highest in 10 years," (Rochester, N.Y.) Democrat & Chronicle (Feb. 26, 2004).

27. See, for example, Cal. Pub. Util. Code §§ 201 *et seq.*

28. See, for example, Mass. Gen. Laws ch. 164, § 124A (protecting low-income, seriously ill customers from termination).

29. It is just as important for consumer groups to consider the helpful role that the state Attorney General or Consumer (or Ratepayer) Advocate can play, although most commissions are more responsive to legislators than to other executive branch agencies.

30. CG&E's opposition and UWUA's reply are available upon request from the National Consumer Law Center.

31. The National Consumer Law Center is currently building a database of sample testimony available to low-income advocates. For more information, contact NCLC's energy unit.

32. For more information, contact NCLC's publications unit at 617-542-9595 or www.nclc.org/publications. The 2004 price for "Access" is $90.

Bibliography

OTHER NCLC PUBLICATIONS

All National Consumer Law Publications can be ordered from Publications, National Consumer Law Center, 77 Summer Street, 10th Floor, Boston, MA 02110, (617) 542-9595, FAX (617) 542-8028, publications@nclc.org. To order by mail, please use the order form at the back of this volume. Visit **www.consumerlaw.org** to order securely on-line or for more information on all NCLC publications.

NCLC BOOKS FOR A GENERAL AUDIENCE

 **NCLC Guide to Surviving Debt:** a great overview of consumer law. Everything a paralegal, new attorney, or client needs to know about debt collectors, managing credit card debt, whether to refinance, credit card problems, home fore-closures, evictions, repossessions, credit reporting, utility ter-minations, student loans, budgeting, and bankruptcy.

 **The Surviving Credit Card Debt Workbook with CD-Rom:** provides strategies for consumers overwhelmed by credit card bills. It contains easy-to-use checklists of warning signs of credit card trouble and step-by-step advice on how to get out of credit card debt. The special advocate's section lists legal remedies and explains legal protections for consumers with credit card problems. The CD-Rom contains sample let-ters and forms, consumer education brochures, and more. (Bulk orders of 20 or more copies for this title only.)

NCLC Guide to Mobile Homes: explains what cosumers need to know about mobile home dealer practices, and what to look for in-depth about mobile home quality and defects, when not to buy a home, what to look for about delivery and installation, how to obtain warranty service, and tips on maintaining a home. Over 30 photographs graphically demonstrate construction details.

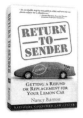

Return to Sender: Getting a Refund or Replacement for Your Lemon Car: describes how lemon laws work, what consumers and their lawyers should know to evaluate each other, how to develop the facts, legal rights, and how to handle both informal dispute resolution proceedings, and more.

National Consumer Law Center Consumer Education Brochures: NCLC has a wide array of brochures, some translated into other languages, that are available at www.survivingdebt.org.

NCLC BOOKS FOR LAWYERS

The Consumer Credit and Sales Legal Practice Series contains 17 titles, each with a CD-Rom that allows users to copy information directly onto a word processor. Each manual is designed to be an attorney's primary practice guide and legal resource when representing clients in all fifty states on that consumer law topic, and is updated annually. The 17 titles are arranged into four "libraries":

DEBTOR RIGHTS LIBRARY

Consumer Bankruptcy Law and Practice: the definitive personal bankruptcy manual, with step-by-step instructions from initial interview to final discharge, and including consumers' rights as creditors when a merchant or landlord files for bankruptcy. Appendices and CD-Rom contain over 130 annotated pleadings, bankruptcy statutes, rules and fee schedules, an interview questionnaire, a client handout, and software to complete the latest versions of petitions and schedules.

Fair Debt Collection: the basic reference in the field, covering the Fair Debt Collection Practices Act and common law, state statutory and other federal debt collection protections. Appendices and companion CD-Rom contain sample pleadings and discovery, the FTC's Official Staff Commentary, *all* FTC staff opinion letters, and summaries of reported and unreported cases.

Repossessions: covers every aspect of motor vehicle, mobile home and household goods repossessions and deficiency claims, and is the only treatise to go well beyond UCC Article 9 to also examine hundreds of other state and federal protections. The CD-Rom reprints numerous pleadings, statutes, and regulations.

Foreclosures: details what you need to protect a home from foreclosure, including how to negotiate workouts, foreclosure defenses, special protections for FHA, VA and RHS mortgages, servicer obligations, tax liens, and even steps to take after a foreclosure. The CD-Rom reprints sample pleadings, HUD, VA, and RHS handbooks, and other key materials.

Student Loan Law: student loan debt collection and collection fees; discharges based on closed school, false certification, failure to refund, disability, and bankruptcy; tax intercepts, wage garnishment, and offset of social security benefits; repayment plans, consolidation loans, deferments, and non-payment of loan based on school fraud. CD-Rom and appendices contain numerous forms, pleadings, interpretation letters and regulations.

Access to Utility Service: the only examination of consumer rights when dealing with regulated, de-regulated, and unregulated utilities, including telecommunications, terminations, billing errors, low-income payment plans, utility allowances in subsidized housing, LIHEAP, and weatherization. Includes summaries of state utility regulations.

CREDIT AND BANKING LIBRARY

Truth in Lending: detailed analysis of *all* aspects of TILA, the Consumer Leasing Act, and the Home Ownership and Equity Protection Act (HOEPA). Appendices and the CD-Rom contain the Acts, Reg. Z, Reg. M, and their Official Staff Commentaries, numerous sample pleadings, rescission notices, and two programs to compute APRs.

Fair Credit Reporting: the key resource for handling any type of credit reporting issue, from cleaning up blemished credit records to suing reporting agencies and creditors for inaccurate reports. Covers credit scoring, privacy issues, identity theft, the FCRA, the new FACTA provisions, the Credit Repair Organizations Act, state credit reporting and repair statutes, and common law claims.

Consumer Banking and Payments Law: unique analysis of consumer law (and NACHA rules) as to checks, money orders, credit, debit, and stored value cards, and banker's right of setoff. Also extensive treatment of electronic records and signatures, electronic transfer of food stamps, and direct deposits of federal payments. The CD-Rom and appendices reprint relevant agency interpretations and pleadings.

The Cost of Credit: a one-of-a-kind resource detailing state and federal regulation of consumer credit in all fifty states, federal usury preemption, explaining credit math, and how to challenge excessive credit charges and credit insurance. The CD-Rom includes a credit math program and hard-to-find agency interpretations.

Credit Discrimination: analysis of the Equal Credit Opportunity Act, Fair Housing Act, Civil Rights Acts, and state credit discrimination statutes, including reprints of all relevant federal interpretations, government enforcement actions, and numerous sample pleadings.

CONSUMER LITIGATION LIBRARY

Consumer Arbitration Agreements: numerous successful approaches to challenge the enforceability of a binding arbitration agreement, the interrelation of the Federal Arbitration Act and state law, class actions in arbitration, collections via arbitration, the right to discovery, and other topics. Appendices and CD-Rom include sample discovery, numerous briefs, arbitration service provider rules and affidavits as to arbitrator costs.

Consumer Class Actions: makes class action litigation manageable even for small offices, including numerous sample pleadings, class certification memoranda, discovery, class notices, settlement materials, and much more. Includes contributions from seven of the most experienced consumer class action litigators around the country.

Consumer Law Pleadings on CD-Rom: Over 1000 notable recent pleadings from all types of consumer cases, including predatory lending, foreclosures, automobile fraud, lemon laws, debt collection, fair credit reporting, home improvement fraud, rent to own, student loans, and lender liability. Finding aids pinpoint the desired pleading in seconds, ready to paste into a word processing program.

DECEPTION AND WARRANTIES LIBRARY

Unfair and Deceptive Acts and Practices: the only practice manual covering all aspects of a deceptive practices case in every state. Special sections on automobile sales, the federal racketeering (RICO) statute, unfair insurance practices, and the FTC Holder Rule.

Automobile Fraud: examination of title law, odometer tampering, lemon laundering, sale of salvage and wrecked cars, undisclosed prior use, prior damage to new cars, numerous sample pleadings, and title search techniques.

Consumer Warranty Law: comprehensive treatment of new and used car lemon laws, the Magnuson-Moss Warranty Act, UCC Articles 2 and 2A, mobile home, new home, and assistive device warranty laws, FTC Used Car Rule, tort theories, car repair and home improvement statutes, service contract and lease laws, with numerous sample pleadings.

Consumer Law in a Box: combines *all* documents and software from the companion CD-Roms of the 17 NCLC titles listed above. Quickly pinpoint a document from thousands found on the CD-Rom through keyword searches and Internet-style navigation, links, bookmarks, and other finding aids.

Internet search of full text of NCLC's 17 legal manuals. Visit www.consumerlaw.org and click on "keyword search" to find a list of all book titles and pages numbers from all NCLC legal manuals that satisfy your search terms.

OTHER NCLC PUBLICATIONS FOR LAWYERS

The Practice of Consumer Law: Seeking Economic Justice: contains an essential overview to consumer law and explains how to get started in a private or legal services consumer practice. Packed with practice pointers for even experienced consumer attorneys and invaluable sample pleadings on the CD-Rom.

STOP Predatory Lending: A Guide for Legal Advocates: provides a roadmap and practical legal strategy for litigating predatory lending abuses, from small loans to mortgage loans. The CD-Rom contains a credit math program, pleadings, legislative and administrative materials, and underwriting guidelines.

NCLC REPORTS is a newsletter that covers the latest developments and ideas in the practice of consumer law, issued 24 times a year. Practice areas covered include: Bankruptcy and Foreclosures; Consumer Credit and Usury; Debt Collection and Repossessions; and Deceptive Practices and Warranties.

Index

Appliance sales by utility companies 33
Arrearages
    deferred payment plans 32–33
    disputed bills 28–29
    landlord's, tenant's liability 27–28
    late charges, *see* Late charges
    prior debts, *see* Prior debts
    termination of service re, *see* Termination of
        service

Bankruptcy filing by consumer 33–34
Bills, *see* Utility bills
Budget billing 23, 100–101

Children, termination of service affecting
        30–31
    cold weather protection 31–32
    state regulations 73–82
Coal, *see* Deliverable fuels
Conservation programs, *see* Energy Efficiency
        Programs
Consumer complaints, *see* Customer
        complaints
Consumer protection laws 48–49
*Consumer's Guide to Intervening in State Public
    Utility Proceedings*, 143–179
Credit scores, use to determine deposits 6–7
Crisis funds 21, 22
Customer complaints
    individual rights 39–41
    seeking larger-scale change 41–42

Deferred payment plans 32–33, 95–99
Deliverable fuels 47–50
    co-ops 48
    consumer protection laws 48–49
    described 47
    help paying or lowering bills 13–19, 21
    LIHEAP customers 48
    loan funds 49–50
    unregulated nature 47, 49–50

Denial of service
    issues in obtaining service 5–12
    selected state regulations 95
Deposits 5–8
    alternatives 8
    bankruptcy, customers who have filed for
        34
    calculation 7
    credit scores, use 6–7
    limits on collection and retention 7–8
    selected state regulations 93–95
    when deposits are required 5–6
Deregulation 2–3
Disabled persons, termination of service
        29–30
    cold weather protection 31–32
    state regulations 73–82
Disconnection of service, *see* Termination of
        service

Elderly customers, termination of service
        30–31
    cold weather protection 31–32
    notification 31
    state regulations 73–82
Electric service, *see* Utility service
Electric utilities
    see also Public utilities
    bills, *see* Heating bills; Utility bills
    discounted rates 17–18
    line extension charges 12
    regulation 1–3
    restructuring 2–3
    termination of service, *see* Termination of
        service
Emergency Food and Shelter Program (EFSP),
    crisis funds 22
Energy efficiency programs 15–19
    water conservation, *see* Water conservation
    weatherization, *see* Weatherization
        programs

Evictions, illegal shut-offs as self-help means 28

Federal Emergency Management Agency (FEMA), crisis funds 22
Federal Poverty Guidelines 141–142
Fees and charges
　late charges, *see* Late charges
　line extension charges 12
　reconnection charges 37–38
Financial hardship
　deliverable fuels 48
　federal poverty guidelines 141–142
　home energy assistance program (LIHEAP) 13–15
　rate reduction programs 17–18
　telephone assistance programs 19–20
　termination of service 29
　weatherization program (WAP) 16–17
Fuel co-ops 48
Fuel funds 21

Gas service, *see* Utility service
Gas utilities
　see also Public utilities
　bills, *see* Heating bills; Utility bills
　discounted rates 17–18
　line extension charges 12
　regulation 1
　termination of service, *see* Termination of service

Heating bills, help paying or lowering 13–19
　crisis funds, 21
Heating oil, *see* Deliverable fuels
Home-heating fuels
　help paying or lowering bills 13–19
　regulated, *see* Utility service
　unregulated, *see* Deliverable fuels

Identification issues 10–12
Investor Owned Utilities (IOUs)
　see also Public utilities; Utility service
　regulation, 1–3

Kerosene, *see* Deliverable fuels

Landlines 43
Landlords
　illegal shut-offs 28

non-payment of utility bills 27–28
RUBS 45–46
selected state regulations 101–102
Late charges 35–37
　disputed bills 36
　pyramiding late charges 36–37
　strategies to avoid 22–23
Levelized billing 23, 100
Lifeline program 19–20
LIHEAP, *see* Low Income Home Energy Assistance Program (LIHEAP)
Line extension charges 12
Link-Up program 19–20
Liquefied petroleum gas (LPG), *see* Deliverable fuels
Low Income Home Energy Assistance Program (LIHEAP) 13–15
　deliverable fuels 48
　state directors, contact information 108–116
Low Income Weatherization Program (WAP) 16–17
　state contact information 103–107
Low-income rate reduction programs 17–18
Low-income telephone assistance programs 19–20

Municipal Utilities (munis)
　see also Public utilities; Utility service
　non-regulation 1
　termination of service 34

Natural gas, *see* Gas utilities
Non-payment of utility bills, *see* Arrearages
Notice of shutoff 25–26
　elderly customers 31
　time frames 26–27, 83–91

Oil, *see* Deliverable fuels

Payment plans
　budget payment plans 23, 100–101
　deferred payment plans 32–33, 95–99
　levelized billing 23, 100
　preferred payment date programs 23, 100
　selected state regulations 95–101
Poverty Guidelines 141–142
Pre-paid phone cards 43–44
Preferred payment date programs 23, 100

Prior debts 8–10
    bills from a prior address 9
    bills of landlord or prior occupant 9
    bills of roommate, spouse, or others 9–10
Propane, *see* Deliverable fuels
Public utilities
    see also Utility service
    appliance sales 33
    billing, *see* Utility bills
    complaints against 39–41
    deregulation 2–3
    electricity, *see* Electric utilities
    investor-owned, *see* Investor Owned
        Utilities (IOUs)
    municipally-owned, *see* Municipal Utilities
        (munis)
    natural gas, *see* Gas utilities
    rates, *see* Utility rates
    regulation, *see* Public Utility Commissions
        (PUCs); Regulation of utility service
    restructuring 2–3
    rural electric, *see* Rural Electric
        Cooperatives (co-ops)
    water, *see* Water utilities
Public Utility Commissions (PUCs)
    see also Regulation of utility service
    individual complaints to 39–41
    intervening in state proceedings 42,
        143–179
    regulation of utility service 1–3
    see king larger-scale change 41–42
    state commissions, contact information
        116–120
Pyramiding late charges 36–37

Rates, *see* Utility rates
Ratio Utility Billing System (RUBS) 45–46
Reconnection charges 37–38
Regulation of utility service
    see also Public Utility Commissions (PUCs)
    bills owed by others or from prior address
        8–10
    denial of service 95
    deposits 5–8, 93–95
    disconnections 25–34, 94–95
    electricity 1–3
    identification issues 10–12
    landlord-tenant procedures 27–28,
        101–102

late charges 35–37
line extension charges 12
natural gas 1
overview 1–3
payment plans 95–101
reconnections 37–38
selected regulations 93–102
state regulations 129–139
telephone service 43–44
water 44–45
Restructuring 2–3
Rural Electric Cooperatives (co-ops)
    see also Public utilities; Utility service
    non-regulation 1

Seasonal termination protections
    cold weather protections 31–32
    hot weather protections 32
    state regulations 61–72
Seniors, *see* Elderly customers
Serious illness protection 29–30, 73–82
    sample certification 125–127
Shutoffs, *see* Termination of service
State regulations
    see also Regulation of utility service
    denial of service 95
    deposits 93–95
    disconnections 94–95
    landlord-tenant procedures 101–102
    payment plans 95–101
    utility regulations 129–139
State utility commissions, *see* Public Utility
    Commissions (PUCs)
Submetering 45–46

Telephone bills, help paying or lowering
    19–20
Telephone service
    see also Utility service
    regulation 43–44
Tenants
    disconnection due to non-payment by
        landlord 27–28
    illegal shut-offs by landlord 28
    selected state regulations 101–102
    submetering issues 45–46
Termination of service 25–34
    age-related protections 30–31, 73–82
    appliance sales, non-payment 33

Termination of service, *continued*
  bankruptcy protections 33-34
  cold weather protection 31–32
  deferred payment plans 32–33
  disabled persons 29–30
  disputed bills 28–29
  elderly customers 30–31
  exceptions to termination protections 27
  financial hardship situations 29
  hot weather protection 32
  illegal shut-offs by landlords 28
  landlord's non-payment 27–28
  limits on times or days 26
  municipal utilities 34
  notice period 26, 83–91
  regulated utilities 25
  restoring service 37–38
  seasonal protection regulations 61–72
  selected state regulations 94–95
  serious illness protections 29–30, 73–82
  shutoff notice 25–27
  time frame 26, 83–91
  water utilities 44–46

UDAP laws 48–49
Utility bills
  arrearages, *see* Arrearages
  budget billing 23, 100–101
  deferred payment plans 32–33, 95–99
  disputed bills 28–29, 36
  heating bills, *see* Heating bills
  help paying or lowering bills 13–23
  late charges, *see* Late charges
  levelized payments 23, 100
  owed previously, *see* Prior debts
  payment period 25–26, 35, 83–91
  preferred payment date programs 23, 100
  RUBS 45–46
  telephone bills, *see* Telephone bills
  water bills, *see* Water bills

Utility commissions, *see* Public Utility
  Commissions (PUCs)
Utility companies, *see* Public utilities
Utility rates
  billings, *see* Utility bills
  low-income discount rates 17–18
Utility Service
  billings, *see* Utility bills
  denial of service, selected state regulations 95
  electricity, *see* Electric utilities
  help with paying or lowering bills 13–23
  line extension charges 12
  natural gas, *see* Gas utilities
  obtaining service 5–12
  provision, *see* Public utilities
  rates, *see* Utility rates
  regulation, *see* Public Utility Commissions
    (PUCs); Regulation of utility service
  submetering 45–46
  telephone, *see* Telephone service
  termination, *see* Termination of service
  water, *see* Water utilities

WAP weatherization program 16–17
  contact information 103–107
Water bills, help paying or lowering 20–21
Water conservation 19, 21
Water funds 21
Water utilities
  see also Utility service
  regulation 44–45
  submetering 45–46
Weather, termination protections based on, *see*
  Seasonal termination protections
Weatherization programs 15–19
  government sponsored programs 16–17
  self-help weatherization 18–19
  state contact information 103–107
Wireless service 43
Wood, *see* Deliverable fuels

ORDER FORM

☐ The NCLC Guide to Surviving Debt (2006 ed.) .... $20 ppd.
(SAVE! $14 each for 5 or more, $12 for 20 or more, $8 for 100 or more.)

☐ The NCLC Guide to the Rights of Utility Consumers (2006 ed.) ..... $15 ppd.
(SAVE! $10 each for 5 or more. $7 each for 100 or more.)

☐ **20 copies** Surviving Credit Card Debt Workbooks with CD-Roms
(2005 ed.) .... $80 ppd.
(Minimum order of 20 copies; $4 for each additional copy over 20)

☐ The NCLC Guide to Mobile Homes (2002 ed.) .... $12 ppd.

☐ Return to Sender: Getting a Refund or Replacement for Your Lemon Car
(2000 ed.) .... $16 ppd.

☐ **Please send me more information about NCLC books for lawyers.**

Name _____

Organization _____

Street Address _____

City _____ State _____ Zip _____

Telephone _____

E-mail _____

Mail to: National Consumer Law Center, Inc.
Publications Department
77 Summer Street, 10th Floor
Boston, MA 02110-1006

Telephone orders
(617) 542-9595
or fax (617) 542-8028
for credit card orders

☐ Check or money order enclosed, payable   ☐ MasterCard   ☐ VISA   ☐ AMERICAN EXPRESS Cards
to the National Consumer Law Center

Card# ☐☐☐☐☐☐☐☐☐☐☐☐☐☐☐☐☐

Exp. date ☐☐☐☐   Signature _____

(card number, expiration date, and signature must accompany charge orders)

NATIONAL CONSUMER LAW CENTER
77 Summer Street, 10th Floor • Boston, MA 02110-1006
Tel. (617) 542-9595 • FAX (617) 542-8028 • publications@nclc.org

Order securely online at
www.consumerlaw.org